# A Student's Guide to the History and Philosophy of Yoga

# A Student's Guide to the History and Philosophy of Yoga

Peter Connolly

equinox

LONDON OAKVILLE

Published by

UK: Equinox Publishing Ltd., Unit 6, The Village, 101 Amies St., London SW11 2JW
USA: DBBC, 28 Main Street, Oakville, CT 06779

www.equinoxpub.com

First published 2007



British Library Cataloguing-in-Publication Data
A catalogue record for this book is available from the British Library.

| | | |
|---|---|---|
| ISBN-10 | 1 84553 155 8 | (hardback) |
| | 1 84553 156 6 | (paperback) |
| ISBN-13 | 978 1 84553 155 3 | (hardback) |
| | 978 1 84553 156 0 | (paperback) |

Library of Congress Cataloging-in-Publication Data

Connolly, Peter, 1951–
A student's guide to the history and philosophy of yoga/Peter Connolly.
p. cm.
Includes bibliographical references and index.
ISBN 1-84553-155-8 (hb) — ISBN 1-84553-156-6 (pbk.) 1.
Yoga—History. 2. Yoga. I. Title.
B132.Y6C638 2007
181'.45—dc22

2006023689

Typeset by S.J.I. Services, New Delhi
Printed and bound by Lightning Source UK Ltd, Milton Keynes, and Lightning Source Inc., La Vergne, TN

# CONTENTS

# ABBREVIATIONS

| | |
|---|---|
| *AU* | *Aitareya Upaniṣad* |
| *AV* | *Atharvaveda* |
| *BG* | *Bhagavad Gītā* |
| *BAU* | *Bṛhadāraṇyaka Upaniṣad* |
| *BSBh* | *Brahmasūtra* |
| *CU* | *Chāndogya Upaniṣad* |
| *HYP* | *Haṭha Yoga Pradīpikā* |
| *KU* | *Kaṭha Upaniṣad* |
| *MaitriU* | *Maitrī Upaniṣad* |
| *Manu* | *Mānava Dharma Śāstra* |
| *MundU* | *Muṇḍaka Upaniṣad* |
| *RV* | *Ṛgveda* |
| *SU* | *Śvetāśvatara Upaniṣad* |
| *TU* | *Taittirīya Upaniṣad* |
| *YS* | *Yoga Sūtra* |

# SANSKRIT LETTERS AND THEIR PRONUNCIATION

The following list gives Romanized versions of the letters in the Sanskrit alphabet. Examples of the letters in the actual devanagari script can be found at the front of Monier-Williams' *Sanskrit–English Dictionary*. The pronunciation examples are taken from this work. Letters are given in the order of the Sanskrit rather than the English alphabet.

a – mica, rural, or as the 'u' in but
ā – tar, father
i – fill, lily
ī – police
u – full, bush
ū – rude
ṛ – merrily
ṛi – marine
lṛ – revelry
lṛi – revelree
e – prey, there
ai – aisle
o – go, stone
au – Haus (as German)
ṃ – pure nasal (anusvāra)
ḥ – an aspirated sound (visarga)
k – kill, seek
kh – inkhorn
g – gun, get, dog
gh – loghut
ṅ – sing, king, sink
c – dolce (as in music), a 'ch' sound
ch – churchill
j – jet, jump
jh – hedgehog (hejhog)
ñ – singe
ṭ – true
ṭh – anthill
ḍ – drum
ḍh – redhaired
ṇ – none
t – water
th – nut hook
d – dice
dh – adhere
n – not, nut, in
p – put, sip
ph – uphill
b – bear, rub
bh – abhor
m – map, jam
y – yet, loyal
r – red, year
l – lull, lead
v – ivy
ś – sure
ṣ – shun, bush
s – saint, sin, hiss
h – hear, hit

NOTE Sanskrit consonants have an 'a' sound built into them which is pronounced unless another vowel is attached or they are combined with another consonant. So when you recite the alphabet, the consonants go 'ka, kha, ga, gha, na', etc. Those consonants transliterated with a dot below them are pronounced with the tongue at the top of the mouth.

Contact Peter via his company Turning Point Consulting
(E: info@turningpointconsulting.co.uk
W: www.turningpointconsulting.co.uk
T: 01243 837779)

# INTRODUCTION

The word 'yoga' conjures up in the minds of many Westerners images of people performing exercises and adopting unusual, sometimes contortive postures. Such exercises and postures do have a place within the practice of yoga, but it is much more than that. Indeed, the early literature on yoga describes and defines it as a form of mental rather than physical discipline. Yoga[1] is also associated with the Indian subcontinent and the religions of Hinduism and Buddhism. So much so, that one of the most eminent writers on the subject of yoga during the twentieth century, Mircea Eliade, argued that yoga was the product of the Indian psyche, of the Indian soil. Certainly, what we now know as yoga did originate in and was developed in India. There is some disagreement, however, about whether yoga is an Indian version of a mystical tradition, other examples of which can be found in other cultures, or whether it is distinctive and unique. I shall not debate this issue here. Rather, I will assume throughout this book that yoga *is* a distinctively Indian form of mysticism, and return in a later chapter to the issue of whether the various traditions of spirituality that are frequently referred to as 'mystical' have anything in common.

This book has grown out of and is designed, in part, to serve a course on yoga philosophy that was created for the British Wheel of Yoga, an organization which seeks to promote a non-partisan, in-depth study of Indian yoga traditions. As such, it reflects the emphases present in that course. Hence, the yoga teachings of the Upaniṣads, the *Bhagavad Gītā* and the *Yoga Sūtra* constitute the core of this work as they do of the British Wheel of Yoga syllabus. I have not, however, completely ignored the wider dynamics of the Hindu tradition. How could I, since that tradition is the context within which yoga developed? Equally, I have referred to the Buddhist tradition on many occasions. This is inevitable for a number of reasons. In the first place, Buddhism offers us one of the best examples there is of a yogic tradition. Indeed, I would go so far as to say that Buddhism is intrinsically yogic in character. In the second place, Buddhism developed alongside the religion of the Brāhmans that eventually became what we now know as Hinduism and each influenced the other, not always symmetrically. In fact, I shall argue that, in terms of borrowing, Hindu yoga owes more to Buddhist yoga than Buddhist yoga owes to its Hindu counterpart.

In a work of this kind the author has to make a decision about whether to adopt a neutral, even-handed approach to the presentation of material and interpretations that are controversial in scholarly circles or whether to tell it as he understands it. I have adopted the latter approach, though I do mention alternative views at various points. The reasoning behind this decision is partly based on my desire to convey to the reader something of how I teach the material in the lecture room. That teaching is designed as much to encourage the students to become independent thinkers and researchers as it is to provide information about yoga philosophy. Indeed, my understanding of yoga training in general is that it encourages such independence of thought. All writers of books and articles on yoga make claims about its history and its nature. My advice to students is nearly always to demand that an author convinces them by providing good reasons for accepting the claims made. In the absence of good reasons, maintaining a sceptical attitude is probably the best course to adopt.

This advice raises the issue of what might be called 'approaches' or 'lenses' or 'perspectives' or 'filters'. It is the issue of how the material is to be introduced and treated. Different approaches concentrate on and accord significance to different aspects of a situation or phenomenon. In what follows I shall draw primarily on three perspectives: the phenomenological, the philosophical and the historical. Each attempts to 'make sense' of the material under investigation in a different way and requires the reader to reflect on it from a different angle. Each approach offers a kind of method for interpreting the available evidence and even for deciding which evidence to select in the first place. For example, a psychologist studying material on yoga will tend to select that which is primarily psychological in nature and will seek to explain it in psychological terms. In short, one's choice of perspective and method will have a profound influence on the kinds of conclusions one arrives at.

A phenomenological approach seeks to make sense of and convey to the reader 'that which is presented', i.e. to explain the phenomenon 'in its own terms' as far as possible. This usually involves the attempt to pursue an empathy with the authors or traditions being investigated, and the development of typologies that link various aspects together and also go below the surface to identify patterns and connections that are not always obvious from a 'that which is presented' position.

An excellent example of phenomenological typology can be found in a work by Andrew Rawlinson entitled *The Book of Enlightened Masters: Western Teachers in Eastern Traditions.* In this book, Rawlinson introduces a typology of spiritual traditions that he constructed on the basis of the accounts provided by various texts on spirituality and interviews with modern spiritual teachers. It has two axes: hot–cool and structured–unstructured, which he describes thus:

> *Hot* is that which is other than oneself; that which has its own life. It is not something that one has access to as of right. It is powerful and breath-taking, and is associated with revelations and grace. It is very similar to Otto's numinous.
>
> *Cool* is the very essence of oneself; one need not go to another to find it. Hence, one does have access to it as of right. It is quiet and still, and is associated with self-realization.
>
> The meaning of *Structured* is that there is an inherent order in the cosmos and therefore in the human condition. There is something to be discovered out there and there is a way of discovering it. A map is required to find the destination.
>
> By contrast, *Unstructured* teachings say that there is no gap between the starting point and the finishing post. Method and goal are identical. We are not separate from reality/truth/god and so no map is required. Everything is available now and always has been.[2]

Schematically these axes can be represented thus:

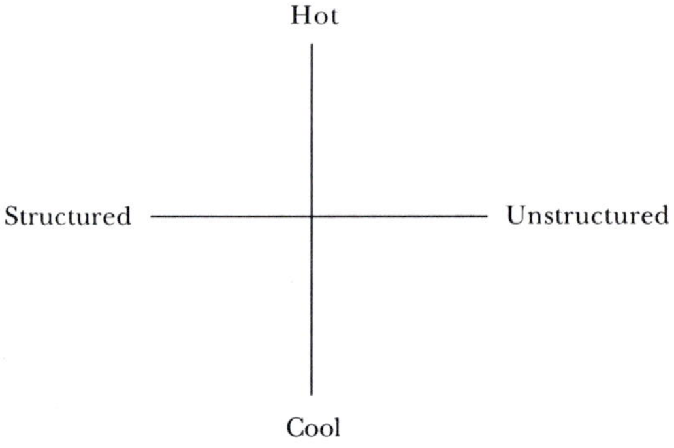


This arrangement gives us four quadrants: hot–structured, cool–structured, hot–unstructured and cool–unstructured. The primary characteristics of each, according to Rawlinson, are:

## HOT–STRUCTURED

These traditions stress the importance of initiatory knowledge, hierarchy, the exercise of will and the manipulation of the laws of the cosmos in the service of self-transformation. Images used by such traditions include the magician and the gambler and the idea of a jump rather than a journey. Examples would include Hindu Tantra, Buddhist Vajrayāna, the Siddha tradition, Vedic ritualism, Kabbalah, Hermeticism, Alchemy and Shamanism.

## HOT–UNSTRUCTURED

These traditions stress the characteristics of bliss, discipline, love, obedience, submission and wisdom. Images include the lover and the martyr. Examples include ecstatic Hindu devotionalism, e.g. Caitanya, Pure Land Buddhism, Sufism, Christian mysticism, e.g. St Teresa.

## COOL–STRUCTURED

These traditions stress the characteristics of dispassionate awareness, order, progress, effort and concentration. Images include those of the craftsman and the yogin and the idea of work rather than grace. Examples include Patañjali's *Yoga Sūtra*, Theravāda Buddhism, Zen, early Vedānta, i.e. the Upaniṣads, Sāṃkhya, Aurobindo, Plotinus.

## COOL–UNSTRUCTURED

These traditions stress the fact of Being, the possibility of knowing the truth at any moment (you do not even have to jump) and the absence of any kind of 'path'. Images include those of the sage and the hermit, and the idea of 'letting go'. Examples include Advaita Vedānta, Mādhyamaka Buddhism, Mahāmūdra, Taoism, Tibetan Buddhist Dzogchen and Zen.

It is clear from the examples provided that different forms of yoga are located in different quadrants, and this, in turn, indicates that there are some quite significant differences between the various schools of yoga and that the notion that they are all ultimately teaching the same thing is false. I shall draw upon some of these distinctions when discussing the various forms of yoga in the following chapters.

Another typology I shall employ in the following chapters focuses on the subject of liberation or salvation (soteriology: doctrine of salvation).[3] It is organized in terms of the four key questions that any doctrine of salvation must answer: (1) 'From what am I being saved?' (2) 'By what means is this salvation accomplished?' (3) 'To what condition do I move into when I am saved?' (or, What is the difference between the unsaved and saved states?) and (4) 'From what source(s) does soteriologically significant information derive?' Answers to these questions vary from tradition to tradition, though all soteriological teachings will answer them in some way or other. The chart on p. 7 sets out some of the main variants.

Traditions vary significantly in their answers to question 1. The Christian concepts of sin and alienation from god are quite different from the Indian ideas of karma and saṃsāra, though their teachings about how such conditions can be transcended (question 2) are, structurally, remarkably similar: by effort, by grace or by some combination of the two.

Likewise, a similar range of responses is found in the Christian tradition as in the Hindu to question 3; either there is some kind of realization of unity or a recognition of difference between soul and god. In the first case, salvation or liberation is fundamentally epistemological in character: the cosmos does not change though our perception and experience of it does. The unliberated state is understood as one where we do not realize our unity with everything else, including god; the liberated state as one where we do realize this. Once liberated, we can, for example, love our neighbour as ourselves because we realize that our neighbours are ourselves. In the second case, the aspirant experiences god and recognizes that the soul and god are different. As the medieval devotee Rāmprasāda puts it, 'I do not want to be sugar, I want to taste sugar.' In other words, he did not want to be god; he wanted to experience god. There is an ontological (doctrine of being or existence) dimension to this as the changes brought about at liberation involve more than just a change in perception; there is a kind of relocation that takes place too. So, for example, the soul moves (often at death) *from* involvement with matter *to* association with god. Christians do not have an atheistic version of salvation such as is found in various forms of Buddhism, Hinduism and Jainism, but their cosmology (in many versions) is essentially god plus souls plus matter, i.e. not that different from the views of the Hindu school of Sāṃkhya or of the Jains with god added on.

The schematic version of this typology is as in the figure on the facing page.

Answers to the third question, 'To what?', often mix together two different aspects of the enquiry: ontology (doctrines of being or existence) and theology (doctrines about god or gods). In terms of ontology, the three most commonly adopted views are, as the diagram indicates, monism, dualism and pluralism. Ontological monism is the doctrine that at the most fundamental level of existence all is one being. Dualism is the view that at the most fundamental level there are two separate beings, e.g. god and the universe (here souls would be understood to be parts of god) or souls and the universe, as in Sāṃkhya and Jainism. Pluralism is an extension of dualism, with more than two kinds of ultimate beings (god plus souls plus universe for example). Because there are many individual souls in Sāṃkhya and Jainism, they could be regarded as subscribing to pluralistic ontologies. The reason why they are usually described as dualistic is that all the souls (puruṣa in Samkhya; jīva in Jainism) are identical to each other.

In terms of theology, the three most commonly encountered views are polytheism (many gods), monotheism (one god) and atheism

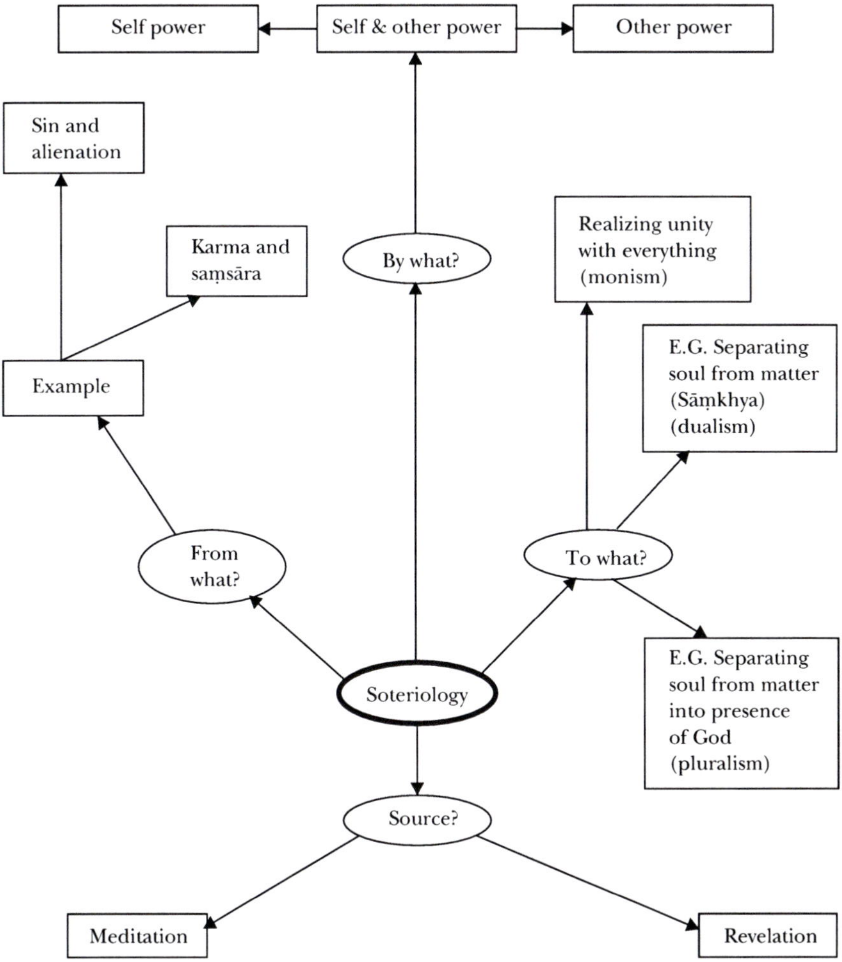


(no gods). The point to note about these alternatives, both ontological and theological, is that the options in each category are mutually exclusive. One cannot be a polytheistic monotheist or a monotheistic atheist. Likewise, one cannot be a monistic dualist or a monistic pluralist. One can, however, combine any theology with any ontology. I mention this because many writers have tended to assume that certain ontologies go with certain theologies, e.g. dualism or pluralism with monotheism. This is *not* the case. Schematically, we can represent these options in two columns. Any cross-column combination is possible; no within-column combinations are possible without falling into logical incoherence. In other words, one can be, for example, a polytheistic monist, or a polytheistic dualist, or a polytheistic pluralist.

| *Ontology* | *Theology* |
|---|---|
| Monism | Polytheism |
| Dualism | Monotheism |
| Pluralism | Atheism |

Phenomenological approaches emphasize accurate description, and hence share much with the work of social and cultural anthropologists. Philosophers take a rather different tack. They tend to be wary and evasive when requested to provide a definition of philosophy, and none that I know of would win universal assent. So all that I will offer here is what I will call a 'working definition', i.e. this is what I have in mind when I use the term 'philosophy'. That definition has two components. On the one hand, philosophers tend to be sceptical. They are disinclined to accept claims unless good reasons are provided in their support. To this end, philosophers demand not only that evidence be provided but also that the interpretation of the evidence is inferentially sound, i.e. logically valid. On the other hand, philosophers seek to respond to their own demands by presenting their own arguments in a rigorous and systematic manner. So, in my understanding, philosophy combines a sceptical mind (which manifests in a questioning attitude towards the claims being made by others) with a commitment to present ideas in a systematic and well-supported way.

Much traditional yoga teaching has a noticeable philosophical bent. Yoga teachers differed among themselves about the most effective ways to pursue liberating knowledge and what was revealed about the nature of the world once that knowledge had been acquired. They often debated with each other about these issues, and the debates, as much as any other factor, pushed these teachers in the direction of becoming philosophers. Crucial to these debates was the issue of epistemology, the study of knowledge and how we get it. Most yoga schools agreed that we acquire what we call knowledge in three main ways: perception (pratyakṣa), inference (anumāna) and testimony (śabda), though they disagreed about the status that can be legitimately applied to these sources. The third was the most contentious, with the most brāhmanically orthodox accepting its authority (as they wanted scripture to have a status equal to or even superior to that ascribed to perception and inference), and the less orthodox taking a more sceptical stance.

Moreover, the terms themselves were used in different ways by different teachers. The Vedāntin Śaṅkara, for example, often uses the term 'perception' to refer to scripture – he argues that scripture records the perceptions of the ancient sages and should thus be accorded the same status as one's own direct perception.

The Buddha provides us with an excellent example of early philosophical thinking about yogic matters generally and epistemology in particular. His approach is essentially twofold: *first* he considers a range of positions taken by others on the subject of knowledge and identifies the errors upon which they are built; *then* he outlines what he considers to be a sound basis for any theory of knowledge.

In the *Saṅgāravasutta* of the *Majjhima Nikāya*[4] the Buddha classifies śramanas and brāhmaṇas into three types with regard to epistemology:

1. the traditionalists – who base their teaching on tradition, authority or report;
2. the rationalists – who base their teaching on reasoning and logic;
3. the experientialists – who have personal insight into truth.

He places himself in the third category. Each of these categories contains a number of sub-groups (essentially different reasons for holding that a view is well-grounded).

## THE TRADITIONALISTS

In the *Bhaddiyasutta*[5] the Buddha identifies ten inadequate reasons for holding views/beliefs/opinions. Six of these relate to authority or tradition and four to reasoning or inference. The six inadequate reasons that relate to authority or tradition are:

- report
- tradition
- hearsay
- proficiency in the collections (i.e. scriptural knowledge)
- because it ought to be so[6]
- the thought 'the recluse (teacher) is revered by us'.

The Buddha's position on authority is that authority or tradition is useless if it cannot be traced back to someone's personal experience. An extended treatment of this can be found in the *Tevijjasutta* of the *Dīgha Nikāya (Dialogues of the Buddha)*. Another is found in the *Caṅkīsutta*.[7]

An extract which illustrates the Buddha's style goes:

> 'Bhāradvāja, even although something be thoroughly believed in, it may be empty, void, false; on the other hand, something not thoroughly believed in may be fact, truth, not otherwise ... Preserving a truth, Bharādvāja, is not enough for an intelligent man inevitably to come to the conclusion: 'This alone is the truth, all else is falsehood.' ... if a man has faith and says: 'Such is my faith,' speaking thus he preserves a truth, but not yet does he inevitably come to the conclusion: 'This alone is truth, all else is falsehood.'

In other words, if a person believes in some report or tradition they should say that they *believe* it to be true rather than claiming that it *is* the truth.

## THE RATIONALISTS

The four unsatisfactory reasons for holding a view that relate to reasoning are:

- logic
- inference
- after considering reasons
- after reflection on and approval of some theory.

The Buddha is not against reasoning as such, only against claiming too much for it and using it to arrive at dogmatically held positions. Buddhaghosa (5th century CE) identified four kinds of reasoners:

1. those who reason on the basis of a tradition (essentially theology);
2. those who reason on the basis of memory;
3. those who reason on the basis of meditational experience;
4. those who are pure reasoners.

Number 1 is reasoning based on an insecure foundation as any tradition is likely to contain errors. Numbers 2 and 3 are instances of reasoning carried out on the basis of experience, and the Buddha's criticism tends to focus not on the experience itself but on the process of extrapolating from it. Thus:

1. One who remembers one or two (prior) births and argues that since it was he who existed in the past in such and such a place, therefore the soul is eternal, is one who reasons on a premises based on retrocognition.
2. He who, because of his jhānic experience, argues that since his soul is happy in the present, it must have been so in the past and it will be so in the future and accepts the theory that the soul is eternal, is an intuitionist reasoner.

In both cases, the reasoner has gone beyond the evidence of his experience and made an unjustifiable inference which, according to the Buddha, results in false statements being believed in.[8]

In the case of the pure reasoners there is a double mistake:

- first of all their *a priori* reasoning (reasoning on the basis of accepted principles) is really reasoning about what ought to be or what must be;
- then they make unwarranted deductions.

So the Buddha could find no confidence in beliefs based on authority or tradition alone; nor in those based on authority plus reasoning; nor in those based on limited experience plus reasoning; nor in those based on reasoning alone. In fact, the Buddha seems to be against holding any beliefs/views whatsoever. In the *Dīghanakhasutta*[9] three attitudes to views or beliefs are set out:

1. I agree with every view.
2. I agree with some views and not others.
3. I agree with no view.

This text is rather difficult to read but the essential message is that the first two positions lead to 'dispute, vexation and worry'. The third position is, however, 'close to detachment, close to the absence of fetters, close to the absence of delight, close to the absence of craving, close to the absence of grasping'. Nevertheless, this third position can also be binding and create dispute if held to dogmatically. Thus, whilst the Buddha advocates holding no views he does not advocate dogmatically holding to the view that all views are false. What he does seem to be encouraging is a kind of mental state which seeks to minimize everything that causes dispute, vexation and worry.

When the Buddha is questioned on epistemological issues, therefore, his response tends to take one of two forms:

- he retains a noble silence;
- he redefines the question in Buddhist terminology.[10]

## THE EXPERIENTIALISTS

The Buddha puts himself in this category. There are, however, different kinds of experientialists. The materialists (Cārvāka/Lokāyata) were empiricists; the only experience they accepted was sense experience. The Buddha, on the other hand, made reference to meditational experience and the knowledge gained thereby. He recommends attaining the fourth meditational plane (jhāna) and then, being wary of making inappropriate inferences, directing one's mind to obtaining the three knowledges he acquired on the night of his awakening:

- of former existences;
- of the causes of rebirth;
- of the destruction of the cankers (āsava).

For the Buddha, this is the way to find a firm foundation for a teaching about the nature of things. It is, of course, at this point that the Buddha parts company with philosophy, and he may well be susceptible to the criticism he directed at others of going beyond the evidence. It is one thing to describe one's experiences in meditation but quite another to claim veridicality for them – and the Buddha's claim that he sees the world as it really is (yathābhūtam) is just that. Certainly, much will hinge on whether he is making a truth claim ('this is the way things really are') or whether he is saying 'this is the way things appear to me'. Only in the latter case is there, in the Buddha's own words, 'the preservation of a truth'.

The Buddha's example shows us that a person can be a yogin *and* a philosopher. Likewise, I would encourage the reader of this book to be a phenomenologist (seeking to understand the material, as far as possible, in its own terms) *and* a philosopher (seeking to question claims that are made and demanding that good reasons are offered in their support). The reader also needs to be able to appreciate some of the issues raised by attempts at historical reconstruction.

'Reconstruction' is a central notion in modern historical studies. Contemporary historians draw upon as many sources of information as possible in order to understand why and how things came to be as they are. They also seek to offer analyses and explanations of events. This is in marked contrast to the work of earlier historians, i.e. pre-twentieth century, who had tended to emphasize the role of human intentions in their reconstructions and adopt a primarily narrative approach.[11] My treatment of Indian philosophy will follow these modern developments in historical study and seek, where appropriate, to explain why the traditions developed as they did, as well as recording the kinds of changes that occurred.

History has to do with chronology, placing people, events and human creations in a temporal relation with each other. Such chronology is of two main types: relative and absolute. Relative chronology is essentially the process of determining what came before what. When we establish a relative chronology we can say, for example, that teacher X lived before teacher Y, or that scripture P was composed before scripture Q. This can often be determined by internal criteria alone, e.g. the language in which the texts are written. If we want to make a specific claim, such as 'teacher X lived from 483 to 403 BCE and teacher Y from 324 to 250 BCE' or that 'scripture P was written in 720 and scripture Q in 640', we require some kind of external corroboration such as an inscription or a reference in a work for which we do have a precise date. Specific dating of this kind is called establishing an absolute chronology, because in addition to the relative order we also have fixed points of reference.

For many of the influential texts and personalities in the history of Indian philosophy only a relative chronology can be established with any degree of confidence. Absolute chronologies are often the subject of considerable debate. This is hardly surprising, as, if two texts offer essentially the same teachings, the likelihood is that one borrowed from the other, and the question of 'who borrowed from whom?' becomes significant for the activity of reconstruction.

Furthermore, if one of the texts is, for example, Brāhmanical and the other Buddhist, an extra dimension is added to the debate. The positions taken in these debates have particular significance for the novice student, who often has an inflated respect for the views expressed by authors of books and not infrequently takes claims to be facts. One noticeable trend in these debates is that, generally, Indian scholars and those who follow Indian spiritual traditions set their absolute chronologies considerably earlier than do their Western counterparts. Hence, if establishing a chronology is important for our purposes, a useful rule of thumb is to consult as wide a range of sources as possible and ensure that the work of writers from both camps is consulted. Like philosophers, historians demand that claims are supported by relevant evidence and/or argumentation.

# Chapter 1
# BACKGROUND TO YOGA PHILOSOPHY

In order to understand the practices of mental and physical culture that go under the label of yoga it is useful to be aware of features in the Indian world view that make it different from its Western counterparts and provide a rationale for many of the teachings of different yoga schools. The Indian understanding of time, of human destiny and of the kinds of connections that exist between language, the physical world and the various realms within the physical world are all different from what is generally accepted in the West, and these differences can have quite a profound effect on how we make sense of yoga.

## TIME

For most Europeans, Antipodeans and Americans ('Westerners' for short), time is linear. It began with the creation of the universe, whether that is understood in terms of the big bang or the act of a creator god, and is moving forwards to some final end. In India, the predominant view is that time is cyclical. This creation is just one of many that have come into existence and gone out of existence over millions and millions of years and one of many that will come into existence and go out of existence over millions and millions of years. One version of this cyclical view (there are many) takes the basic unit of time as a day in the life of the creator god Brahmā, who lives for 100 years and then passes out of existence for the same period of time before returning again to create the universe once more. A day of Brahmā is called a *kalpa,* a time during which he is awake. At the end of each day Brahmā sleeps for as long as he was awake, a period called *pralāya.* Each day of Brahmā is made up of 1,000 great ages (*mahāyuga*), and each great age is itself made up of four ages (*yuga*). These ages are known as the *Krita, Treta, Dvāpara* and Kali Yugas, corresponding to the four throws, from highest to lowest, on a four-sided die.

The Krita Yuga is the perfect age, the Golden Age. During the Krita Yuga, the *dharma,* the social regulations instituted by the brāhman, i.e. priestly, class, is at its height and the cow of dharma is said to stand on four legs. This age lasts for 1,728,000 human years. Treta Yuga is the Silver Age. Virtue (= conformity to dharma) is reduced by one quarter during this age and the cow of dharma stands uncertainly on three legs. The Treta Yuga lasts for 1,296,000 human years. Dvāpara Yuga is the Bronze Age, a dangerous time, when good and evil, ignorance and knowledge are in the balance, and the cow of dharma stands unsteadily on two legs. The Dvāpara Yuga lasts for 864,000 human years. Kali Yuga, the present age, is the Iron Age. Virtue and knowledge are at one-quarter strength and the cow of dharma wobbles precariously on one leg. The Kali Yuga lasts for 432,000 human years. The *Vishnu Purāṇa* describes it thus,

> 'When society reaches a stage where property confers rank, wealth becomes the only source of virtue, passion the sole bond of union between husband and wife, falsehood the source of success in life, sex the only means of enjoyment, and when outer trappings are confused with inner religion ...' then we are in the Kali Yuga.[1]

This kind of vast, almost mind-blowing, cosmology is found in Buddhist and Jain traditions as well as Hindu, though there is considerable variation in the detail. For example, in the *Brahmajāla Sutta* of the Buddhist Pāli Canon, the Buddha presents Brahmā (the Hindu creator god) as the first being who comes into existence at the beginning of a new age because of his previous good deeds. Because no other beings are around Brahmā feels lonely and wishes for companionship. Just then, other beings come into existence because of their previous good deeds. Seeing these other beings, Brahmā thinks, mistakenly, that his wish has created them. They, seeing that he was there before them, assume that he brought them there, that he created them. The fact is, explains the Buddha, all this is accomplished through the impersonal working of the law of karma (action).

## HUMAN DESTINY

The law of karma is a presupposition, an assumption that is accepted by most schools of Indian religious thought. In other words, it is not something that is demonstrated to exist; it is simply believed to exist. Many texts, Buddhist, Hindu and Jain, describe the workings of the law of karma in varying degrees of detail, but the means by which people can check for themselves whether the universe actually works according to this principle are never provided. The law of karma is accepted in the Hindu tradition, for example, because the Upaniṣads claim that this is the way the world works. It is accepted in the Buddhist tradition because the Buddha claimed to have perceived its workings during his experience of enlightenment. Much of yoga philosophy and practice only makes sense if it is understood against the backdrop of the 'law of karma'.

In essence, the idea of a law of karma is that the universe is constructed in such a way that all of our actions generate consequences according to their moral character. These consequences are known as the 'fruit' (phala), and the phrase 'karma-vipāka', the ripening of action, is often used to refer to the experience of the consequences of former actions. If this view of the universe is accepted and one reflects on the state of a person at the moment of death, it is obvious that not all of the karmic fruit generated by the person throughout a lifetime will have ripened. Hence, the power of that unripened karmic fruit will pull the entity that generated it back into some condition through which the as-yet-unexperienced fruit can find expression. This is saṃsarā (rebirth or reincarnation, depending on how one understands the nature of the entity that created the fruit in the first place).

For most Hindu schools, as well as the Jains, that entity is understood as some kind of self (ātman or jīva), whereas for the Buddhists the 'entity' is an illusion—the karma is all there is. The central concern of all schools of yoga is the termination of this process, which is regarded as inherently unsatisfactory or painful (duḥkha). The most common terms employed to refer to the termination of samsara are *mokṣa* (release), *nirvāṇa* (extinction or cooling) and *kaivalya* (isolation or aloneness). All schools use the term mokṣa on occasions, though the preferred term for Buddhists is *nirvāṇa* and for Jains *kaivalya*. These preferences reflect something of the metaphysics of each school. For the Jains, release is understood as the separation of the jīva from everything that is not itself, namely ajīva.

For the Buddhists, release is understood as the eradication or extinction of the craving and ignorance that fuel saṃsāra, whilst for Hindus of the Vedānta school it is understood as either a realization of cosmic oneness, a merger of the individual self with god or the attainment of proximity to god by the individual self.

In broad outline then, all these schools understand human destiny in terms of two options: the round of rebirth or reincarnation, and escape from that round. Although the details might differ from school to school, the common thread is that in order for escape to occur there has to be a radical reorientation on the part of an individual: from identification with the bodymind to either identification with a self, in the case of Hindus and Jains, or just seeing the self for the illusion that it is, in the case of Buddhists.

## CORRESPONDENCES

The idea that there are parallelisms bordering on identity between different realms of the universe and between words and things is far more prevalent in India that it is in the West. The orthodox brāhmanical (priestly) traditions tend to identify correspondences, or what Mircea Eliade called 'homologies', both between mental states and the levels of the cosmos and between words and things. Buddhists tend to accept the former but not the latter, so I shall explain these correspondences primarily from the brāhmanical perspective.

In the literature of the Veda (= Saṃhitā [the four Vedas], Brāhmaṇa, Āraṇyaka and Upaniṣad collections) we are told that there are three primary levels of existence in the universe: the adhidaivika (the realm of the gods, the cosmic), the adhyātmika (the realm of the self), and the adhibhautika (the realm of the material elements). Each of these levels, particularly the first two, reflects the others in terms of fundamental structure. So, for example, the wind (vāyu) is a cosmic phenomenon and a deity. Breath (prāṇa) is the wind at the level of the self (ātman) (e.g. at *RV* 10.9.3). The individual level is a microcosm of the macrocosm.

This kind of homology is also found in accounts of yogic practice. In Buddhism, for example, each of the rūpa and arūpa jhānas (meditations on form and formless states) corresponds to and offers the meditator access to the worlds or realms (loka) of form and formlessness. In other words, because the universe is organized in this way meditational experience can yield knowledge about the cosmos. It is this kind of correspondence that underpins claims to omniscience found in a number of yoga texts. Indeed, if the universe were not organized in this way it would be difficult to make sense of claims to knowledge about it made on the basis of yogic experience.

In the brāhmanical tradition, these kinds of correspondences are pervasive. They are also linked with another kind of correspondence, that of the gods and other fundamental principles of existence. For example, prāṇa (breath) is identified with āyus (life or vitality) in *Ṛgveda* 1.66.1, with Virāj (the co-creator of the universe according to *RV* 10.90), Sūrya (the sun), Prajāpati (father of beings), Mātariśvan (the aerial space) and Vāyu (wind) in *Atharvaveda* 11.4. Vāyu, in turn, is identified with ātman in *Ṛgveda* 10.168.4, which itself is identified with vāta (air) in *Ṛgveda* 7.87.2, 10.16.3 and 10.92.13. There are many other examples. In short, for many of the Rigvedic poets these terms can be used interchangeably. This, in part, is because many of the Vedic thinkers tended to trace all principles of existence back to a single origin or source, the most prominent of which were agni (fire), ātman (self, though the word had a variety of meanings in the early Vedic literature), brahman (the expansive), prāṇa (breath), puruṣa (person) and vāc (speech).

Some of these concepts cluster together more than others. Crudely, for the situation is complex, ātman, prāṇa, puruṣa and vāyu tend to go together and so too do brahman, vāc, virāj, the udgītha (high chant of the *Sāmaveda*) and the uktha (high chant of the *Ṛgveda*). Puruṣa and prāṇa have a particular association with form (rūpa) whilst brahman and vāc are particularly associated with sound (nāma or śabda). In *Ṛgveda* 10.90, we are told that three-quarters of puruṣa remained in heaven whilst one-quarter became everything that exists here. Similarly, in *Ṛgveda* 1.164 we are told that vāc divided herself into four parts, only one of which is accessible to humans.[2] In some places prāṇa and vāc are presented as partners or co-principles, e.g. *Vajasaneya Saṃhitā* 8.37; *Śatapatha Brāhmaṇa* 7.5.1.7. This link is preserved in later literature in various ways, the most common being the idea of nāma-rūpa (name and form)—what we might think of as 'individuality'. Name/sound and form/material are two sides of the same coin, two complementary aspects of reality. All forms have a corresponding sound, all sounds have a corresponding form.

This correspondence between sound and form is what underpins the efficacy of the Vedic sacrificial ritual. If you know the sounds you can control the forms. Knowledge of the sound aspects of reality gave the priests control over the form aspects. This is how the priests subjected the Vedic gods to their will. Such an understanding of the relationship between sounds/words and things/beings is fundamentally magical. Indeed, I would suggest that it is the essence of a magical view of the world. Sorcerers in almost all magical traditions use spells and incantations (words) to work their magic on the world of things (forms). In yoga, some kinds more than others, we often encounter the use of mantras, chants that are deemed to have specific effects—both psychological and physical—that derive from the nature of the particular sounds being employed. Mantras can have these effects because the universe is believed to be structured in terms of the kinds of correspondences outlined above. This is why Westerners often have difficulty in understanding how mantras work. The dominant Western view is that the relationship between words and things is essentially arbitrary: 'that which we call a rose by any other name would smell as sweet' is how Shakespeare put it in *Romeo and Juliet.*

These, then, are some of the presuppositions that lie behind many yogic teachings and practices. They are rarely stated explicitly, a fact that can sometimes cause puzzlement among Western students of yoga. There are others, some of which you, the readers, may be able to identify for yourselves. Any development of a truly Western form of yoga will have to address the issues raised by these presuppositions. Will Western practitioners of yoga want to subscribe to or be comfortable with a cyclical view of time and the idea of an ideal system of social regulation? Will they want to accept the 'law of karma' and the resultant saṃsāric process as an accurate account of the fundamental forces that determine human life and experience? Will they accept the kind of macrocosm–microcosm correspondences that ancient yoga texts presume to exist, and, perhaps most significantly, will they accept an understanding of language that puts it in a non-arbitrary relationship with the world of things? Would a system of yoga that rejected these presuppositions and claims still be yoga? To answer this question we need to determine what we mean by 'yoga' and how it differs from other kinds of spirituality. We will return to this issue in a later chapter. With these background concepts and issues in mind, we can proceed to investigate yoga in the context of the texts in which it is first mentioned.

# Chapter 2
# YOGA IN THE TEXTS OF THE VEDA

The texts of the Veda (Veda means 'knowledge') are commonly divided into four groups. The first of these is Saṃhitā (the four collections of Vedic hymns: the *Ṛg, Yajur, Sāma* and *Atharva Vedas*). The second is Brāhmaṇa (commentaries and interpretations of the hymns along with guidance on the conduct of rituals and some philosophical speculations). Third is Āraṇyaka (technically 'forest books', for use by brāhmans who had retired to the forest and who wished to conduct alternative versions of the sacrificial ritual). The final group is Upaniṣad (literally 'sitting down near' the teacher—hence 'secret/esoteric teachings that are not to be overheard by eavesdroppers'). Some texts employ only a twofold division into Saṃhitā and Brāhmaṇa, the latter understood to contain not only the Brāhmaṇas but the Āraṇyakas and Upaniṣads as well. This is hardly surprising as the divisions between these types of text are far from sharp. Indeed, the final section of the *Śatapatha Brāhmaṇa* is called the *Bṛhad Āraṇyaka Upaniṣad* (generally regarded as the oldest of the Upaniṣads), and the oldest Upaniṣads all have pronounced Āraṇyaka features.[1]

A reader of the Saṃhitās and the Upaniṣads notices a radical shift of emphasis and the introduction of many new concepts in the latter. S.N. Dasgupta has even claimed that 'The passage of the Indian mind from the Brāhmanic to the Upaniṣad thought is probably the most remarkable event in the history of philosophic thought.'[2] Although something of an overstatement, this comment does draw our attention to the significant differences that exist between Saṃhitā and Upaniṣadic thought.

The religion of the Saṃhitās has three prominent features: a polytheistic conception of deity; an emphasis on the importance of sacrificial ritual; and an understanding of post-mortem experience that postulates eternal existence in one or other heavenly realms. A consideration of these themes allows an informed judgement to be made about the relationship between the thought of the Saṃhitās and that of the Upaniṣads, particularly in terms of what they have in common and where they are different.

## POLYTHEISM

In the early Vedic period[3] the gods were principally known under two general titles: asura (sovereign or majestic one) and deva (shining one). By the end of the epic period (400 BCE—400 CE) the meaning of asura had changed to 'demon' whilst 'deva' remained a title for the gods. An interesting point about this development is that in Iran, where the Zoroastrian Avestan texts have much in common with the Vedic Saṃhitās, the reverse occurred. The Avestan for asura is 'ahura' and for deva it is 'daeva'. In Iran, ahura came to mean lord or god, whilst daeva came to mean demon, from which we get the English terms daemon and demonic. The primary divinity in the Iranian pantheon came to be Ahura Mazda, the wise lord, whose counterpart in India was Varuṇa, lord of the moral order (ṛta) who can see into human hearts. Varuṇa, however, fell from prominence in India and in the Purāṇic period[4] became lord of the deep waters; and Indra, who was classed as a demon in Iran, came to be, for a time, the undisputed king of the gods.

Most of the Vedic gods can be identified with one of the three realms of 'the triple world' of sky, atmosphere and earth, though some elude this classification and scholars have suggested a variety of classificatory solutions to this problem. Here I shall simply opt for a 'miscellaneous' category for those divinities who seem to be associated with neither earth, atmosphere nor sky.

### SKY GODS

| | |
|---|---|
| Dyaus- | the sky |
| Varuṇa- | lord of the moral order (ṛta) |
| Mitra- | 'the friend', the benign power of the sun |
| Sūrya- | the sun |

| | |
|---|---|
| Savitṛ- | 'the stimulator', bestows life span, psychopomp (guide of spirits after death) |
| Pūṣan- | 'the prosperer', bountiful power of the sun |
| Uṣas- | the dawn |
| Viṣṇu- | the benevolence of the sun |
| 2 Aśvins- | 'lords of horses', removing distress and illness |
| Candra- | the moon |

ATMOSPHERIC GODS

| | |
|---|---|
| Indra- | king of gods, lord of storm |
| Trita Aptya- | connected with lightning and rain, Indra's ally |
| Apām Napāt- | 'son of waters', the lightning |
| Vāyu/Vāta- | the wind |
| Rudra- | the 'howler', destructive, bringer and healer of disease |
| Parjanya- | the rain cloud |
| Mātāriśvan- | who brought fire down from heaven |
| Āpaḥ- | the waters, the cleansers |
| Ahi Budhnya- | 'serpent of the deep', 'a personification of the writhing cloud'? |
| Aja Ekapad- | 'one-footed unborn/goat', the lightning? |
| Maruts/Rudras- | children of Rudra, storm gods, sometimes 21 in number, sometimes 180 |

TERRESTRIAL GODS

| | |
|---|---|
| Pṛthvī- | earth |
| Agni- | fire |
| Bṛhaspati/ Brahmaṇaspati- | the divine priest, connected with Agni |
| Soma- | god of the soma plant, later identified with the moon |
| Sindu- Vipaś- Sutaudrī- Sarasvatī- | rivers |
| Samudra- | the sea |

MISCELLANEOUS GODS

| | |
|---|---|
| Dhatṛ- | the 'creator' |
| Vidhatṛ- | the 'disposer' |
| Dhartṛ- | the 'supporter' |
| Trātṛ- | the 'protector' |
| Netṛ- | the 'leader' |
| Tvaṣṭr- | the 'fashioner' |
| Prajāpati- | lord of creatures, sometimes the creator |
| Viśvakarman- | the all-creating |
| Hiraṇyagarbha- | the golden embryo |
| Rohita- | the red one, originally an epithet of the sun |

The *Ṛgveda* also mentions Aṃśa, Aryaman, Bhaga, Daksa and Mārtāṇḍa, all of whom are members of the group called Ādityas, children of Āditi (primordial vastness). These gods should therefore be added to the list of sky gods. The number of Ādityas, however, varies from place to place. In *RV* 10.72.8 eight Ādityas are mentioned, Mitra, Sūrya and Varuṇa being the other three.

In the Brāhmaṇa literature, the three classes of gods are called Ādityas, Maruts and Vasus, ruling respectively the sky, atmosphere and earth. In these lists, however, the numbers have been reduced to twelve, eleven and eight respectively.

In most cases, the natural phenomena that the gods represent can still be identified in the hymns to them. By the end of the epic period, however, they had become anthropomorphized and presented as divine humans living in a heavenly realm. The Vedic hymns thus present us with what might be called 'a primitive polytheism'. It seems unlikely to me that the early Vedic poets regarded their gods as manifestations of some divine monistic reality, though a number of writers have argued that this is the case.[5] On the other hand, we can identify certain tendencies in the Vedic hymns which might have provided inspiration for such a view and the foundations for its future development. One of these is what F. Max Muller called 'henotheism', a view in which one god is understood to be the true identity of all the others: one-god-at-a-time-ism. He considered this to be a distinct stage in the evolution of religious consciousness. His evolutionary notions have been rejected by most scholars, though the phenomenon itself can be clearly discerned in the Vedic hymns, as this extract from one of the oldest sections reveals:

> Hero of Heroes, Agni! Thou art Indra, thou art Viṣṇu of the mighty stride, adorable: Thou, Brahmaṇaspati, the Brahman finding wealth: thou, O Sustainer, with thy wisdom tendest us.
>
> Agni, thou art King Varuṇa whose laws stand fast; as Mitra, Wonder-Worker, thou must be implored. Aryaman, heroes' Lord, art thou, enriching all, and liberal Aṃśa in the synod, O thou God.
>
> Thou givest strength, as Tvaṣṭar, to the worshipper: thou wielding Mitra's power hast kinship with the Dames. Thou, urging thy fleet coursers, givest noble steeds: a host of heroes art thou with thy great store of wealth.
>
> Rudra art thou, the Asura of mighty heaven: thou art the Maruts' host, thou art the lord of food. Thou goest with red winds: bliss hast thou in thine home. As Pūṣan thou thyself protectest worshippers.
>
> Giver of wealth art thou to him who honours thee; thou art God Savitar, granter of precious things. As Bhaga, Lord of men! thou rulest over wealth, and guardest in his house him who hath served thee well.
>
> (*RV* 2.1.3-7)[6]

The other tendency is towards tracing all gods and phenomena back to a single principle and is found primarily in the later texts of the Saṃhitās, namely *Ṛgveda* 1 and 10, and sections of the *Atharvaveda.* Examples are to be found in *Ṛgveda* 1.164, *Ṛgveda* 10.90 and *Atharvaveda* 11.4. Hence,

> They call it (the One Real) Indra, Mitra, Varuṇa, Agni. Then there is the heavenly bird Garutmant (Sun). The inspired priests speak of the One Real (ekam sat) in many ways. They call it Agni, Yama, Mātāriśvan.
>
> (*RV* 1.164.46)[7]

> It is the Man [puruṣa] who is all this, whatever has been and whatever is to be. He is the ruler of immortality, when he grows beyond everything through food. Such is his greatness, and

> the Man is yet more than this. All creatures are a quarter of him; three quarters are what is immortal in heaven.
>
> (*RV* 10.90.2, 3)[8]

> Homage to prāṇa in whose control is this all, who hath been lord of all, in whom all stands firm.
>
> Breath (prāṇa) clothes (anu-vas) human beings (praja), as a father a dear son; breath is lord of all, both what breathes and what does not.
>
> Breath is Virāj, breath is the directress, breath all worship, breath is the sun [Sūrya], the moon; breath they call Prajāpati.
>
> Breath they call Mātariśvan; breath is called the wind [vāyu]; in breath what has been and what will be, in breath is all established (pratiṣṭha).
>
> (*AV* 11.4.1, 10, 12, 15)

It is clear from the above that one of the most prominent features of the Upaniṣadic world view, the monistic ontology, was already being developed in pre-Upanisadic Vedic literature. I have argued elsewhere that at the centre of these developments was the concept of prāṇa (breath/vital energy),[9] a concept which underwent significant marginalization in the early Vedānta but which became central again in many forms of tantric yoga. This is not, however, to claim that the Upaniṣads can be understood as simply continuing to develop ideas that were initially formulated in the context of early Vedic religion. The Upaniṣads show clear signs of influence from outside sources, and this is particularly apparent with regard to the adoption of yoga practice as a means of attaining their metaphysical goals. This issue will be explored more fully below.

## THE SACRIFICE

In its earliest, and perhaps pre-Indian form, the Vedic sacrifice appears to have been a kind of hospitality rite where the gods were invited to participate in a ritual meal, which was probably celebrated around a simple fire with a grass-strewn space set aside for the divine guests. The evidence of the *Ṛgveda* suggests, however, that by the time the hymns were collected together the sacrifice had already become more complex than the simple hospitality rite, and that three fires were being used. Similarly, the earliest form of sacrifice probably required the services of just one priest. By the end of the Vedic period up to 16 could be involved. In the early period, the priest was a celebrant who officiated at the rite; by the end of the Vedic period he had become a magician. As A.B. Keith puts it, when commenting on the role of the priest in the earlier period,

> Great as the position of the priest was in the Vedic community he does not claim as yet to be powerful enough to constrain the gods to his will.[10]

This started to change when the idea developed that the sacrifice could be used to 'persuade' the gods to deliver specific benefits to individuals and the community. Eventually, the sacrifice came to be regarded, at least by the priests, as the most important of all human activities. Their reasoning seems to have developed along the following lines:

- if the sacrifice generates enough power to coerce the gods it could do an awful lot of damage if it got out of control;
- on the other hand, if a misperformed sacrifice could have so much destructive power, then surely a perfectly performed one could have the opposite effect, could help to sustain the natural order;
- so sacrifices need to be performed regularly in order to preserve the structure of the cosmos, which, by the late Vedic period, was beginning to be understood as the result of an initial sacrifice that was performed by the gods (see *RV* 10.90, the *Puruṣa Sūkta*, for the fullest expression of this view).

The principal idea underlying all forms of sacrificial ritual seems to be that it creates a link between sacred and profane modes of existence that can be exploited in some way for the benefit of the sacrificer and those represented by him (performers at sacrificial rituals have tended to be mainly male, and in India this was often justified on grounds of purity: females are inherently less pure than males, primarily because of menstruation).[11] Various theories about the nature of sacrifice have been offered by scholars of various persuasions, and I shall not discuss them here. Rather, I shall simply base my comments on the work by Henri Hubert and Marcel Mauss, whose analyses I find generally persuasive. For them, the first part of the sacrificial ritual is concerned with what they call 'sacralization', that is, creating a situation in which sacred power can be channelled into the profane world.

In many cultures, and later in India, such a situation is often identified with one or more places (sacred spots) that frequently have a temple built on them. In the nomadic culture of the early Vedas, however, it was created by setting aside an area of ground and rendering it fitting for the receipt of sacred power by separating it from the land around by marking it off with fire, one of the principal manifestations of the god Agni. In Vedic times this space was called a 'vihāra', a term later employed to refer to a temple. Within this, the three fires necessary for all public sacrifices were set up. Also within the vihāra was the vedi or altar, which could be a mound or a pit. When animal sacrifices were being performed, a stake, called a yupa, was set up next to the vedi.

These public (śrauta) sacrifices were of two kinds: regular and occasional. The former were required by changes in the month and seasons—enabling an ongoing participation in the maintenance of order; the latter were for specific purposes, often the benefit of some patron (yajamāna) who was paying for it. On these occasions the size of the yupa was linked to the size of the patron, its length being the same height as him when he stood with upraised arms. The patron's preparation for the ritual has certain features in common with yoga practice. In order to leave his impurities behind (necessary because the sacred power could damage an impure person) he bathed, shaved, fasted, avoided sexual activity and sought to generate 'tapas', purificatory heat. Such purification sacralizes the patron and makes him a suitable recipient of sacred power. Because of their role, priests have to maintain a high level of purity, and here we may have the basis for some of their later claims to high status.

The high point of the ritual comes when the offering is sacrificed. This 'opens the door', as it were, to the influx of spiritual power and the offering becomes saturated with it. The offering is then consumed and the sacred power absorbed by the participants. The process of desacralization then begins. This prepares the participants for re-entry into the profane world and involves various kinds of cleansing procedures to ensure that no vestiges of the sacred spill over into the profane realm.

We can thus understand the sacrificial process in terms of a standard curve that moves from the profane to the sacred and back again to the profane:

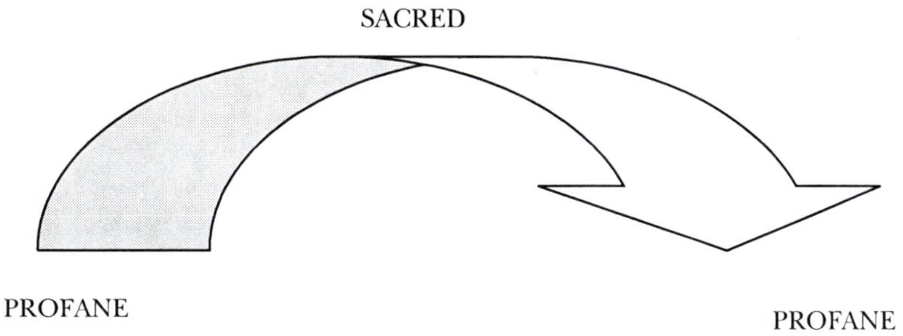


This curve will vary according to the type of sacrifice being performed. Sacrifices of the initiatory type are typified by a long upward curve (the idea is to imbibe the maximum amount of spiritual power), followed by a steep downward curve, so that the gains are preserved. Sacrifices of the expiatory type, where the sacrificers and/or patrons wish to shed negative spiritual power (sin), have the opposite: a steep upward curve for sacralization and a long downward curve to ensure that all the negative power is left behind.

The priests who officiated at these sacrifices formed three, and later four, main groups. Each group was connected with one of the four Vedas. Chief of the hymn-singing priests was the hotṛ, who sang hymns of praise from the *Ṛgveda*. Chief of the priests concerned with the sacrificial activity was the advaryu, who recited formulas from the *Yajurveda*. Chief of the sāman-singing priests was the udgātṛ, who chanted chants from the *Sāmaveda*. Chief of the overseeing priests was the brāhman, who uttered mantras from the *Atharvaveda*.

A.B. Keith tells us that the 'later ritual', presumably that dealt with in the Brāhmaṇas, requires 16 priests to participate in the soma ritual. These are arranged in four groups of four (see table overleaf).

However, he reckons that the Nesṭṛ, the Brāhmaṇācchansin, the Potṛ and the Agnīdhra should really be grouped with the Hotṛ. Nevertheless, even despite this long list, an important priest in many other sacrifices, the Agnīdh—assistant to the Advaryu—is not accounted for.

| *Hotṛ* | *Advaryu* | *Udgātṛ* | *Brāhman* |
|---|---|---|---|
| Maitrāvaruṇa (also called Praśāstṛ and Upavaktṛ) | Pratiprasthātṛ | Prastotṛ | Brāhmaṇācchansin |
| Achāvaka | Neṣṭṛ | Pratihartṛ | Potṛ |
| Grāvastut | Unnetṛ | Subrahmaṇya | Agnīdhra |

## LIFE AFTER DEATH

The Vedic view of life after death has little in common with the later Indian notion of perpetual rebirth (saṃsāra) fuelled by the fruits of action until the attainment of release (mokṣa). Rather, the Vedic aspiration was for a deceased person to join the ancestors (pitṛ) in a heavenly realm ruled by Yama, lord of the dead.

For the Vedic seers, a human being was composite, created out of different parts that return to their source when a person dies. The number, precise nature and ultimate destiny of these various parts is not, however, always specified in the Vedic hymns, and scholars continue to debate the details. The broad outline is, nevertheless, reasonably clear.

The material parts of a person go back to the elements from which they arose, whilst the immaterial ones proceed to the realm of the ancestors. Making sense of the passages in which this process is outlined can be problematic, not least because a number of the key terms undergo changes of meaning in later forms of Indian religion. For example, *Ṛgveda* 10.16 suggests that the eye goes to the sun, the spirit (ātman) goes to the wind and the other parts go, according to their natures, to the sky, the earth, the waters and the plants. In later Vedāntic thought, ātman becomes an immutable essence, the unchanging reality behind the ephemeral flux of forms, the inner controller within all living beings. In this Ṛgvedic passage, however, it still has clear associations with the verbal root from which it is derived: √ an, to breathe, and with other vitalistic terms such as vāyu (wind), prāṇa (breath), vāta (air), asu (breath) and āyus (life). In this context it is perfectly appropriate for ātman to return to its source in the wind. Likewise, in almost all later Indian religious thought, manas (mind) is part of the illusory ephemera of saṃsāra or a constituent of non-sentient material nature (prakṛti). In *Ṛgveda*

10.16, however, we are told that the manas goes with the asu and the aja (unborn part) to the realm of immortality where they rejoin the tanū. This last is the reflexive pronoun, the self, and the core of individuality. It is sometimes, and on occasions mistakenly, translated as 'body'. The entity that survives death and becomes immortal is thus, like its pre-mortem counterpart, a composite one.

In the realm of Yama, the deceased enjoy a most felicitous existence. Wishes are fulfilled, food is delightful, water is fresh, light abounds and movement is effortless (*RV* 9.113). The *Atharvaveda* is more earthy in its descriptions. The deceased meet fathers, mothers, wives and children (*AV* 6.120; 8.3), and sexual gratification is abundant (*AV* 3.29; 3.56; 4.34; 10.14; 10.135). They enjoy the company of the gods and join them in receiving sacrificial offerings (*RV* 10.15; 10.56). As H.D. Griswold describes it,

> Being assimilated to the gods and leading the same kind of life, the Fathers (pitṛ) receive almost divine honours, and in one passage (10.56.4) are apparently called gods. They constitute a special group of deities or at least of demi-gods.[12]

There is, however, the possibility of a less benign destiny. A couple of Rigvedic hymns, 6.5 and 7.104, mention a deep pit, gloomy and bottomless, into which evildoers fall. This, 6.5 tells us, they create for themselves. Likewise, entry into Yama's realm is dependent on a person doing good. The practice of austerity (tapas) can open the way to the world of the fathers (*RV* 10.154) but more efficacious still is generosity. Those who are generous gain immortality (*RV* 1.125; 10.107; 10.117).

In terms of the soteriology model offered in the Introduction, Vedic spirituality can be understood as gaining its knowledge primarily from revelation, framing the problem of the human situation in terms of death, solving the problem mainly by means of effort (Yama has an important role to play by marking out the way) and moving towards a pluralistic (though there are hints of monism) solution where the blessed deceased dwell with gods and other ancestors in a heavenly realm. In Rawlinson's model, it would be Hot–Structured: magical techniques are employed in a systematic manner.

## THE UPANIṢADS

The Upaniṣads constitute the fourth and final part of the Veda; hence, they are often referred to as the Vedānta (Veda's End). The philosophical school known as Vedānta is that which bases its teachings on the Upaniṣads. There are many Upaniṣads, many more than the traditional number of 108, though it is generally recognized amongst scholars that only a few are genuinely Vedic. The influential Vedāntic theologian Śaṅkara comments on or refers to twelve Upanisads: *Aitareya, Bṛhadāraṇyaka, Chāndogya, Īśā, Kaṭhaka/Kaṭha, Kauṣītakī, Kena, Māṇḍūkya, Muṇḍaka, Praśna* and *Śvetāśvatara.* R.E. Hume adds the *Maitrāyaṇīya/Maitrī* to his list of what he calls *The Thirteen Principal Upanisads,* Paul Deussen adds the *Mahānārāyaṇa* to his list in *The Philosophy of the Upanisads,* and Sarvapelli Radhakhrishnan adds the *Jabala* and *Paingala* to his collection of *The Principal Upanishads.* So the number of genuinely authoritative Upaniṣads is small, though somewhat variable. Deussen offers a relative chronology of the texts on his list, and this is accepted by Hume apart from the *Śvetāśvatara*—which he places in the third group along with the *Maitrī* and the *Māṇḍūkya.*[13]

Deussen's list, incorporating Hume's emendation, is:

**Early Prose Upaniṣads** (all pre-Buddhist)
*Bṛhadāraṇyaka*
*Chāndogya*
*Taittirīya*
*Aitareya*
*Kauṣītakī*
*Kena* (on the borderline)

**Middle (Verse) Upaniṣads**
*Kaṭhaka/Kaṭha*
*Īśā*
*Muṇḍaka*
*Mahānārāyaṇa*

**Later Prose Upaniṣads**
*Praśna*
*Maitrāyanīya/Maitrī*
*Māṇḍūkya*
*Śvetāśvatara* (verse)

Deussen comments that the Upaniṣads of the first group are usually closely interwoven with their respective Brāhmaṇa and Āraṇyaka texts whereas this feature is absent from those in the second group. The third group, apart from the verse *Śvetāśvatara*, exhibit many of the features of later Sanskrit prose: complexity, elaboration and repetition. Subsequent Upaniṣads tended to be attached to the *Atharvaveda* and were not regarded as authoritative by most commentators.

Each Upaniṣad was preserved and transmitted by one of the Vedic schools (śākha), e.g. Aitareyins, Jaiminīyas:

| *TIME* | *Ṛgveda* | *Sāmaveda* | *Yajurveda (Black)* | *Yajurveda (White)* | *Atharvaveda* |
|---|---|---|---|---|---|
| Early Prose | Aitareya (Aitareyins) | Chāndogya (Tāṇḍins) | Taittirīya (Taittirīyakas) | Bṛhadāraṇyaka (Vājasaneyins) | |
| | Kauṣītaki (Kauṣītakins) | Kena (Jaiminīyas) | | | |
| Middle Verse | | | Kaṭhaka (Kaṭhas) | Īṣā (Vājasaneyins) | Muṇḍaka |
| | | | Mahānārāyaṇa (Taittirīyakas) | | |
| Later Prose | | | Maitrāyanīya (Maitrāyanīyas) | | Māṇḍūkya |
| | | | Śvetāśvatara (Kaṭhas) | | Praśna |

This arrangement highlights the linkages between different Upaniṣads and, most interesting in terms of yoga philosophy, shows that the Upaniṣads in which yoga is described in most detail: the *Kaṭha, Maitrī* and *Śvetāśvatara* are all attached to the *Black Yajurveda.*

Despite the fact that all of these texts are regarded as śruti (revelation) and therefore treated as infallible, Western commentators are generally agreed that they do not all teach the same thing and that one can often detect different hands at work even in the same Upaniṣad. Nevertheless, there are some dominant themes. Perhaps the most significant is what we might call the karma-saṃsāra-mokṣa complex. The Upaniṣads are the earliest texts to introduce the notions of saṃsāra (wandering—here from life to life), karma (action) as a moral principle that is built into the universe, and mokṣa, release from this process.

In the earliest Upaniṣads, the new doctrines of karma and saṃsāra are combined with or introduced through a reinterpretation of the older Vedic notion of two pathways that a person can follow after death. The first of these is the way of the gods (devayāna), also called the path of light (arcirmārga); the second is the way of the ancestors (pitṛyāna), also called the path of darkness (dhūmamārga). If, after death, a person follows the path of the gods then the destination is the realm of brahma (brahmaloka), also called the realm of truth (satyaloka). From this realm there is no return. Hence, brahmaloka became identified with the attainment of release from rebirth. However, if a person follows the path of the ancestors the destination becomes the realm of the moon (candraloka). From here beings return to the earth after enjoying the fruits of their previous good actions. The *Bṛhadāraṇyaka Upaniṣad* (*BAU* 6.2.15-16) also mentions a third way that is taken by those who know nothing of the other two. Such beings become 'crawling and flying insects and whatever there is here that bites'. The text itself is a little more complicated than this and is worth quoting in full, not just for the provision of all the information but also because it reminds us that modern accounts of Upaniṣadic teaching often omit awkward bits and present the teachings in a modified form that is likely to be easily understood by modern Western audiences.

> 15. Those who know this, and those too who in the forest truly worship (upāsate) [with] faith (śraddhā), pass into the flame [of the cremation-fire]; from the flame, into the day; from the day, into the half month of the waxing moon; from the half month of the waxing moon, into the six months during which the sun moves northward; from these months, into the world of the gods (deva-loka); from the world of the gods, into the sun; from the sun, into the lightning-fire. A Person (puruṣa) consisting of mind (mānasa) goes to those regions of lightning and conducts them to the Brahma-worlds. In those Brahma-worlds they dwell for long extents. Of these there is no return.
>
> 16. But they who by sacrificial offering, charity, and austerity conquer the worlds, pass into the smoke [of the cremation-fire]; from the smoke, into the night; from the night, into the half month of the waning moon; from the half month of the waning moon, into the six months during which the sun moves

> southward; from those months, into the world of the fathers; from the world of the fathers, into the moon. Reaching the moon, they become food. There the gods—as they say to King Soma, 'Increase! Decrease!'—even so feed upon them there. When that passes away for them, then they pass forth into this space; from space, into air; from air, into rain; from rain, into the earth. On reaching the earth they become food. Again they are offered in the fire of man. Thence they are born in the fire of woman. Rising up into the world, they cycle round again thus. But those who know not these two ways, become crawling and flying insects and whatever there is here that bites.[14]

What this passage does not provide is details of the mechanism underlying a person's choice of path. That is provided elsewhere in the text, in passages such as 4.4.5-6:

> According as one acts, according as one conducts himself, so does he become. The doer of good becomes good, the doer of evil becomes evil. One becomes virtuous by virtuous action, bad by bad action...
> Where one's mind is attached—the inner self goes thereto with action, being attached to it alone. Obtaining the end of his action, whatever he does in this world he comes again from that world, to this world of action.[15]

What is more, it is the moral quality of one's acts that determines the situation into which one is born. *Chāndogya Upaniṣad* 5.10.7 states:

> those who are of pleasant conduct here—the prospect is, indeed, that they will enter a pleasant womb, either the womb of a Brāhman, or the womb of a Kshatriya, or the womb of a Vaiśya. But those who are of stinking conduct here—the prospect is, indeed, that they will enter a stinking womb, either the womb of a dog, or the womb of a swine, or the womb of an outcaste (caṇḍāla).[16]

By employing the two concepts of karma and saṃsāra, the Upaniṣads are able to explain both the nature of the human condition and the reason why there is such diversity in the life experiences of human beings: different actions produce different results and hence destinies. They seek to go beyond simple explanation, however, and offer a way to go beyond the cycle of rebirth. Behind the phenomena of saṃsāra, we are told, lies a unitary reality from which all diversity arises. This is variously named, though the two most frequently used terms are ātman (from the verb √an, to breathe) and brahman (from the verb √bṛh, to expand). The way to escape from the round of rebirth is to acquire a knowledge of this unitary reality. The earliest Upaniṣads provide little by way of information about the means by which one gains such knowledge, however. There is mention of a kind of meditation (upāsana—see *BAU* 1.4.14, 2.1.3 and 2.1.10), but it is not explained exactly how this relates to the acquisition of liberating knowledge. The impression one gets from the earliest Upaniṣads is that this knowledge (jñāna) is obtained through a careful analysis of the nature of the world, a method reminiscent of what later came to be known as jñāna yoga (the discipline of knowledge or philosophical reflection).[17] Not until the middle Upaniṣads are we informed that the method par excellence for achieving liberating insight is that of 'yoga'.

The earliest mention of the term 'yoga' as a kind of spiritual practice in Indian religious literature is found in the *Taittirīya Upaniṣad* (*TU* 2.4). *Taittirīya* 2 is a famous passage that presents the doctrine of the five persons or layers (later called 'sheaths', kośa) that make up the individual. Outermost of these is the person made of food (anna-maya-puruṣa); within that and having the same form as it, is the person made of breath (prāṇa-maya-puruṣa); within that and having the same form as it, is the person made of mind (mano-maya-puruṣa); within that and having the same form as it, is the person made of understanding (vijñāna-maya-puruṣa), and within that, also having the same form, is the person made of bliss (ānanda-maya-puruṣa). Each of these persons has five parts: head, right side, left side, torso and lower part.[18] Yoga, this text informs us, is the torso (ātman) of the person made of understanding. Some writers, Karel Werner is a notable example,[19] take this usage to indicate an understanding of yoga that is a genuine prefigurement of later forms of yoga such as that found in Patañjali's *Yoga Sūtra*, but the case for this view, whilst ingenious, is hardly conclusive.

The first unambiguous references to a recognizable system of yogic thought and practice in the Upaniṣads come in two sections of the *Kaṭha Upaniṣad*: 3.3-9 and 6.6-15. In the first of these passages the mind is likened to the reins of a chariot, which is the body, having the senses as the horses. Controlling the mind is the intellect (buddhi), which is likened to a charioteer. Above the intellect is the lord of the chariot, the self (ātman).[20] The theory underlying this image is that there are various kinds of forces that the mind has to deal with. Often, these arise from the senses, though they can also arise from the mind itself. For most people, the power of sensory inputs, memories and imaginings is so influential that their lives cannot be said to be controlled by the intellect. The yogin is one who, through the intellect and mind, brings the body and senses under control. This, of course, is not an easy task. Many of us have experienced the difficulties involved in self-control when we have sought to achieve some goal that involved concentration and discipline. Study provides a good example; it requires high degrees of concentration and can be exhausting. Most of us can only do it in short bursts.

In the middle Upaniṣads, knowledge (jñāna) is presented as being dependent on a person's ability to achieve a certain level of mental concentration, an achievement that is accomplished through the practice of yoga, which, as *Kaṭha* 6.11 informs us in the earliest formal definition of yoga, is 'the firm holding back of the senses' (indriya dhāraṇām). This leads to the state of being undistracted (apramatta). By the time of the *Maitrī Upaniṣad*, different stages of mental concentration were being recognized. *Maitrī* 6.18 outlines a sixfold yoga practice consisting of breath control (prāṇāyāma), sense withdrawal (pratyāhāra), concentration (dhyāna), deeper concentration (dhāraṇā), contemplation (tarka) and absorption (samādhi). There are a number of points to note about this list. In the first place, five of the six components of this list are found in Patañjali's later eightfold yoga, tarka being the one omitted. Patañjali's other three components are restraints (yama), disciplines (niyama) and posture (āsana). Patañjali puts these three at the beginning of his list as they are essentially preparatory for the mental practices that follow. Tarka was omitted, probably to keep the number of components to eight, mirroring the eightfold path of the Buddhists. The second noteworthy point about these lists is that the order of dhyāna and dhāraṇā is reversed in Patañjali's version. This probably indicates not that one or other author got the order wrong but that these terms had not acquired fixed meanings at the time these texts were compiled. Such a conclusion is supported by the treatment of the same terms in the Buddhist context. The eighth step of the Buddhist eightfold path is right concentration (samyak samādhi [Sanskrit], sammā samādhi [Pāli]) and, like Patañjali's eight-limbed yoga, it contains a number of stages within it. The point to note is that these stages are often referred to as dhyānas (Pāli, jhāna), which points to the fluidity of the terminology at this stage of the traditions' development.

So, where and when did yoga originate?

As noted above, Surendranath Dasgupta claims that 'The passage of the Indian mind from the brāhmanic to the Upaniṣad thought is probably the most remarkable event in the history of philosophic thought.'[21] Although it is something of an overstatement, Dasgupta's comment draws our attention to the significant shift in thinking about spiritual matters that is evident in the two sets of texts. The gods are much less prominent in the Upaniṣads than they are in the Vedas; so too is the sacrifice. Even more striking is the change in ideas about post-mortem existence. No longer do the material parts of a person go back to their natural homes and the immaterial ones to join the ancestors in heaven. Now, all those who do not have a direct experience of the invisible source of everything return to the world to be born again and again. What is more, at least some of those who were introducing the new ideas were highly critical of the older forms and their proponents.

For example, in *Chāndogya Upaniṣad* 6, Uddālaka challenges head on the claim found in Vedic texts such as *Ṛgveda* 10.72.2-3, *Śatapatha Brāhmaṇa* 6.1.1 and *Taittirīya Brāhmaṇa* 2.2.9 and also, interestingly, in *Chāndogya Upaniṣad* 3.19 and *Taittirīya Upaniṣad* 2.7.1, that being arose out of non-being:

> 'In the beginning, my dear, this world was just Being (sat), one only, without a second. To be sure, some people say: "In the beginning this world was just Non-being (asat), one only without a second; from that Non-being Being was produced".'
>
> But verily, my dear, whence could this be? said he. How from Non-being could Being be produced? On the contrary, my dear, in the beginning this world was just Being, one only, without a second.[22]

Two points are worth noting about this passage: first, that, like a number of other Upaniṣadic teachers, Uddālaka is critical of traditional Vedic teachings; the second is that other Upaniṣadic teachers are happy to affirm the very same teachings. In other words, some sections of the Upaniṣads are much more radical, much less

Veda-affirming than others. Indeed, this pattern of both affirming and challenging Vedic orthodoxy can be seen to operate throughout most of subsequent Brāhmanical religious history.

Consider also the following passage from the *Muṇḍaka,* a middle period Upaniṣad:

> Unsafe boats, however, are these sacrificial forms,
> The eighteen,* in which is expressed the lower work.
> The fools who approve that as the better,
> Go again to old age and death.
>
> Those abiding in the midst of ignorance,
> Self-wise, thinking themselves learned,
> Hard smitten, go around deluded,
> Like blind men led by one who is himself blind.
>
> Manifoldly living in ignorance,
> They think to themselves, childishly: 'We have accomplished our aim!'
> Since doers of deeds (karmin) do not understand, because of passion (rāga),
> Therefore, when their worlds are exhausted, they sink down wretched.
>
> Thinking sacrifice and merit is the chiefest thing,
> Naught better do they know—deluded!
> Having had enjoyment on the top of the heaven won by good works,
> They re-enter this world, or a lower. (*MundU* 1.2.7-10)[23]

This is savage stuff. For brāhmans who think themselves wise, there can be few insults more offensive than being called a deluded fool who thinks like a child, blindly following others who are blind. Indeed, the Buddha, who is critical of the brāhmans on many occasions, is never quite this severe. The higher knowledge that leads to freedom from rebirth, according to the *Muṇḍaka,* is only available to those who live on alms in the forest, practising austerity (tapas) with faith (śraddha), i.e. to world renouncers. This is a major shift, and we can understand why Dasgupta was impressed by it. Exactly

*The four Vedas plus their Brāhmaṇas, Sūtras and Aṅgas.

why and how it happened is, however, more difficult to determine than is the fact that it did happen.

A number of writers have offered theories that can explain at least some of the reasons. I will briefly comment on four of them here. Two of these are part of more general theories of human development and two are specific to the evolution of Indian spirituality.

The two general theories are those offered by Jared Diamond and Julian Jaynes. Diamond points out that 'the first farmers in many areas were smaller and less well nourished, suffered from more serious diseases, and died on the average at a younger age than the hunter-gatherers they replaced'.[24] The reasons for this are complex, but include the facts that a settled lifestyle keeps people close to their waste products (nomads just leave them behind) and the diseases that these bring. They are also in more enclosed spaces with animals and the diseases that this brings. Reductions in food variety, through over-exploitation of local flora and fauna, and over-reliance on abundant though nutrient-deficient crops also had adverse effects. Social differences increase too. Some become very wealthy and powerful whilst other become impoverished, a situation that creates a variety of unpleasant consequences for human beings.[25] In short, early agricultural life was, in many ways, more dismal than its nomadic predecessor. Suffering increased, and so too, probably, did the desire on the part of many people to escape from it. In the period during which the Upaniṣads were composed and Buddhism, Jainism and other world renouncer groups appeared, most Indians had abandoned nomadic lifestyles and adopted a settled existence in villages and cities. It would not be surprising to find, given Diamond's comments, that spiritual teachings also underwent significant changes in response to the new kinds of problem. The emphasis on duḥkhānta (the end of suffering) that is a prominent feature of most yoga systems would be just the kind of change that someone who had read Diamond's hypothesis would expect.

The other general theory was put forward by Julian Jaynes in the 1970s. He argues that something significant happened to human consciousness in the period between the composition of the *Iliad* and the *Odyssey* in the West and the Vedas and Upaniṣads (which he takes as happening around the same time) in India. What we encounter in the *Iliad* and the Vedas, he suggests, are human beings who make decisions in a manner that is quite different from that adopted by modern people. Then, the stress of decision making prompted the right hemisphere of the brain to communicate an answer to the left by means of auditory hallucinations that were experienced as the voices of gods. Hence these texts are full of people who are the recipients of direct communications from deities. This feature is far less prominent in the *Odyssey* and the Upaniṣads. Instead, we find that people tend to make decisions by working out the best course from a range of alternatives or deciding that some piece of traditional wisdom is faulty and needs to be challenged. Such independence from tradition, with all its advantages for problem solving and planning, came at a price: disconnection from what was perceived as divine authority, and a consequent experience of uncertainty and anxiety. So, since the divine no longer came to humans, humans had to start seeking out and making connection with the divine. Herein lies the birth of religious mysticism, which is essentially a human quest to find divinity within the self. The Upaniṣads, Buddhism, Jainism and other traditions of yoga all exhibit this mystical orientation. That they began to arrive on the Indian scene when they did is, according to Jaynes, no coincidence—for it was part of a much more general change that was happening around the same time in different parts of the world.

The two theories that are specific to the development of Indian religion have not been articulated as such by individual authors. Rather, they are implicit in the ways that scholars explain the changes and continuities within the religious traditions of India. I call these two theories the Developmental Explanation and the Interaction Explanation. Simply put, scholars who favour the Developmental Explanation tend to account for the changes on the Indian religious scene in terms of the gradual evolution of Vedic ideas, either as elaborations of, as modifications of or as reactions against traditional views. Such scholars tend to be sceptical of the kind of claim made by Dasgupta. They point out, rightly, that many Upaniṣadic ideas are already explored in embryonic form in the Brāhmaṇas and Āraṇyakas. For example, the idea that the merit accrued through sacrificial rituals is finite and its exhaustion will lead to rebirth on Earth was already prefigured in Brāhmaṇa texts where a fear of dying again (punar mṛtyu) was expressed. The guiding principle of the developmentalists is that we should look for the antecedents of all doctrines in the Vedic corpus before embarking on speculations about non-Vedic, possibly indigenous, religious traditions being their source. The evidence for such traditions is largely inferential whereas the Vedic texts offer something concrete and explicit.

Those who favour the Interaction Explanation will often acknowledge the continuities but nevertheless argue that they are not the whole story. Much, of course, depends upon dating. This is a highly controversial issue and is far from being conclusively resolved. Here I will simply offer some contextualization for the debate and offer an outline of my own thoughts on the matter.

Until the 1920s, when Sir John Marshall discovered the remains of an ancient civilization in the Indus Valley of northwestern India, the dominant view was that various groups of people who called themselves Aryan (noble) migrated into India and gradually spread out in an easterly direction along the plain of the Gaṅgā (Ganges). Later Indian culture was assumed to be the creation of the Aryans. Marshall's discovery changed all that. The Indus remains were taken as indicating the existence of a developed civilization in India prior to the arrival of the Aryans. In the 1950s, Sir Mortimer Wheeler suggested that the demise of the Indus civilization could be attributed to successive waves of Aryan 'invasions'. The Indus civilization lasted for around 1000 years, roughly from 2500 to 1500 BCE,[26] so these invasions would have taken place around 1500 BCE. Modern scholars have tended to reject Wheeler's invasion hypothesis, arguing that the Indus civilization had collapsed long before the Aryans arrived. Large quantities of marine molluscs have been found up to 150 miles upstream from the mouth of the Indus, suggesting that some kind of natural disaster that raised the sea level hit the civilization around 1800 BCE. This would have caused the destruction not only of buildings and crops but also of the entire economic foundation of the civilization. In this scenario there was no civilization to invade; the cities had already been abandoned.

There are, however, some indications that not all of the urban areas had been abandoned when the Aryans arrived. The *Ṛgveda* describes the god Indra as a sacker of fortresses (pura). Moreover, these fortresses are said to be occupied by dark-skinned, snub-nosed people called Dāsa or Dasya (Dās in modern Hindi), a word that later came to mean 'slave' or 'servant'. The Dāsas are described as being phallus worshippers; they have the phallus for a god (śiśna deva).[27] The interesting thing about this material is that it has direct connections with what we know about the Indus civilization and the people who became the servant class (śūdra). Carved phallic stones that are highly reminiscent of the liṅga-yoni figures associated with Śiva-Śakti have been found all across the Indus region. This strongly suggests that many people in the Indus civilization did, indeed, have a phallus (plus vulva) as a god. The researches of scholars such as George Dumezil and others point to the social organization of Aryan society being originally tripartite in nature: warriors, priests and stockbreeders/artisans. In India, from the time of the later *Ṛgveda* (e.g. *RV* 10.90) it was fourfold: warriors, priests, stockbreeders/artisans/farmers and servants. What seems to have happened is that the Aryans subdued the local population and essentially enslaved them. Whether this was by 'invasion' or 'migration' is unclear. We may also note that the traditional life cycle of Aryan males into student, householder and retired was also expanded into a fourfold system in India with the addition of a further, optional, stage of renouncer (saṃnyāsin), the activities of whom are often centred on the practice of yoga.

When this information is put alongside other finds from the Indus Valley such as seals depicting figures seated in yoga-like postures and having some affinity with the god Śiva, lord of yoga (yogeśvara) and the least orthodox of the high gods of later Hinduism, then it looks as though yogic spirituality may have been in India before the coming of the Aryans. Such speculation is given weight by the fact that Buddhism, the most yogic of all the major religions, denies brāhmanical authority and claims a source for its teachings that is independent of the Veda. And here we come to the heart of the Interactionist Explanation: rather than look to the Vedas for the origins of all later Indian spirituality, think in terms of Vedic spirituality interacting with native or indigenous spiritualities. The problem with this view is that there is very little by way of direct evidence to support it. One is primarily inferring the existence of native spirituality from a) snippets of evidence such as that mentioned above, and b) incompatibilities between Vedic teachings and those of other religious groups such as the Buddhists and the Jains. Furthermore, even if it could be demonstrated that śramanic (renouncer) religions like Buddhism and Jainism are non-Vedic in origin, that does not prove that they were non-Aryan. To claim that a tradition is non-Vedic is one thing; to claim that it originated in pre-Aryan native culture is another.[28]

So, did yoga originate in Vedic circles, eventually finding expression in the Upaniṣads and going on to become disseminated out to the wider culture and adopted by religions such as Buddhism, or did it already exist in India, ready to be appropriated by both

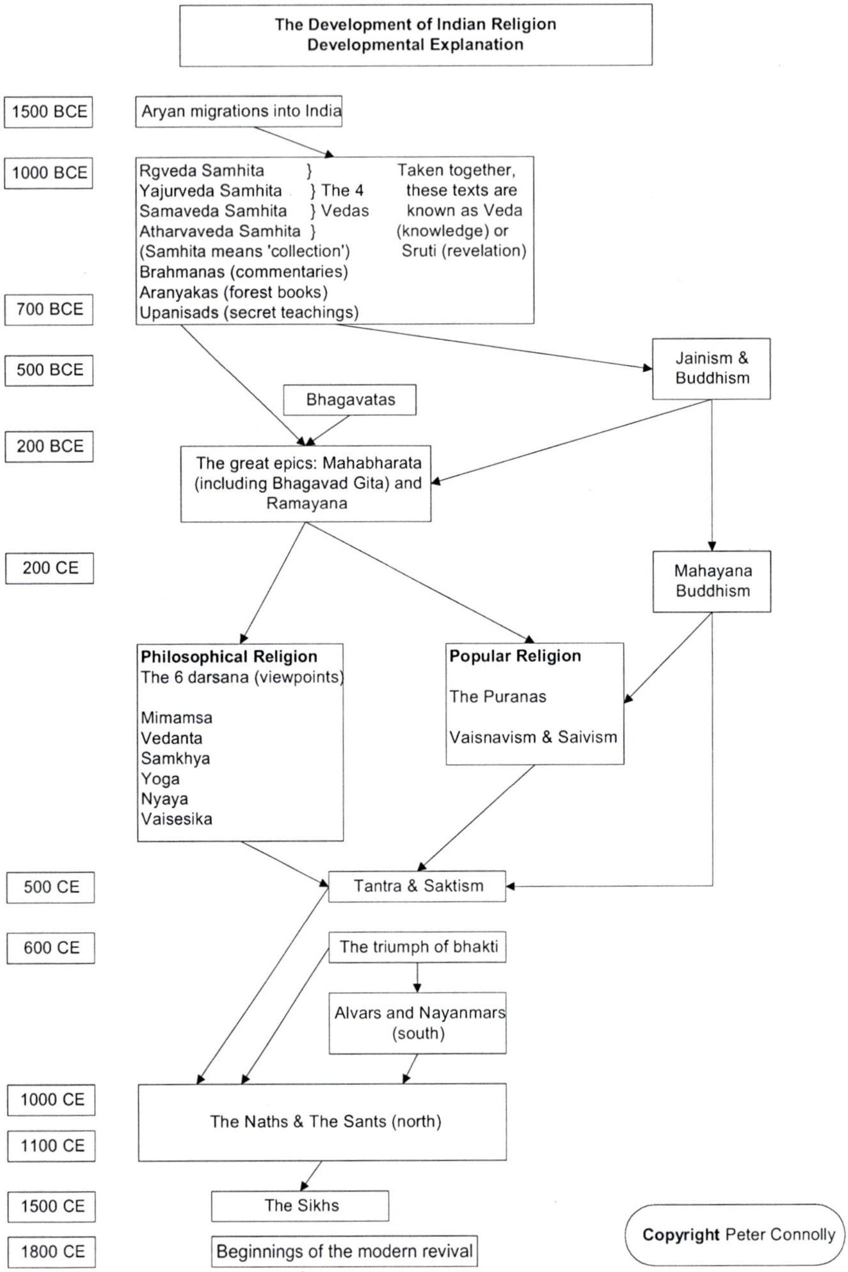
The Development of Indian Religion
Developmental Explanation
1500 BCE
Aryan migrations into India
1000 BCE
Rgveda Samhita }
Yajurveda Samhita } The 4
Samaveda Samhita } Vedas
Atharvaveda Samhita }
(Samhita means 'collection')
Brahmanas (commentaries)
Aranyakas (forest books)
Upanisads (secret teachings)
Taken together, these texts are known as Veda (knowledge) or Sruti (revelation)
700 BCE
500 BCE
Jainism & Buddhism
Bhagavatas
200 BCE
The great epics: Mahabharata (including Bhagavad Gita) and Ramayana
200 CE
Mahayana Buddhism
Philosophical Religion
The 6 darsana (viewpoints)
Mimamsa
Vedanta
Samkhya
Yoga
Nyaya
Vaisesika
Popular Religion
The Puranas
Vaisnavism & Saivism
500 CE
Tantra & Saktism
600 CE
The triumph of bhakti
Alvars and Nayanmars (south)
1000 CE
1100 CE
The Naths & The Sants (north)
1500 CE
The Sikhs
1800 CE
Beginnings of the modern revival
Copyright Peter Connolly

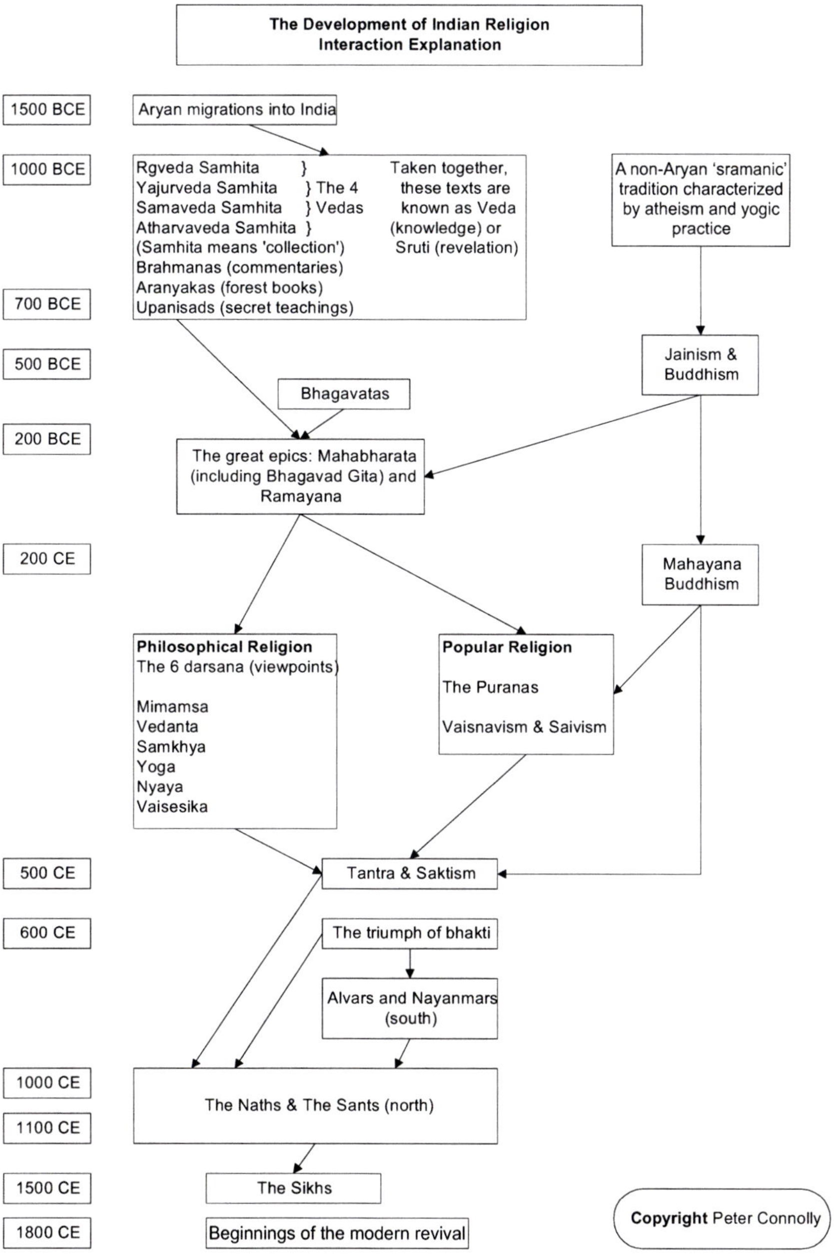
The Development of Indian Religion
Interaction Explanation
1500 BCE
Aryan migrations into India
1000 BCE
Rgveda Samhita }
Yajurveda Samhita } The 4
Samaveda Samhita } Vedas
Atharvaveda Samhita }
(Samhita means 'collection')
Brahmanas (commentaries)
Aranyakas (forest books)
Upanisads (secret teachings)
Taken together, these texts are known as Veda (knowledge) or Sruti (revelation)
A non-Aryan 'sramanic' tradition characterized by atheism and yogic practice
700 BCE
500 BCE
Jainism & Buddhism
Bhagavatas
200 BCE
The great epics: Mahabharata (including Bhagavad Gita) and Ramayana
200 CE
Mahayana Buddhism
Philosophical Religion
The 6 darsana (viewpoints)
Mimamsa
Vedanta
Samkhya
Yoga
Nyaya
Vaisesika
Popular Religion
The Puranas
Vaisnavism & Saivism
500 CE
Tantra & Saktism
600 CE
The triumph of bhakti
Alvars and Nayanmars (south)
1000 CE
1100 CE
The Naths & The Sants (north)
1500 CE
The Sikhs
1800 CE
Beginnings of the modern revival
Copyright Peter Connolly

brāhmanical and non-brāhmanical groups alike? Much depends on the dating of the *Kaṭha Upaniṣad.* If the *Kaṭha* pre-dates the Buddha then it is possible that he borrowed ideas about yoga from it. If, on the other hand, the Kaṭha is contemporary with or even later than the Buddha he cannot be thought to have borrowed from it, particularly since his teachings on yogic meditation are far more detailed than those found in the *Kaṭha,* and also because, in the period before his enlightenment, he was taught meditation by two forest-dwelling teachers: Āḷāra Kāḷāma and Uddaka Rāmaputta. Alternatively, we might want to address the issue in terms of the more general theories mentioned above and look to changes in food production and human cognition as primary factors. There are no clear-cut answers, but the wise student will bear all the relevant points in mind as he or she explores the origins of yoga.

In terms of our model of soteriology, the Upaniṣadic teachers get their information primarily by means of meditation and they frame the problem of the human condition in terms of bondage to saṃsāra. This problem is overcome primarily by human effort (austerity and meditating in the forest), though there are some passages that indicate the beginnings of a grace doctrine, e.g. *Kaṭha* 2.23; *Muṇḍaka* 3.2.3, and on liberation one realizes one's identity with the ātman/brahman. In terms of Rawlinson's model, the Upaniṣads present us with a primarily Cool and increasingly Structured approach.

## THE UPANIṢADS OF THE *BLACK YAJURVEDA*

The Upaniṣads of the *Black Yajurveda* offer the most explicit accounts of yoga in the Principal Upaniṣads, though their concerns are much wider than that. The following comments are designed to assist the student with the reading of these texts, which can be difficult for those unfamiliar with the style of the Upaniṣads.

### The *Taittirīya Upaniṣad*

This is the only old Upaniṣad of the *Black Yajurveda,* through which a number of scholars have seen 'non-Vedic influences insidiously making their way into the Vedic pantheon'.[29] If this is the case, we might well find that the Upaniṣads of the *Black Yajurveda* are important vehicles for introducing non-Aryan ideas (such as yoga?) into the brāhmanical tradition.

## THE STRUCTURE OF THE TEXT

The *TU* is divided into three chapters (vallī—lit. 'creeper; offshoot?'):

1. śikṣā vallī—instruction or pronunciation, divided into 12 anuvāka (lessons);
2. ānanda vallī—bliss, divided into 9 anuvāka;
3. bhṛgu vallī—name of a brahman, 'son' of Varuṇa, not divided into anuvāka.

Whether these are sections of a single work or whether each is essentially independent of the others is a matter of debate among scholars. If the former is the case, we would look for common themes, common terminology and philosophical coherence; and, perhaps, a sense of progression. If the latter is the case, we would look for evidence of each vallī being self-contained, differences in terminology and an absence of coherent fit between them. The chapters themselves may also be unitary or composite. To determine this we would look for breaks in the presentation, sections that seem independent of their surroundings, conflicting statements, etc.

## ŚIKṢĀ VALLĪ

General points: this vallī is very Vedic in character. There is no mention of rebirth (saṃsāra) nor of liberation from it (mokṣa). Rather, the aspirations seem to be for traditional Vedic goals; hence 1.3.4 concludes with 'These are the great combinations. He who knows these combinations, thus expounded, becomes conjoined with offspring, with cattle, with pre-eminence in sacred knowledge, with food, with the heavenly world (suvarga loka).' Similar sentiments are expressed in the teacher's prayer at the beginning of 1.4, the student's precepts in 1.11 and the various invocations such as that at the beginning of 1.12.

At the same time, contained within this vallī are a number of statements that have a distinctly Upaniṣadic ring about them. 1.6 contains most of these. 'The space within the heart' (antar hṛdayākāśa) is mentioned in *BAU* 2.17; 4.2.3; 4.4.22; *CU* 8.1.1-3;

*MundU* 2.2.6; *MaitriU* 6.22.27-8 and 30; 7.11. In the *TU* passage, and in *MundU* 2.2.8, the person made of mind (manomaya puruṣa) abides in this space. In *BAU* 2.17, it is the person made of intelligence (vijñānamaya puruṣa); in *BAU* 4.2.3 and *MaitriU* 7.11, it is the union of Indra and Virāj; whilst in *BAU* 4.4.22 it is the person made of intelligence among the senses (vijñānamaya prāṇeṣu), who is the great unborn self (mahān aja ātman). This theme is paralleled in the concept of the ātman as inner controller (antaryāmin) as found, for example, in *BAU* 3.7 and *Māṇḍūkya Upaniṣad* 6 (see also the references to the inner self (antar ātman) in *KU* 5.12; 6.17; *MundU* 2.1.9 and *MaitriU* 6.1).

There is also, in *TU* 1.6, a mention of one who practises the ancient yoga. *TU* 1.5 prepares the way for this statement through the introduction of the four utterances that facilitate the traversing of the universe: bhūr, bhuva, svar, mahas—linking Vedic mantras with yogic practice. Note, though, that this fourfold pattern does not match the more dominant fivefold symbolism that characterizes the rest of the Upaniṣad, e.g. 1.3; 1.7; 2.1-5; 3.2-6, perhaps indicating an independent origin. Another typically Upaniṣadic theme is that of Indra entering or exiting the body by way of the top of the skull. Prāṇa is said to enter the body by way of the head in *Śatapatha Brāhmaṇa* 7.5.1.22 and the ātman by the same route in *AU* 1.3.12. According to *MaitriU* 6.21, the atman also departs this way when it is liberated from the body. Finally, the idea that the self (manomaya puruṣa/Indra) can become lord of the body and all its faculties has clear connections with the antaryāmin concept and can be seen as a prefigurement of *KU* 3.3ff.

## ĀNANDA VALLĪ

The opening of this vallī links directly with 1.6. The brahman is equated with the manomaya puruṣa, which is said to be knowledge, truth/reality and infinity/bliss. Also in this verse is an equation between the brahman and the ātman, which are both, by implication, equated with the manomaya puruṣa.

From the ātman comes the whole of creation, with humanity last. This evolution or transformation is linked in the following verses with an outer to inner reverse pattern. The puruṣa at the end of the series of transformations is identified initially with the outer or physical person (annarasamaya ātman—the self made of the essence of food). Then we are taken through the five layers of the person to the self made of bliss (ānandamaya ātman). This is not, however, a straightforward reversal of the creation process but only an implied parallelism.

The *TU* is best known for this passage on the five selves and most references to the *TU* by modern writers are to it alone. The rest of the Upaniṣad, except for 2.8, which sets out the gradations of bliss, is rarely mentioned.

#### BṚGHU VALLĪ

The first section of this vallī, 1.6, is reminiscent of *BAU* 4.1, where a number of incomplete (one-footed) definitions of brahman are considered. In that passage, speech (vāc), breath (prāṇa), the eye/sight (cakṣus), the ear/hearing (śrotra), the mind (manas) and the heart (hṛdaya) are all considered as possible candidates for the status of supreme principle (brahman) but each is stated to be just a part of brahman. Here, the components are the same as the five selves of the preceding vallī: anna, prāṇa, manas, vijñāna and ānanda, though five of the *BAU* group are mentioned at the beginning of 3.1. The end of 10.4 and the whole of 10.5 are interesting, partly because they link the self in the individual with the self in the sun (gateway to the world of brahma) by identifying them as the same, and partly because they state that one who has such knowledge at the time of death passes through the five selves and gains the ability to take any desired form and eat any desired food. One wonders whether the author of this vallī had been fasting and having food fantasies.

### The *Kaṭha Upaniṣad*

The *Kaṭha Upaniṣad* is regarded by many Indologists as the oldest of the verse Upaniṣads, probably composed sometime around the time of the Buddha (5th to 4th centuries CE).[30] In all likelihood, it is a composite text, being a compilation of two essentially independent works. The first and oldest of these comprises books (vallī) one to three; the second books four to six. The second part may have been composed to supplement the first.

#### FIRST VALLĪ

Naciketas, a young brāhman, wins three boons from Yama (king of the dead) because of the obligation he accrues through Naciketas residing at his house for three nights without refreshments (see 1.7, 8).

The first boon is straightforward: return to and reconciliation with his father.

The second boon picks up on a concern often expressed in the Brāhmaṇa literature: that of a falling away from the heavenly world, a re-death (punar mṛtyu). The boon guarantees that this will not happen and guarantees immortality to Naciketas—a very Vedic aspiration (though, of course, liberation from saṃsāra is not too dissimilar). The means of gaining this immortality (sacrifice) is also very Vedic.

The third boon seems somewhat peculiar in the light of the second. The actual boon is for information about what happens after death, and for some reason Yama is reluctant to divulge it (1.21-25). This is indicative of a secret teaching, and the strategy of discouraging interest actually serves to intensify it. Yama's response to Naciketas's question does not, in fact, answer it. As Deussen points out,[31] 'it is directed towards the knowledge of the Ātman as the true essence of man and along with it, towards eternal release'. In short, the third boon is employed as a vehicle for introducing distinctive Upaniṣadic ideas.

## SECOND VALLĪ

2.1 contrasts the good (śreyas) with the pleasant (preyas). The wise man chooses the good; the fool the pleasant. 5 and 6 are reminiscent of *MundU* 1.2.7-8. Verse 7 switches abruptly into a comment about the ātman and the need for a special teacher. The ātman is located in 'the cavern' or 'secret place' (guhahitam), which Radhakrishnan identifies with the space within the heart. One who meditates on that self (ātman) as god transcends both joy and sorrow (2.12). Oṃ is the sound-form of the ātman and knowledge of it brings the fulfilment of all desires (2.16). This ātman is eternal, indestructible, etc. and dwells in the hearts of beings. 2.23 indicates that knowledge of the ātman is dependent on His grace. He reveals Himself only to one whose mind has been stilled. Here we have a clear statement of a works/grace doctrine. Meditation is necessary but not sufficient.

THIRD VALLĪ

This opens with a reference to two entities who are not clearly specified. Hume and Deussen translate this first verse quite differently. Knowers of brahman call them light and shadow (inseparable?). Verse 3 switches to the metaphor of a chariot—the control of which is symbolic of yoga. This section introduces a number of terms and concepts that are later associated with the semi-heterodox Sāṃkhya school, e.g. buddhi, avyaktam, puruṣa (this last is, of course, used in the *Ṛgveda*, though here it has a rather different meaning—notwithstanding the fact that the equation of puruṣa with ātman, so common in the Upaniṣads, serves to link the new ideas with the older orthodoxy). Puruṣa and ātman are here being employed as equivalents and knowledge of it frees a person from 'the jaws of death'.

FOURTH VALLĪ

This opens with a statement that the knowledge of the ātman is to be obtained by focusing the attention inwards. One who knows the ātman within does not suffer and feels no fear (see *TU* 2.7). Verse 6 links this doctrine with Vedic teachings, e.g. *RV* 129, and offers metaphors explaining how the ātman can be hidden within the body. Verses 10-11 make it clear that this is not a dualistic teaching. The world is also part of the ātman. The ātman residing in the heart (the size of a thumb) is the natural, untransformed and, in fact, changeless reality. Here we hit a significant philosophical problem. If the self is changeless (as 3.15 claims) how can the changing world be a part of it? This is less of a problem for the dualistic Sāṃkhya. In a monistic context it requires some kind of illusionistic rather than realistic status for the world. The image of the chariot, the emphasis on the self being located within the individual (4.12-13) and the danger of getting lost in sense impressions (4.14) all point to the need for interiorization: the practice of yoga.

FIFTH VALLĪ

The opening verse alludes to the metaphor of the chariot. The one who controls the chariot (body) and its horse (senses) is liberated at death. Note the absence of the jīvan mukti concept here. Verse 2, as Deussen points out, is an interpolation from *RV* 4.40.5, which is probably included to emphasize the continuity of this teaching with that found in the saṃhitās. 3-5 return to the subject of the ātman within the body and declare that it is the source of life as manifested in the process of breathing. The remaining verses of this vallī address the issues of:

1. the fate of the ātman after death (i.e. an answer to Naciketas's third question);
2. the relationship of the ātman to the world;
3. the source of true happiness.

The answer to 1 is rebirth into animate or inanimate forms, the specification of which is determined by two factors: one's former actions (karman) and one's knowledge (śrutam), i.e. what one has learned/heard from one's teachers.

The answer to 2 is that the ātman, which is the brahman (supreme principle), is the source of the world and, in fact, its being. The world is a transformation of the ātman, who, nevertheless, remains external to it—the doctrine of panentheism (that the world is part of god/the divine being).

The answer to 3 is that only the knower of the ātman is truly happy. Not until the middle of the next vallī, however, are we told that knowledge of the ātman brings release (6.8).

## SIXTH VALLĪ

The opening verse reiterates the monistic teaching, whilst the second identifies the brahman (= ātman) with prāṇa, knowledge of which bestows immortality. Verse 4 is somewhat problematic. It states that one who obtains knowledge of the prāṇa (= ātman/brahman) whilst alive becomes fit for embodiment in the creations (of the ātman). This seems strange to say the least. Hume proposes the emendation of sargeṣu (creations) to svargeṣu (the heavenly worlds), which would certainly make more sense. What remains puzzling is the fact that in 6.8 it is stated that one who knows the puruṣa (= ātman/brahman/prāṇa) is released and attains immortality.

One way of resolving this incongruity is adopted by Radhakrishnan, who, following the medieval theologian Śaṅkara, translates 6.4 as 'If one is able to perceive (Him) before the body falls away (one would be freed from misery); (if not) he becomes fit for embodiment in the created worlds.'[32] Another way is to recognize that some Upaniṣadic teachers or redactors did not want prāṇa to stand as a synonym for ātman/brahman. A good example of how the supreme status of prāṇa can be challenged by the addition of verses following a statement of its supremacy can be found in *CU* 7, where vss. 16ff. have been added later.[33] This kind of addition may have happened here with v.4.

The import of v.5 is unclear; v.6 returns to a discussion of yoga, which, again, (as in 3.3-13) employs Sāṃkhya terminology. 6.11 offers the earliest definition of yoga in Upaniṣadic literature: indriyadhāraṇām, the control or concentration of the senses. The last line of this verse has evoked different interpretations. Śaṅkara suggests 'an arising and passing away', i.e. yoga is a transitory state. Verse 14 is possibly a suggestion of jīvan mukti (liberation in life), particularly if 15-17 are taken as referring to a meditational practice (see *MaitriU* 6.21). *CU* 8.6.6 also refers to a channel leading upward from the heart to immortality, but here such a journey seems a possibility only at death.

Overall, the *Kaṭha Upaniṣad* presents us with statements on the major recurring themes of the Upaniṣads:

- the identity of ātman and brahman;
- a monistic cosmology;
- the presence of the ātman in the heart of all beings;
- rebirth according to action for beings who are ignorant of ātman;
- yoga as the method for gaining knowledge of the ātman;
- knowledge of the ātman being the key to happiness and release from rebirth.

## The *Maitrāyaṇa (Maitrī) Upaniṣad*

### THE DIVISION OF THE TEXT

This text is divided into seven lessons (prapāṭhaka), the sixth being by far the longest. Lessons 1-4 present Śākāyanya's teaching to King Bṛhadratha. This is Śākāyanya's version of Maitri's teaching (to him?). Maitri, in turn, ascribes this teaching to Kratu Prajāpati (a seer [ṛṣi]). Hume agrees that this teaching ends at 4.6. However, only at the end of 6.30 does the text explicitly bring Śākāyanya's teaching to a close. Deussen intimates that 6.18-30 may be the concluding section of the core text (1–4.6), which would then consist of 1–4.6 plus 6.18-30. Certainly, 6.18-30 deals with the same theme as lesson 4: the way to escape from the world and attain communion with brahman. But the question about the way this is to be achieved (4.1) is answered very differently in 4.3ff and 6.18-30. It may be that the latter is a continuation of the former or that it offers an alternative to it or even that 4.3ff is an interpolation.

As Deussen points out, the core text is structured around three questions:

1. how does the ātman enter the body?
2. why does the ātman enter the body?
3. how does one attain communion with brahman?

**The first lesson** serves as a contextualization for these questions by setting out the undesirability of continuing to exist in a perishable world.

**The second and third lessons** seek to answer questions 1 and 2.

First, Bṛhadratha is told that the way to escape the perishable world is to obtain knowledge of the ātman (2.1), which is, in fact, brahman (the supreme) (2.2).

Second, we are informed, through the question of the Vālakhilyas, that the ātman is different from the body. Note, however, that in this section we have a change in terminology—Kratu Prajāpati refers to the puruṣa and the kṣetra-jñā rather than the ātman. This puruṣa is described as being 'pure, clean, void, tranquil, breathless, selfless (nirātmananta), endless, undecaying, steadfast, eternal, unborn, independent'.[34] This is a good description of the Sāṃkhya puruṣa, though here it is single rather than multiple (as is usually the case with the Vedic schools of Sāṃkhya described in the 12th book of the *Mahābhārata*). The description of the individual also draws heavily on Sāṃkhya terminology. The account of creation, however, draws on earlier Upaniṣadic teachings. The motive for creation is loneliness. So creation comes into existence because of desire rather than as god's play (līlā) or projection rooted in ignorance as is the case in much of the later Vedānta.

What we have here then, is an attempt, which is further developed in the later Vedānta, to combine Vedic and Sāṃkhya teachings (assuming that Sāṃkhya was non-Vedic in origin). Note, however, that there is the suggestion that Prajāpati creates a material world which is separate from himself and into which he enters (2.6).

**Lesson 3** introduces the concept of the elemental or individual soul (bhūtātman), which is different from the immortal soul. This account is unclear, however, and the exact relation between the two is not well explained. The body is made of the sense faculties (tanmātras) and the great elements (mahābhūtas); the bhūtātman dwells within it, not knowing the immortal ātman (amṛtatman = inner self/person—antarpuruṣa). Ultimately, the latter has control over the former (3.7). Note that 6.10 suggests that the bhūtātman is part of prakṛti.[35] It is the bhūtātman that transmigrates (3.2). In the Sāṃkhya system the place of the bhūtātman would be taken by the ahaṃkāra (I-maker or ego) or the internal instrument (antaḥkaraṇa = buddhi, ahaṃkāra and manas).

**Lesson 4** deals with question 3. The initial answer is to follow the varṇāśramadharma (duty according to social class and stage of life) and, in the later stages, practise knowledge (vidya), penance (tapas) and meditation (cintā). This will take the ascetic beyond the manifestations of brahman (the gods etc.) to 'the highest, immortal, incorporeal brahman' (4.6), which is the puruṣa.

**Lesson 5** is another attempt to combine Vedic and Sāṃkhya ideas. Verse 1 is reminiscent of Ṛigvedic praises which make all the gods manifestations of just one of them, e.g. *Ṛgveda* 2.1. Max Muller called this pattern 'henotheism': one-god-at-a-time-ism. Verse 2 is typical of Vedic versions of Sāṃkhya found in *Mahābhārata* 12.

**Lesson 6** is as long as the rest of the Upaniṣad put together. Deussen divides it into five subsections:

1. 1-8
2. 9-17
3. 18-30
4. 31-32
5. 33-38.

6.1-17 can, in fact, be treated as a single section since the same terminology and concerns run throughout, notwithstanding the various tensions between one part and another. The lesson opens with a distinction being made between two forms of the ātman: as breath or vitality (prāṇa) and as the sun (āditya). This is reminiscent of the adhyātma/adhidaivata (individual/cosmic) distinction found in a number of earlier Upaniṣads and the Vedic hymns. Indeed, it is a parallelism found in many aspects of brāhmanical religion, probably having its roots in the mimetic magic of the Vedic sacrificial ritual: this corresponds to that, therefore, by manipulating this, the control of that can be achieved. This kind of distinction is taken up again later when the two forms of brahman are introduced. Although of Vedic origin and developed within the context of the Vedic world picture, this distinction (or one similar to it) is crucial for advocates of a monistic philosophy who wish to accommodate concepts that originated within a dualistic system.

These two subsections have a very Vedic character—expressed through Vedic quotations, references to Vedic gods, the employment of Vedic concepts, the characterization of meditation on the ātman as a sacrifice and the identification of the ātman with agni (fire/the fire god) as well as with the sun. References to prāṇa as the ātman and to brahman as food are also reminiscent of earlier Upaniṣads such as the *Kauṣītaki* and *Taittirīya* respectively. Once again, there is also the attempted integration of Vedic and Sāṃkhyan ideas. Reference to the renouncer (saṃnyāsi) in v.10 may have a link with lesson 4 where following the varṇāśramadharma is recommended. Renunciation is the fourth of life's stages for a twice-born male and, at least according to the Laws of Manu (*Mānava Dharma śāstra*), the most influential of the dharma śāstras, only to be entered after the birth of a grandson.

**Speculation:** These frequent attempts to integrate Vedic and Sāṃkhyan teachings may have been included because of criticisms from the orthodox, who were suspicious of the new ideas and regarded them as subversive foreign imports. Even at the time of Śaṅkara (8th century CE) the Sāṃkhyans were regarded as heterodox by some orthodox theologians—strange if Sāṃkhya really had evolved in Vedic circles.

18-30 can be read as giving more detail on vidya, tapas and cintā (4.4) but, given the fragmentary nature of the text, these verses are possibly better understood as an alternative answer to question 3. Verse 18 outlines a sixfold yoga. This is the most detailed account of yoga practice in the principal Upaniṣads. Five of the components are also found in Patañjali's eightfold yoga: prāṇāyāma, pratyāhara, dhyāna, dhāraṇā and samādhi. Note that here the order of dhyāna and dhāraṇā is the reverse of Patañjali's—suggesting that these terms did not acquire fixed meanings until quite late. Note too that knowledge of brahman either destroys sins (= karmic accretions) or at least prevents them in the future.

**The practice of yoga** results in the experience of selflessness (nirātmakatvam), which, in turn, leads to the state of isolation or aloneness (kevalatvam): the preferred term for indicating release by the Jains, Sāṃkhyans and Patañjali, compiler of the *Yoga Sūtra*. Verse 25 offers a definition of yoga, the practice of which leads to the extinction of the aśraya (the storehouse of karmic seeds). This, along with the reference to becoming selfless, suggests Buddhist influence. It also supports the idea that knowledge of brahman destroys existing karma as well as preventing future accretion (v.18); cf. 6.34. The end of v.28 may also indicate śramanic influence, though it could be taken to suggest that only those in the last two āśramas can experience yoga.[36]

Verses 31ff. touch on the theme of the origin of phenomena from the ātman, reminiscent of *Kena Upaniṣad* 1 and *MundU* 1.1 and 2.1. Also expounded are the ideas that the sacrifice that takes place within the body (i.e. meditation) is equivalent to the external sacrifice, and that the mind is the cause of saṃsāra (i.e. the world itself is not problematic; only a misunderstanding of and attachment to it cause problems). Again, this is very much in line with unorthodox (Buddhist, Jain, Sāṃkhya etc.) ideas.

Connections with other Upaniṣads of the *Black Yajurveda* are also maintained: four of the 'sheaths' of the *TU* are mentioned at the beginning of v.38, and the person the size of a thumb who resides in the heart (*Kaṭha Upaniṣad* and *Śvetāśvatara Upaniṣad*) is mentioned at the end.

**Lesson 7** is essentially a polemical section. The first part emphasizes that the ātman is everything; everything comes from it, yet, in itself, it is characterless and is concealed in the space within the heart. 8ff. suggests that these verses were composed during the epic period when northern India was politically and religiously fragmented. Those who challenge the authority of the Veda are labelled 'demons' (asura) and the story in v.10 is designed to discourage the orthodox from investigating the non-Vedic doctrines that were competing for their allegiance.

The threefold form of ātman as agni, prāṇa and āditya is reiterated in v.11 (see 6.17), though note that 6.1 and 6.9 refer only to prāṇa and āditya.

7.11.8 links the four states of the ātman set out in the *Māṇḍūkya Upaniṣad* with the four quarters of puruṣa as described in *Ṛgveda* 10.90, equating the turiya state with the three-quarters of puruṣa that exists beyond creation. Note, however, that the reason given for the ātman creating the universe—to experience truth and falsehood (satya and anṛta)—conflicts with that found in 2.6: Prajāpati was lonely.

PROMINENT THEMES IN THE *MAITRĪ UPANIṢAD*

**One theme,** much reiterated in lesson 6, is the two forms of brahman:

- higher (para) and lower (apara)
- soundless (aśabda) and sound (śabda) (6.22)
- unformed/formless (amūrta) and formed (mūrta) (6.3)
- timeless (akala) and in-time (kala) (6.15)
- peaceful (śanta) and abounding/opulent (samṛddha) (6.36)

The two, or three, forms of ātman: as prāṇa, āditya (and agni), are connected to this idea in 6.3, where the amūrta brahman is equated with light (jyotis) and light with the sun (āditya). The general idea can be traced back to early Upaniṣads (e.g. *BAU* 2.3.1) and even to the older adhyātma/adhidaivata distinction. In the *Maitrī* it is first presented in a non-explicit fashion in 4.5-6. The question of how one should regard the gods etc. is answered by the statement that they should be treated as manifestations of brahman.

**Not exactly a theme,** but characteristic of the Upaniṣad as a whole, is the employment of Sāṃkhya terminology in the description of the individual and of the cosmos. Puruṣa, kṣetrajñā, buddhi, ahaṃkāra are all used in 2.4-5. The description of the ātman in 2.7 is also reminiscent of the Sāṃkhya puruṣa, who is also characterized as a spectator, rather than the ātman of earlier Upaniṣads, who is described as the inner controller (antaryāmin), though note that the *Śvetāśvatara* (which is also influenced by Sāṃkhya), e.g. 1.9, also emphasizes the inactive nature of the ātman.

Prakṛti, guṇas, tanmātras, mahābhūtas and rajas and tamas (two of the three Sāṃkhya guṇas) are all mentioned in lesson 3. Lesson 4 mentions tamas and sattva (the third guṇa), and lesson 5 all three guṇas plus kṣetrajñā, buddhi, ahaṃkāra and liṅga. 6.10ff. uses puruṣa, pradhāna, prakṛti and indriyas; so too does 6.30.

## The *Śvetāśvatara Upaniṣad*

Deussen places this Upaniṣad with the middle (verse) texts such as the *Īṣā* and the *Muṇḍaka*. Hume locates it in the same period as the later prose Upaniṣads such as the *Maitrī* and the *Māṇḍūkya*, whilst some writers are of the opinion that it may well be a product of the late epic period.[37]

THE MAIN THEMES ARE:

1. *the rulership of god,* both from the outside and the inside. See, for example, 1.3; 1.9-10; 2.1-4; 3.17-18; 4.11-16; 5.1-5; 6.1-2; 6.7; 6.12.
2. *the importance of knowing god,*
   god:
   a) brings release (1.8; 1.11; 2.15; 4.16; 5.13; 6.13)
   b) destroys illusion (1.10)
   c) satisfies desire (1.11)
   d) brings immortality (3.7; 3.10; 3.13; 4.15 (?); 4.17; 4.20; 5.6)
   e) brings freedom from sorrow (2.14; 3.20)
   f) brings peace (4.14).
3. *god's relation to the world,*
   a) god is all (4.1-4; 4.11; 6.5-6 (?)—but see 1.7-12)
   b) god is creator (3.2).
4. *the means of liberation,*
   a) grace (1.6; 6.10; 6.18)
   b) meditation (1.10; 2.8-11).

*Summary and Comment*

FIRST ADHYĀYA (CHAPTER)

1-3 Through a Question and Answer technique, the text presents the view that god (deva) is the cause and ruler of all *and* that the soul (ātman) is powerless.

4-6 God contains all the (Sāṃkhya) tattvas within himself. The soul thinks it is separate from god and a causal agent. This produces bondage. 'When favoured by Him it attains immortality.'

7-12 Within god are three ultimates: god (deva), soul (ātman) and nature (pradhāna/prakṛti). God and soul are unchanging, nature is changing. God is a knower, the soul is ignorant. God rules over both soul and nature. Knowledge of god brings release, cf. 2.15; 5.13; 6.13.

13-16 Some hints on acquiring the knowledge of god.

SECOND ADHYĀYA

1-7 These verses contextualize yoga practice, making it Vedic in character. For the remainder of the adhyāya the Veda-oriented references are absent.

8-17 The practice of yoga; the goal of yoga; the pervasiveness of god. Note that the term 'indriyāni' for senses is indicative of lateness. Older Upaniṣads use 'prāṇa' for senses. Note too that only the preparatory stages of yoga are mentioned here. Verse 17 mentions god entering into (aviveśa), which suggests a degree of separateness between god and the world.

THIRD ADHYĀYA

1-4 Rudra is identified as the one god, the ruler of the world, the source of all.

5-6 Rudra is best known as an outsider god with destructive tendencies. He is the lord of the Maruts or Gaṇas, the storm divinities. Here is a request to see his benign (Śiva) form.

Verse 7 is problematic. It seems to state that Brahman is higher than Rudra—which conflicts with other statements in the Upaniṣad, e.g. 4.13ff, which seem to identify Rudra with the Vedic puruṣa and the ātman as the inner controller (antaryāmin). As Hume points out, however, 'this' (tataḥ) could refer to 'this world'.'

7-20 equates the lord (Īśā) with the person (puruṣa) of *RV* 10.90 and the inner ruler (antaryāmin) who abides in the hearts of all creatures. Knowledge of god brings freedom from sorrow and arises through god's grace (prasāda) (v. 20).

FOURTH ADHYĀYA

1-4 introduces a number of Vedic riddles. The two birds mentioned in v.6 and also at *MundU* 3.1.1-2 are taken, in the Vedānta tradition, to refer to the bound soul and the free soul. In *RV* 1.164.20, from where this verse originates, the meaning was probably different. The mention of god as an illusionist (māyī) suggests Buddhist influence, possibly from the teachings of the Mādhyamaka school (post 2nd century CE). Note that Deussen's version omits v.11 and that subsequent verses in his text are one in advance of those in others.

Verse 10 Prakṛti (the creative—a favourite Sāṃkhya term for nature/matter) is described as illusion (māyā), which is under the control of god.

Verse 14 Peace comes from knowing the auspicious (Śiva) form of god, the illusionist. The kindly one (Śiva) is the great self (mahātma) who resides in the heart of creatures (as the inner controller—antaryāmin). The last verse (21 or 22) is a typical Vedic invocation to Rudra.

### FIFTH ADHYĀYA

The opening verses, particularly 4 and 5, are reminiscent of *Bhagavad Gītā* 18.59-61 in stating that god controls everything. Beings do not have control over their destinies, god does. Since these are some of the latest verses in the *Gītā* the suggestion is that this text is also quite late. The remaining verses do little more than reiterate the main themes of the Upaniṣad, even quoting some earlier verses—suggesting that this section was added later.

### SIXTH ADHYĀYA

This chapter is replete with Sāṃkhya terminology (e.g. tattva [principle], guṇa [quality/constituent]) and enumerations (one, two, three, eight) but contextualized in a monistic and theistic framework (classical Sāṃkhya is dualistic and atheistic). At the same time, the ontology of this chapter echoes ch.1, where god, souls and the universe appeared to be distinct. The use of the term kṣetra-jñā (field-knower) for the ātman is reminiscent of the *Bhagavad Gītā*, which also struggles with the same ontological issues. Also like the *Gītā*, this chapter emphasizes methods for gaining release (here, as in the *Gītā* and later parts of the *Mahābhārata*, known as Sāṃkhya-Yoga) alongside god's grace (deva-prasāda).

The equal emphasis on devotion (bhakti) to god and one's teacher (guru) is typical of the later Vedānta. At the level of metaphysics, this Upaniṣad works with the same issues as the *Gītā*: the harmonization of Vedāntic monism, Sāṃkhya dualism and monotheism, and does it in much the same way. The *Gītā* does more, however. It applies this metaphysic to social organization.

# Chapter 3
# THE ŚRAMANIC TRADITIONS: JAINISM AND BUDDHISM

## BACKGROUND

The Vedas, Brāhmaṇas and Āraṇyakas mention a number of unorthodox religious figures including munis (sages/ascetics), vrātyas (outsiders) and yatis (hermits). An entire Vedic hymn, *RV* 10.136, is devoted to the muni who can ride the winds and drink poison. The *Taittirīya Āraṇyaka* describes one ascetic group called Vātaraśanāh, whose members are said to have lived a celibate life, who could disappear at will and were able to teach brāhmaṇas the way beyond sin.[1] Somewhat later, Greek writers who accompanied Alexander of Macedon on his Indian adventures, distinguish between brāhmaṇas and śramanas, two groups described by Patañjali the grammarian (2nd century BCE) as eternal opponents. We have already noticed elements of such antagonism in the context of the Upaniṣads. The Buddha himself is sometimes referred to as a muni (as in Śakyamuni—sage of the Śakyas) and as a śramana (Pali—sāmana).

In addition, the Pāli Buddhist texts refer to a number of śramana teachers, including Āḷāra Kalāma and Uddaka Rāmaputta, who taught the Buddha how to attain highly rarefied states of meditation; Pūraṇa Kassapa, who denied the doctrine of karma; Ajita Kesakambalin, who taught annihilation at death; Sañjaya Belaṭṭhaputta (the eel-wriggler), who would affirm no doctrine, either positive or negative; and Pakudha Kaccāyana, who taught that the world was composed of seven permanent elements. Mahāvīra (leader of the Jains) is mentioned on a number of occasions, as is his one-time disciple Makkhali Gosāla, leader of the

Ajīvakas. There were probably many other groups and teachers as well. The term 'śramana' is the one that scholars tend to employ to refer to all of these. The one thing they all seem to have in common is that they renounce the householder life. Some brāhmaṇas were also renouncers ('living with faith in the forest' as the *Bṛhadāraṇyaka Upaniṣad* puts it), but most were householders, so the distinction is a useful one within limits. Religious life at the time of the Buddha and Mahāvīra was, then, quite diverse. Most of these groups faded away with the demise of their teachers, but two of them went on to become major religions in their own right: Jainism and Buddhism.

## JAINISM

A Jain is a follower of the Jina (the victor), who is also known as Mahāvīra (great hero). The person to whom these titles are normally attached was one Vardhamāna Jñātṛ, an older contemporary of the Buddha. The two main sub-groups within Jainism, the Digambaras (sky-clad, i.e. naked) and the Śvetāmbaras (white-clad) agree that he was born in 599 BCE, though the former place his death in 509 and the latter in 527. Vardhamāna is said, by Jains, to have been the twenty-fourth tīrthaṅkara (ford-maker) of the present age. His predecessor, Pārśva, is claimed to have lived between 872 and 772 BCE. Vardhamāna's parents were disciples of Pārśva, so rather than thinking of Vardhamāna as founding a new religion, we should probably regard him as a reformer or re-invigorator. Ariṣṭanemi, the twenty-second tirthaṅkara is reported as living 84,000 years before Pārśva, so at this point any contact with the possible history of the movement is lost and we enter fully into the realm of myth.[2] Each of the two main sub-groups possesses its own scriptural collection. The Digambaras appear to have preserved the oldest existing Jain texts: the *Ṣaṭkaṇḍāgama* and the *Kasāyapāhuḍa*, though the remainder of their canon is later than the bulk of the Śvetambara collection, the twelve Aṅgas.

The title 'Jina' indicates that Vardhamāna has conquered saṃsāra and is now free. He was one who led the way and showed others how to do the same, so he is a tīrthaṅkara, a ford-maker. Liberation from rebirth is the hardest possible thing to achieve, hence he is a great hero (Mahāvīra). The Jain understanding of bondage and liberation is, in important ways, quite different from that found in the Upaniṣads. Although the Jains accept the idea of a permanent self that constitutes the essence of personal identity, they do not accept the Upaniṣadic teaching that this self is unitary and the same in all beings. Rather, they claim that each individual organism has its own unique self, which the Jains call a jīva (living spirit—from the verb √jīv, to live). Each individual jīva experiences individual bondage and individual release. Bondage occurs when a jīva becomes enmeshed in matter (ajīva) and liberation when it becomes free of matter.

In the liberated state, jīvas possess infinite perception (ananta darśana), infinite knowledge (ananta jñāna), infinite bliss (ananta sukha) and infinite energy/power (ananta vīrya). By contrast, the bound jīvas—those subject to saṃsāra—have none of these characteristics, because they are covered by a film of karmic matter. The Jain notion of karma is more materialistic than any other version found in Indian religious traditions. For the Jain, all actions attract matter to the jīva. Such matter adheres to the jīva until it is dissolved through expression, i.e. through some kind of experience, or through penance. The body–mind complex is understood to be essentially material (ajīva) in nature and not part of one's true identity. Only the jīva is the real you. Everything that people normally take to be themselves, such as body, mind, feelings, etc., are, in the Jain view, simply ajīva. Jīvas are constrained by matter in various ways, which are reflected in the eightfold classification of matter found in Jain teachings:

1. matter that obscures knowledge;
2. matter that obscures perception;
3. matter that obscures the bliss of the jīva with feelings;
4. matter that obscures the goodness of the jīva;
5. matter that determines the length of life;
6. matter that determines the nature of the body;
7. matter that determines the social and environmental situation of the jīva;
8. matter that prevents the jīva engaging in good action when it wishes to.

In a conception that has parallels with the doctrine of five layers found in the *Taittirīya Upaniṣad*, the Jains understand the jīva to take on the size and shape of the body it inhabits. Thus an elephant has an elephant-shaped jīva; a human, a human shaped jīva; an ant, an ant-shaped jīva; and a microbe, a microbe-shaped jīva. The amount of suffering experienced by any particular jīva is primarily determined by the kinds of constraints that restrict it. Thus the number of senses possessed by an organism provides a good indicator of the degree to which it is enmeshed in matter.

At the lowest level are the nigodas, which possess only respiration and nutrition. These beings are incredibly small and experience great pains. 'The whole space of the world is closely packed with them like a box filled with powder. The nigodas furnish the supply of souls in place of those that have reached mokṣa.'[3]

Next in the Jain hierarchy are the plants and elementary lives (jīvas that inhabit the four elements of earth, water, fire and air). These have only the sense of touch.

Then there are the worms, which have touch and taste.

Then ants, etc. with touch, taste and smell.

Then bees, etc. with touch taste, smell and sight.

Then vertebrates with touch, taste, smell, sight and hearing.

Finally, we have humans, gods and the inhabitants of the hell realms, who have touch, taste, smell, sight, hearing and mind (manas).

For those of you who were wondering, this classification does not accord with that of modern scientific biology, which is a bit of a problem for Jains as their scriptures tell them that the teachings must be accepted as true in all aspects.[4]

The prime objective of Jain yoga is not so much knowledge, though that comes automatically with the attainment of liberation, as the eradication of all karmic matter from the jīva. This is achieved in two main ways: nirjara (wearing down) and samvara (keeping back or stopping). Nirjara is accomplished primarily through the practice of various kinds of penance. Self-inflicted suffering is understood to burn off the effects of karma just as effectively as its expression in life. Nirjara, however, only addresses the karmic accretions that have already been created. New accretions (āsrava; Pali—āsava) must also be prevented. For this there are the seven techniques of samvara:

1. vrata (vows)—non-injury, truthfulness, non-stealing, sex control and disregarding the objects of desire;
2. samiti (rules of conduct)—using well-worn paths to avoid injury to insects, etc., gentle speech, almsgiving/receiving only proper alms;

3. gupti (restraints)—of body, speech and mind;
4. dharma (habit)—e.g. forgiving, humility, cleanliness;
5. anuprekṣa (meditation)—on transitoriness, human responsibility, the difference between jiva and non-jiva and other aspects of Jain teaching;
6. parīṣahajaya (developing indifference to discomfort);
7. caritra (right conduct).

These practices show Jainism to have a particular emphasis on non-violence (ahiṃsā) and on penance. Indeed, the Jain path is probably the most demanding of any found in India. Digambaras are more austere than Śvetambaras, however. Going naked under the Indian sun is a penance in itself. They are also more restrictive. Women are not allowed to enter the order and must be reborn as men in order to gain liberation. There is not, however, a strict division between the monastic order and the laity, who can take on many of the monastic practices for limited periods. Progress towards liberation, which the Jains call kaivalya (aloneness/isolation), is described in terms of 14 stages called guṇasthānas.[5] At the fourth stage a jīva is sufficiently pure to live as a Jain layperson; at the sixth stage the jīva is ready for the monastic life and the final path to freedom.

With reference to our model of soteriology, Jainism gets its knowledge through meditation and frames the human problem in terms of bondage to saṃsāra. Liberation is achieved through effort[6] and is experienced as a radical separation between spirit (jīva) and matter (ajīva). In Rawlinson's model it is a clear example of a Cool–Structured tradition.

## BUDDHISM

Buddhism is the most successful of all the śramanic traditions. Under the patronage of the emperor Aśoka (269–232 BCE) Buddhist missionaries travelled to all points of the compass with the Buddha's message. The main route was through the northwestern part of India into Afghanistan and Central Asia. From there it travelled along the silk route into China. Since the time of Alexander of Macedon (356–323, Alexander the Great to the Greeks; Alexander the Barbarian to the Persians) the northwest of India had been ruled by descendants of the Greeks, many of whom found

Buddhism quite attractive. Greek converts went on to create some of the most beautiful Buddhist art in a style called Gandhāra, a blend of Greek and Indian traditions. Further west, however, the Buddhists had little success, or at least little lasting success. In the early third century CE the Sassanian dynasty ousted the remnants of Greek rule and re-established Zoroastrianism. Further west, the emperor Constantine converted to Christianity in 337 CE and the Roman world followed suit.

To the east, the Buddhists fared rather better. On the southeastern route from India the Theravāda (Way of the Elders) form of Buddhism was established in Śrī Laṅka, Burma, Thailand, Kampuchea (Cambodia) and Laos. In some form or other, it still exists in these countries today. On the northeastern route, in a variety of forms, it was established in Nepal, parts of Central Asia, China, Korea, Japan and Vietnam. In a later wave of missionary activity it was also established in Tibet, and from there spread to Bhutan and Mongolia. It still retains a foothold in most of these countries, though in many of them that foothold is rather precarious.

Wherever Buddhism is found, there will be an emphasis on what are known as The Three Jewels or Three Refuges: Buddha (the awakened one), Dharma (the teaching) and Saṅgha (the community). Tantric Buddhists sometimes add a fourth: Guru (teacher). Each plays an important role in Buddhist soteriology.

## The Buddha

Most of the information that we have about the person who started the tradition known to us in the West as Buddhism comes from a collection of scriptures known as the Pāli Canon, because it is written in an ancient Indian language called Pāli[P], a kind of vernacular version of Sanskrit[S]. This has been preserved and transmitted down the ages by the Theravāda (Skt. Sthaviravāda, Elder Way) school. It has three main sections, called baskets (Piṭaka): Vinaya (rules), Sutta (Skt. Sūtra, discourses) and Abhidhamma (Skt. Abhidharma, higher teachings). The first two sections are older than the third and were probably shared in most of their parts by all the early Buddhist schools. The Pāli Abhidhamma can be regarded as the distinctively Theravādin interpretation of the Vinaya and Sutta collections.

The Vinaya and Sutta collections tell us about a young man known as Siddhatta Gotama, who renounced the world in order to seek a solution to the problem of suffering. After exploring a variety of ineffective methods he began to meditate until he was able to see the world as it really is and woke up to the truth. The effect of this 'waking up' (bodhi) was that he became free from the round of rebirth and experienced the undecaying peace he called nibbāna (Skt. nirvāṇa). For the next 40 years he travelled around northern India helping others access the insight he had gained. This is the kernel of the story. Establishing the fine detail of the story is a little more problematic. At this point in time the definitive 'Life of the Buddha' is still waiting to be written. What follows, then, is just a brief sketch, which includes a few pointers to assist further personal study. For convenience, the story of the Buddha can be divided into seven sections:

1. birth events;
2. early life;
3. renunciation of the world;
4. austerities;
5. enlightenment;
6. teaching;
7. death.

### BIRTH EVENTS

The traditional Theravāda dating of Siddhatta Gotama is 583–463 BCE, and until recently scholars have tended to use these dates as a marker on which they could base a relative chronology of other early Indian texts. So, for example, Max Muller's date of approximately 1000 BCE for the *Ṛgveda* is based on his assessment of how long before the Buddha the early Vedic texts were composed. However, research by scholars such as Richard Gombrich has pointed to a more recent date for the death of the Buddha: somewhere in the last decade of the fifth century BCE.[7] The implication is that Siddhatta lived during but not before the fifth century, i.e. 499–400. Consequently, all dating that has been done in relation to the Buddha's dates will have to be revised accordingly.

The earliest account of the Buddha's birth is probably that found in the Sutta of Wondrous and Marvellous Events.[8] An almost identical account is found in the birth story of a former Buddha named Vipassin.[9] Just as there were many tīrthaṅkaras before Mahāvīra in the Jain tradition so there have been many Buddhas before

Siddhatta in the Buddhist tradition. The formulaic nature of these stories suggests that they are hagiography rather than biography. Hagiographies are the life stories of holy people that are written by their followers. They are usually more concerned with making claims about what the tradition can offer and the dissemination of its view of reality than with historical truth, and are probably best understood as more mythic than historical in nature. Often, hagiographies address one or more issues that were being disputed at the time of their composition and put the compiler's answer(s) into the mouth of the saint/founder. They are, then, a kind of propaganda.

This sutta tells of how the being destined for enlightenment (bodhisatta, Skt. bodhisattva) took up abode in the Tusita heaven to prepare for birth in the human realm. From there he entered the womb of his mother, Māyā, wife of Suddhodana, leader of the Śakya clan. At birth, the bodhisatta is said to have been untouched by blood or birth fluids of any kind (which were regarded as polluting) and washed by two streams of water, one hot, one cold, that fell from the sky. The infant took seven steps and declared that this would be his last birth. Seven days later, his mother died and was reborn in the Tusita heaven. Subsequently, Siddhatta was nursed by his aunt, Mahāpajāpatī Gotamī, who, according to some accounts, became the first Buddhist nun.

## EARLY LIFE

There are three stories from Siddhatta's early life recounted in the Canon:

- The visit of the sage Asita, who recognized that the infant before him would become a Buddha and that, unfortunately, he would die before that blessed day.[10]
- Whilst his father was ploughing, Siddhatta sat under a tree and began to meditate. He attained a state of jhāna (Skt. dhyāna) that was characterized by detachment, rapture and bliss. In later Buddhist schemes of meditational states this one is the first of the rūpa jhānas (meditations in the realm of form).[11]
- Siddhatta is said to have been delicately nurtured, to have worn fine clothes and to have had three palaces, one for each season. In one version,[12] he is presented as reflecting on the nature of old age, sickness and death. In another,[13] we are

told that he was a householder at this time. Such stories may well have been constructed to quell people's doubts about the wisdom of renouncing the world: 'The Buddha had everything and found it wanting, so why bother wasting time trying to get worldly success because when you do you too will find it wanting.' This didactic interpretation is supported by the fact that another almost identical account is found in relation to the Buddha Vipassin and a second in relation to a wealthy young man who converted to Buddhism called Yasa.[14]

## SIDDHATTA'S RENUNCIATION OF WORLDLY LIFE

In what is probably the oldest account of this episode, we are told how Siddhatta reflected on the transiency of life and decided to seek that which is not transient, that which is not subject to birth, decay and death.[15] This passage has much in common with those mentioned above in connection with Siddhatta's luxurious life. There is an interesting addition, however. In this passage Siddhatta decides to renounce the world whilst still 'a black-haired lad in the prime of youth', i.e. prior to marriage. This at least raises the possibility that Siddhatta might not have had a wife and child when he renounced the world just as he might not have been a prince with three palaces.

## AUSTERITIES: BETWEEN RENUNCIATION AND ENLIGHTENMENT

Two events are particularly noteworthy in the period between Siddhatta's renunciation of the world and his attainment of enlightenment: his practice of austerities and his practice of meditation under the guidance of two different teachers.

The practice of austerities is rather alien to most people in the industrialized Western world, though it is still a prominent feature in many religious traditions. In India, the rationale for such behaviour generally seems to be twofold. On the one hand, the basic discomforts of life, such as becoming hungry, bored, lonely or experiencing aches and pains, prompt people into a variety of actions to counteract them. The ascetic approaches the matter from a different angle. The ascetic accepts the discomfort, hoping to break through to a state of equanimity in which pleasure and pain are treated alike. On the other hand, there is the law of karma. If someone accepts a version of this idea then asceticism offers a way of bringing the latent effects of karma forward into the present and working them off by deliberately creating suffering. The more karmic effects one can burn up in this way the less dominated by karma and the more free one will become.

Siddhatta practised austerities along with five other ascetics and was the most determined of the group, constantly seeking to extend his ability to deal with pain. He practised holding his breath until he experienced headaches which created the sensation that his head was being crushed with the point of a sword or being held over a fire of coals. He fasted and became so thin and malnourished that when he sought to touch the skin of his stomach he felt his spine; when he sought to touch his spine he felt the skin of his stomach, and when he stroked his arm the hairs fell out. Eventually, he realized that austerities were not the way to escape from suffering.

Also in this period, it is not clear whether before or after his practice of austerities, Siddhatta studied meditation under, first, Āḷāra Kalāma and, second, Uddaka Rāmaputta. Āḷāra taught Siddhatta how to attain the state of no-thing-ness (a state designated by later Buddhists as the seventh jhāna) and offered to share leadership of his group with his student, but Siddhatta refused, realizing that this state was not the end of sorrow that he sought. Later he studied under Uddaka and learned how to attain the state of neither-perception-nor-non-perception (a state designated by later Buddhists as the eighth jhāna). Like Āḷāra, Uddaka offered to share the leadership of his group with Siddhatta, but again the young man declined, realizing that this too was not the way that led beyond sorrow.

## ENLIGHTENMENT

The Pali texts present us with a number of different accounts of Siddhatta's enlightenment. They do, however, present the student of Buddhism with a number of problems, not least of which is that they are not compatible with each other. **One of them** has Siddhatta leaving Uddaka Rāmaputta and settling outside of a small town called Uruvela, 'a delightful spot with a pleasant grove, a river flowing delightfully with clear water and good fords, and round about a place for seeking alms'. After sitting down to meditate on the nature of self, he became enlightened.[16]

**A second account** has Siddhatta practising austerities, coming to the conclusion that asceticism does not lead to enlightenment and deciding to take food. Having eaten, he begins to meditate in the way that he had whilst a boy in his father's field. The five ascetics who were tending him were disgusted at what they perceived to be his fall into a life of abundance and they decided to leave. Siddhatta continued to meditate and eventually obtained the three knowledges that woke him up to the true nature of things. The passage is worth quoting because it presents us with what is probably the earliest description we have in Indian literature of someone progressing through various levels of concentration (jhāna/dhyāna/samādhi) and gaining liberating knowledge as a result.

> Now having taken solid food and gained strength, without sensual desires, without evil ideas I attained and abode in the first trance (jhāna) of joy and pleasure, arising from seclusion and combined with reasoning; and investigation (savitarka, savicāra). Nevertheless such pleasant feeling as arose did not overpower my mind. With the ceasing of reasoning and investigation (nirvitarka, nirvicāra) I attained and abode in the second trance of joy and pleasure arising from concentration, with internal serenity and fixing of the mind on one point without reasoning and investigation. With equanimity towards joy and aversion I abode mindful and conscious, and experienced bodily pleasure, what the noble ones describe as 'dwelling with equanimity, mindful, and happily', and attained and abode in the third trance. Abandoning pleasure and abandoning pain, even before the disappearance of elation and depression, I attained and abode in the fourth trance, which is without pain and pleasure, and with purity of mindfulness and equanimity.
>
> Thus with mind concentrated, purified, cleansed, spotless, with the defilements gone, supple, dexterous, firm, and impassible, I directed my mind to the knowledge of the remembrance of my former existences. I remembered many former existences, such as, one birth, two births, three, four, five, ten, twenty, thirty, forty, fifty, a hundred, a thousand, a hundred thousand births; many cycles of dissolution of the universe, many cycles of its evolution, many of its dissolution and evolution; there I was of such and such a name, clan, colour, livelihood, such pleasure and pain did I suffer, and such was the end of my life.

Passing away thence I was born elsewhere. There too I was of such and such a name, clan, colour, livelihood, such pleasure and pain did I suffer, and such was the end of my life. Passing away thence I was reborn here. Thus do I remember my many former existences with their special modes and details. This was the first knowledge that I gained in the first watch of the night. Ignorance was dispelled, knowledge arose. Darkness was dispelled, light arose. So is it with him who abides vigilant, strenuous and resolute.

Thus with mind concentrated, purified, cleansed, spotless, with the defilements gone, supple, dexterous, firm and impassible, I directed my mind to the passing away and rebirth of beings. With divine, purified, superhuman vision I saw beings passing away and being reborn, low and high, of good and bad colour, in happy or miserable existences according to their karma. Those beings who lead evil lives in deed, word, or thought, who speak evil of the noble ones, of false views, who acquire karma through their false views, at the dissolution of the body after death are reborn in a state of misery and suffering in hell. But those beings who lead good lives in deed, word, and thought, who speak no evil of the noble ones, of right views, who acquire karma through their right views, at the dissolution of the body after death are reborn in a happy state in the world of heaven. This was the second knowledge that I gained in the second watch of the night...

Thus with mind concentrated, purified, cleansed, spotless, with the defilements gone, supple, dexterous, firm, and impassible, I directed my mind to the knowledge of the destruction of the āsavas. I duly realized (the truth) 'this is pain,' I duly realized (the truth) 'this is the cause of pain,' I duly realized (the truth) 'this is the destruction of pain,' and I duly realized (the truth) 'this is the way that leads to the destruction of pain.' I duly realized 'these are the āsavas' . . . 'this is the cause of the āsavas' . . . 'this is the destruction of the āsavas' . . . 'this is the way that leads to the destruction of the āsavas.' As I thus knew and thus perceived, my mind was emancipated from the āsava of sensual desire, from the āsava of desire for existence, and from the āsava of ignorance. And in me emancipated arose the knowledge of my emancipation. I realized that destroyed is

> rebirth, the religious life has been led, done is what was to be done, there is nought (for me) beyond this world. This was the third knowledge that I gained in the last watch of the night. Ignorance was dispelled, knowledge arose. Darkness was dispelled, light arose. So is it with him who abides vigilant, strenuous, and resolute.[17]

**A third account** has Siddhatta meditating on the bank of the Nerañjara river. He is approached by Māra, the spirit of temptation, who encourages him to abandon his quest, but Siddhatta resists. Then Māra sends his armies of lusts, aversions, cravings, hungers, thirsts, cowardice, laziness, hypocrisy, stupidity and the like against the young meditator. In some accounts, these qualities are described as the daughters of Māra. Siddhatta resists them all and goes on to become enlightened. In some versions of the story Māra claims that Siddhatta is not worthy of enlightenment. In reply, Siddhatta touches the earth and calls upon her to bear witness to the fact that he had come to this point through great exertions over many lifetimes. The earth then quakes to indicate her agreement with the young man's claim.[18]

## TEACHING

After his enlightenment, the Buddha sat and reflected on his experience. He thought,

> Mankind is intent on its attachments, and takes delight and pleasures in them... it is hard [for them] to see the principle of causality, origination by way of cause. Hard to see is the principle of the cessation of all compounded things, the renunciation to clinging to rebirth, the extinction of all craving, absence of passion, cessation, *nirvāṇa*.[19]

Such thought led the Buddha to wonder whether it was worth trying to teach what he had learned. At that point, a god, Brahmā Sahampati, appeared and pointed out that there were some beings who only had a little dust in their eyes and would benefit from a proclamation of the dhamma. The Buddha then decided to give teaching a go and thought about who to contact first. Āḷāra and Uddaka were dead, but his supernormal vision revealed that the five ascetics were in a deer park at Vārāṇasī (Banares). So he went there. On his arrival, he taught first two of the ascetics and then the other three. All became arhats (worthy ones, who are liberated in life). These were the first members of the Buddhist community (Saṅgha). Soon the number of arhats had reached 60 and the Buddha sent them out to spread the doctrine.

Most of the *Sutta Piṭaka* is concerned with the Buddha's 40-year period of teaching and contains most of what we know about his life and his understanding of the human situation. The London-based Pāli Text Society has commissioned translations of the entire Piṭaka, and some of the works contained within it are available in more than one version. There are also many anthologies of Pāli texts that the interested student can consult. See the Bibliography for some examples.

#### DEATH

The main account of the Buddha's death that we find in the Pāli Canon is typical of hagiographical treatments. A variety of miracles take place and the Buddha is shown to be in control of even this event by the fact that he chooses to die rather than being taken by death. Even after his death the miracles continue with his funeral pyre refusing to light until all his arhats had arrived.[20]

### Dhamma

The Buddha wandered around northern India for 40 or more years after his enlightenment, teaching and preaching to a variety of audiences. Most of the suttas in the *Sutta Piṭaka* are accounts of these teaching episodes. The same point is often made in a different way according to context and time, and sometimes one version contains details not found in others. There is, nevertheless, a core teaching that can be identified. 'Two things do I teach,' said the Buddha, 'suffering and its removal.' The details of this teaching are summarized in the form of the Four Noble Truths (ariyasatta):

1. suffering (dukkha);
2. the origin of suffering (dukkha samudaya);
3. the cessation of suffering (dukkha nirodha);
4. the path (magga) that leads to the cessation of suffering.

### SUFFERING

About suffering the Buddha says,

> Now this monks, is the Ariyan truth about Ill [dukkha], death is Ill: likewise sorrow and grief, woe, lamentation and despair. To be conjoined with things which we dislike; to be separated from things which we like—that also is Ill. Not to get what one wants—that also is Ill. In a word, this body, this fivefold mass which is based on grasping, that is Ill.[21]

In short, embodiment as a living organism inevitably brings suffering.

### THE ORIGIN OF SUFFERING

For the Buddha, suffering is caused by many factors working together, though he often emphasized the centrality of craving or thirst (tanha). The way these factors create suffering is usually described in the suttas in terms of dependent origination (paṭicca samuppāda [P] / pratītya samutpāda [S]). The essence of this idea is that no phenomenon exists by itself, independent of everything else. Rather, everything depends on other things for existence. Everything in our worldly experience (Buddhists call these 'conditioned states') has come into existence because previous states already existed, and is linked to and dependent on other simultaneously existing states. All conditioned states, says the Buddha, are impermanent (anicca), ill (dukkha) and without self or a permanent, unchanging essence (anattā).

There are various formulations of this process of origination in the suttas. Some have twelve 'links' in the 'chain',[22] some have nine[23] and some only six.[24] The following is the sixfold version:

> While staying at Savatthi the Exalted One said:-
> In him, brethren, who contemplates the enjoyment that there is in all that makes for grasping, craving grows. Grasping is conditioned by craving. Becoming is conditioned by grasping. Birth is conditioned by becoming. Decay-and-death is conditioned by birth. Grief, lamenting, suffering, sorrow, despair come to pass. Such is the uprising of this entire mass of ill.

> It is just as if there should be a blazing bonfire of ten or twenty or thirty or forty loads of faggots; thereon a man should throw from time to time dry grasses, should throw dry cow-dung, should throw dry faggots. Verily such a great bonfire so fed, so supplied with fuel, would burn for a long while.
>
> Even so in him who contemplates the enjoyment that there is in all that makes for grasping, craving grows, and is the condition of grasping; so becoming, birth, decay-and-death follow, grief, lamenting, suffering, sorrow, despair come to pass. Such is the uprising of this entire mass of ill.
>
> In him, brethren, who contemplates the misery that there is in all that makes for grasping, craving ceases. When craving ceases, grasping ceases, so also becoming, birth, decay-and-death, grief, lamenting, suffering, sorrow, despair cease. Such is the ceasing of this entire mass of ill.
>
> It is just as if there should be a blazing bonfire of ten, or twenty, or thirty, or forty loads of faggots; thereon no man should from time to time throw dry grasses, dry cow-dung, dry sticks. Verily that great bonfire, when the first laid fuel were come to an end, and it were not fed by other fuel, would without food become extinct.
>
> Even so in him who contemplates the misery that there is in all that makes for grasping, craving ceases, and hence grasping ceases, becoming, birth, decay-and-death, and sorrow cease. Such is the ceasing of this entire mass of ill.

## THE CESSATION OF SUFFERING

The end of the last passage makes it clear that for the Buddha suffering, which, like everything else in this world, is conditioned and therefore impermanent, can be overcome. Indeed, the eradication of suffering (dukkhānta [P] / duḥkhānta [S]) is the primary aim of all systems of yoga. It is worth mentioning here that in yogic thought generally death is not believed to be the end of suffering because as long as there are still karmic fruits to be experienced death simply leads to rebirth.

We can recognize then that the Buddha's analysis of suffering, the essential features of which are shared by other yogic systems, is fundamentally metaphysical in nature. We can all agree on the empirical facts of suffering and even that desires and cravings contribute to suffering, but the teachings of karma and rebirth are not amenable to ordinary or even scientific evaluation. One accepts them as true either because certain texts teach them as truths or because one is able to access some kind of mystical state of consciousness that validates them for oneself. In other words, if the universe is not regulated by a law of karma, if beings are not reborn, then death may, in fact, be the end of suffering. In short, the yogic solution to the problem of suffering only works if the yogic analysis of its nature and causes are accurate. That said, even if they are not accurate, there may be other benefits to be gained from adopting a lifestyle based on yogic teachings.

For the Buddha, there is a state that is not subject to suffering, a state that he calls the unconditioned. Unlike conditioned states, the unconditioned is permanent (nitya) rather than impermanent (anitya) and happy (sukha) rather than painful (duḥkha), though even this state (often called nibānna/nirvāṇa by the Buddha) is without abiding substance. It too is anattā/anātman. On this point the yogic teaching of the Buddha departs most significantly from that found in the Upaniṣads.

The Upaniṣadic ātman is a substance (sat) and it is active, directing every individual from within as the inner controller (antaryāmin) and creating the universe. Nirvāṇa has none of these features. One of the Pāli texts, the Udāna, describes it as follows:

> There exists, monks, that sphere where there is: (i) neither solidity, nor cohesion, nor heat, nor motion; (ii) nor the sphere of infinite space, nor the sphere of infinite consciousness, nor the sphere of nothingness, nor the sphere of neither-perception-nor-non-perception; (iii) neither this world, nor a world beyond, nor both; (iv) nor sun-and-moon; (v) there, monks, I say there is no coming or going, nor maintenance, nor falling away, nor arising; (vi) that, surely, is without support (patiṭṭhā), it has no functioning, it has no object (ārammaṇa); just this is the end of dukkha.[25]

The attainment of this state is what, in Buddhist teaching, brings about the cessation of suffering.

THE WAY THAT LEADS TO THE CESSATION OF SUFFERING

The most well-known version of the Buddhist path to salvation from suffering is the noble eightfold path (ariya aṭṭaṅgika magga / ārya astāṅga mārga). There are, however, a number of training schemes mentioned in the Pāli Canon which either lead to enlightenment or contribute to it in some way. Many of these schemes contain practices found in others; so they can be regarded as various ways of explaining the nature of the spiritual life according to Buddhism. Eventually, a list of 37 factors contributing to awakening (bodhi pakkhiyā dhammā) was compiled. There are four references to this list in the *Sutta Piṭaka*, though they are not called bodhipakkhiyādhammā in these places.[26]

The situation in which this list is introduced is the announcement to the Buddha of Mahāvīra's death and a schism among his followers. The Buddha's response is to identify the items that are accepted by all his followers. In these accounts the 37 items are arranged under seven headings:

1. **The four foundations or applications of mindfulness** (cattāro satipaṭṭhāna): 1. of body; 2. of feelings; 3. of thoughts; 4. of phenomena.
2. **The four right endeavours or efforts** (cattāro sammappadhāna): 1. Avoid the arising of unwholesome states of mind; 2. Overcome existing unwholesome states of mind; 3. Develop wholesome states of mind; 4. Maintain wholesome states of mind.
3. **The four steps to (mental) perfection or (mental) power** (cattāro iddhipādā): 1. Concentration of intention; 2. Concentration of energy; 3. Concentration of thought; 4. Concentration of investigation.
4. **The five faculties** (pañca-indriyāni): 1. Faith; 2. Energy; 3. Mindfulness; 4. Concentration; 5. Insight.
5. **The five powers** (pañca-balāni): same as the five faculties.
6. **The seven factors or limbs of enlightenment** (satta bojjhaṅga): 1. Mindfulness; 2. Investigation of phenomena; 3. Energy; 4. Rapture; 5. Tranquillity; 6. Concentration; 7. Equanimity.
7. **The noble eightfold path** (ariya aṭṭhaṅgika magga): 1. Right view; 2. Right intention; 3. Right speech; 4. Right action; 5. Right livelihood; 6. Right effort; 7. Right mindfulness; 8. Right concentration.

All of these items can be recognized as forms of yogic practice and many of those from the first six sections reappear in various parts of the eightfold path. I will thus confine my treatment of the path leading to the cessation of suffering to comments about the final section: the noble eightfold path. Many writers present the eightfold path as a relatively unproblematic scheme that will guide an aspirant to the goal of nibbāna. My reading of the situation is somewhat different and I prefer to alert anyone who has an interest in Buddhist soteriology to the nature of the controversy, even though I do not have a definitive solution to offer, than to pretend that the disagreements do not exist. That said, I do find some of the accounts more problematic that others. Of the four alternatives outlined below my preference is for the fourth, which, as it happens, is the most controversial and furthest away from standard accounts. It does, however, answer questions that to my mind the other accounts fail to resolve adequately. I will, therefore, devote more space to describing this account than the others.

Four essentially incompatible interpretations can be identified. The first is well articulated by the eminent Theravādin scholar monk Walpola Rahula. In his introductory text, *What The Buddha Taught*, Rahula writes:

> It should not be thought that the eight categories or divisions of the path should be followed and practised one after the other in the numerical order as given in the usual list... they are to be developed more or less simultaneously. As far as possible, according to the capacity of each individual.[27]

A commonly employed metaphor to convey this understanding of the path is an umbrella with eight spokes. One progresses from the outer rim down each of the spokes to the still centre of nibbāna.

A second interpretation, found in works such as Sangharakshita's *Survey of Buddhism* and Nyantiloka's *Buddhist Dictionary*, is that initially right view means acceptance of the Buddha's teaching by faith. One's right intention should be based on this. Then follows the practice of the moral principles (right speech, action and livelihood), which serve as a foundation for the meditational practice as found in the final three steps of right effort, mindfulness and concentration. Success in the last of these facilitates the experience of 'authentic' right view, right intention, etc. which eventually lead to right knowledge and right release (steps nine and ten in some versions of the path). A similar view is found in Peter Harvey's recent introductory text on Buddhism, where he writes:

> The eight factors exist at two basic levels, the ordinary, and the transcendent or noble, so that there is both an ordinary and an Ennobling Eightfold Path... Most Buddhists seek to practise the ordinary Path, which is perfected only in those who are approaching the lead-up to stream-entry. At stream entry, a person fully enters the Ennobling Eightfold Path.[28]

A third interpretation is that one actually begins one's practice with right speech and follows the remaining steps until, on the basis of right concentration, one gains right view and right intention. This is a view often associated with the fifth-century CE Theravādin scholar Buddhaghosa and his magnum opus, *The Path of Purification* (*Visuddhimagga*). It is clearly quite close in character to the second interpretation mentioned above.

What all these views have in common is the idea that anyone can decide to follow the eightfold path and start practising right away. The fourth view denies that this is possible. It also denies the existence of two paths, an ordinary and an ennobling, and maintains that the path is to be understood as sequential—beginning with right view and ending with the tenth step of right release.[29] This view has been most eloquently articulated by Peter Masefield of the University of Sidney.[30] Right view, according to Masefield,

> is defined as understanding (pajānāti) or possessing knowledge (ñāṇaṃ) of the four truths; it is to see with right insight (paññā) the uprising and cessation of the world as it really is, to have, without dependence on another, no doubt, no uncertainty that whatever uprises is (dukkha) and that whatever ceases is dukkha... Right view is, in short, to see the Dhamma, to see Nibbāna... Such a right view is, moreover, supermundane [lokuttara], anāsava [without karmic consequence] and ariyan [noble] and the means by which one comes to be born of the ariyan birth.[31]

In Masefield's account it is the acquisition of right view that makes one an ariyan, a noble one. Ariyans, in this sense, are those who see the four truths for themselves. Possessors of right view see the path to nirvāṇa but have not yet achieved it. What enables them to follow the path, which would be almost impossible if not completely impossible for ordinary people, is that the acquisition of right view destroys the bulk of one's karmic burden. A passage in the *Sanyutta Nikāya* describes it thus:

> Even so, for the ariyasāvaka [noble hearer] who has attained Right View, for the person possessing paññā [insight], this is quite the greater dukkha, this that has been destroyed, has been put to an end, whilst that which remains is infinitely small and does not amount to one hundredth, does not amount to one thousandth, does not amount to one hundredth thousandth, when set beside the former dukkha that has been destroyed, has been put to an end—that is at most a term of seven (births)—so great a good is (it to have) insight into Dhamma, so great a good is it to acquire the Dhammacakkhu [eye seeing the Dhamma].[32]

Those who have acquired right view (ariya sāvakas, noble hearers) are, according to the Pāli texts, of four types—type being determined by the number of hindrances destroyed and the number of rebirths that the person can expect to experience.[33] The first of these is the streamwinner, who has destroyed the three fetters of personality belief, sceptical doubts, and faith in good works and religious rituals. The streamwinner will be reborn no more than seven times. Second is the once-returner, who has destroyed the same fetters as the streamwinner and weakened lust, ill will and dullness. The once-returner will return to the earthly realm for only one more birth. Third is the non-returner, who has destroyed the streamwinner's three plus ill will and sensuous craving. Any future rebirth for the non-returner will be in a heavenly realm.[34] Fourth is the arahat (worthy one), who has destroyed all the above five as well as the āsavas of kāma (lust), bhava (desire for existence) and avijja (ignorance). Some lists add diṭṭhi (views, i.e. wrong views/beliefs) to these three. The destruction of the āsavas is essentially synonymous with the attainment of nibbāna, and the arahat is one who is liberated in life. There will be no more rebirth once the karmic energy supporting the present life is exhausted.

If Masefield is correct, and the noble eightfold path really does begin with right view as described above, then a person cannot simply decide to begin following the noble path to the cessation of suffering. One has to find a way to obtain right view. It might, therefore, seem strange that the Pāli Canon does not provide guidelines on how to get it. This, according to Masefield, is because the discourses recorded in the Canon are mostly directed at those who already have it. What we do have, though, are descriptions of a number of instances where individuals acquire right view. These descriptions have one thing in common: the individual is a recipient of an orally delivered proclamation of the dhamma by either the Buddha or one of his ariya sāvakas. Interestingly, the state of mind that a recipient enters during such a proclamation is described in terms that are almost identical to those employed in descriptions of the fourth jhāna: 'malleable, devoid of the hindrances, uplifted, devout',[35] which was the state in which the Buddha acquired his own liberating insight.

The message is clear: if you want right view, find someone who already has it (preferably an arahat) and request a teaching on dhamma. Whether such a person wears the robes of a monk or nun would seem to be far less important than whether he or she is an ariyan, i.e. a sāvaka who has gained right view. It is easy to understand why many Buddhists are not attracted to Masefield's analysis, because it tells them that unless they have experienced right view they cannot be following the noble eightfold path that leads to nibbāna. Masefield pulls no punches in pointing out the implications of his research:

> Whilst this [means of acquiring right view] was of obvious benefit to the fortunate individual who became a sāvaka, it had the sinister implication for the Buddhist world that until such a conversion were received, almost as an act of grace on the part of the Buddha, there could be no possibility of anyone, whether monk or layman, following the eightfold way to Nibbāna nor of their becoming free of their past kamma.[36]

## Saṅgha

In much modern writing about Buddhism the term 'saṅgha' is often taken to mean the community of monks and nuns rather than the community of ariya sāvakas. In either case, the integrity of the Saṅgha is protected by the Vinaya (discipline). Within the *Suttavibangha* section of the *Vinaya Piṭaka* are the 227 pāṭimokkha rules that are recited communally at the new and full moon. These rules are the basis of what we would call 'schools' (nikāya) of

Buddhism. If monks and nuns live according to different sets of rules then they cannot recite them together and have to form a new school. The rules regulate the lives of all Saṅgha members and breaches of them must be declared at the fortnightly recitations. Various penances are prescribed for transgressing these rules, though only four transgressions (known as the four forbidden acts) result in expulsion:

1. sexual acts;
2. taking anything not given;
3. harming any living being;
4. falsely claiming miraculous powers.

We know that these rules were set out at an early period in Buddhist history, not least because a very similar set belonging to the Sarvāstivāda school has been preserved in Chinese. The Sarvāstivādin pāṭimokkha has 250 rather than 227 rules, though most of the extra ones have been created by dividing some of the items in the Theravādin list into two. Nuns live under these and eight additional precepts that essentially subordinate all nuns to all monks. Both the *Vinaya Piṭaka* and the *Anguttara Nikāya* (Gradual Sayings) contain a passage where Mahāpajāpatī, the Buddha's aunt and wet nurse, accepts ordination on condition that she and all nuns will embrace these extra precepts. Women in Buddhism can become arahats and attain nibbāna but they remain socially inferior to *all* monks.

These regulations, along with their equivalents in Jainism and the descriptions of the lives of forest dwellers in the Upaniṣads, all point to non-violence and celibacy as the norm for the early practitioners of yoga. However, in the epic period a radically new interpretation of yoga came onto the scene. It is persuasively presented by the warrior king Kṛṣṇa to his friend Arjuna in one of Hinduism's most celebrated texts: the *Bhagavad Gītā*. Before examining that yoga, however, it is worth noting some of the developments in yogic thought and practice that took place within that form of Buddhism known as the Great Vehicle (Mahāyāna).

## MAHĀYĀNA BUDDHISM

Some time after the death of the Buddha a controversy broke out within the Buddhist community over the issue of whether people who claimed to be arahats had really destroyed the āsavas. Karel

Werner suggests that even though most of the early arahats had gained the three and often the six higher knowledges,

> we have at quite an early stage in the Pāli canonical tradition several types of liberated ones who had attained nirvāṇa, but who were not equal to each other in the attainment of higher spiritual powers. Yet they were recognised as arahants who had destroyed their cankers [āsava].[37]

Some of these had attained to only one of the six knowledges: destruction of the āsavas. This is technically all that is needed for the attainment of freedom, but, as Werner points out, it was possible for people to think that they had destroyed the āsavas when they had not, and he cites the cases of Mahā Nāga and Mahā Tissa who believed that they were arahats for 60 years until one of their awakened students realized this and helped them to make the final step.

The Pāli texts refer to those who claimed arahatship on the basis of destruction of the āsavas alone as the 'wisdom liberated' (paññavimutta) or those who are liberated by insight alone (sukha vipassika, suddha vipassika), i.e. they had no proficiency in the jhānas and lacked the knowledge about the nature of saṃsāra that three- and six-knowledge arahats possessed.[38] Consequently, the status of arahats came to be disputed, and for many Buddhists arahatship became a goal that was considerably inferior to that of Buddhahood. Eventually, the idea that 'arahats' could 'fall away' from liberation took hold in many parts of the Buddhist world, and this paved the way for what came to be known as the Mahāyāna (Great Vehicle), which rejected the goal of arahatship and sought Buddhahood for all. The name employed by Mahāyānists for aspirants to this lofty goal was bodhisattva (awakening being), the term used by earlier Buddhist tradition to refer to the Buddha before he came to be enlightened.

The origins of Mahāyāna Buddhism are somewhat obscure and a subject of considerable controversy among those who study the Buddhist tradition. Here I shall simply explain why a once popular account of how the Mahāyāna arose is untenable and outline what seem to me to be the essentials of more recent thinking on the matter.

Sometime around 150 years after the death of the Buddha, perhaps during the early years of Aśoka's reign, the Buddhist Saṅgha held a council at Pāṭaliputra.[39] This is sometimes called the second Buddhist council, though if one accepts that his followers held a council immediately after his death it was the third. At this council the Saṅgha split into two groups: the sthaviras/theras (elders) and the mahāsaṅghikas (great community). The sthaviras were divided into eleven major sub-sects and the mahāsaṅghikas seven. These comprise what are often known as the 18 schools of Hīnayāna (lesser vehicle) Buddhism. The term 'Hīnayāna' was coined by Mahāyānists and is clearly evaluative. Modern scholars have not yet reached a consensus about a more neutral term for referring to these schools collectively, but Śravakayāna (the Way of the Hearers) would seem to be an appropriate one as it is reasonably accurate and descriptive rather than evaluative.

Scholars working in the first six or seven decades of the twentieth century tended to regard the Pāṭaliputra council as decisive for the emergence of the Mahāyāna and looked to the Mahāsaṅghika tradition for its origins with, perhaps, some streams of influence from outside of Buddhism.[40] However, such an approach is highly problematic. In the first place, many Mahāsaṅghika teachings do not square with what we know about the Mahāyāna. For example, the Gokulikas (a Mahāsaṅghika sub-sect) held that only the Abhidharma was the true message of the Buddha, yet Mahāyānists relied on their own sūtra collections as primary sources of the Buddha's teachings and did not even possess an Abhidharma until well into the first millennium CE. Secondly, no Śravakayāna text mentions the Mahāyāna by name and none of the Mahāyāna Sūtras mention any Hīnayāna/Śravakayāna schools or sub-sects. They only use the all-embracing term 'Hīnayāna'.

Another reason why scholars have linked the Mahāyāna with the Mahāsaṅghikas is that the latter tended to give prominence to the role of the laity and a number of Mahāyāna texts suggest that bodhisattvas can transfer merit that they have accumulated over countless lifetimes to other beings who are in need—an expression of compassion and lovingkindness. This too is problematic. Many early Mahāyāna Sūtras, e.g. the Perfection of Wisdom Sūtras (*Prajñāpāramitā Sūtras*) and the Lotus Sūtra (*Saddharmapuṇḍarīka Sūtra*), affirm quite clearly that the dharma is deep, profound and difficult to understand, much as the Buddha did after his enlightenment when he was wondering whether to try to teach it. That the Mahāyāna emerged in response to concerns about or pressures from the laity is thus hardly convincing. In short, there are good reasons for thinking that the Mahāyāna did *not* originate out of Mahāsaṅghika developments.

Andrew Rawlinson, amongst others, has offered a rather different view. He suggests that Mahāyānists arose in many Śravakayāna schools as a kind of alternative movement, not dissimilar to the Pentecostalist tradition in Christianity, which has adherents from most of the Christian denominations. On this account, the reason that Mahāyāna texts do not refer to Hīnayāna 'schools' is that for the followers of the Greater Vehicle *all* non-Mahāyānists were on an inferior path and Mahāyānists themselves came from many different schools. What brought diverse groups of Buddhists together under the banner of Mahāyāna was not affiliation with some new school (that has more to do with matters of monastic rules, see above) but inspiration from a new vision. Mahāyānists, suggests Rawlinson, would meet in small groups in which visionary experiences of the Buddha were commonplace. In such visions, the Buddha presented the dharma to those with ears to hear, and that dharma became the basis of what came to be known as the Mahāyāna Sūtras. Again, we can see parallels within the Christian tradition, where Saint Paul became recognized as an apostle even though he had only encountered Jesus in visionary form. Hence, Mahāyānists hold their own texts to be the primary authority for them, and that is why the emergence of the Mahāyāna is often called 'the second turning of the wheel of dharma'.

## Mahāyāna Teachings

The first thing to be stated here is that the Mahāyānists accepted much of the teaching found in the *Sutta Piṭaka,* and many of their doctrines can be seen to be elaborations or extensions of material that can be found in the suttas. Here I shall simply comment on a few of the more prominent ones.[41]

Given the debasement of the arahat ideal, Mahāyānists avoided unprofitable debates with their fellow Buddhists about who is and who is not a genuine arahat. Instead, they jettisoned arahatship as an ideal altogether and adopted Buddhahood as an ideal for all. Those who accepted this new ideal were called bodhisattvas (literally, awakening beings) or Buddhas-to-be. Earlier tradition had already mentioned other Buddhas, e.g. Vipassin (see above), and other bodhisattvas, e.g. Siddhatta before his enlightenment and Metteya/Maitreya, the Buddha to come. The Mahāyānists also

## SOME IMPORTANT MAHĀYĀNA SŪTRAS

**Prajñāpāramitā Sūtras** (Perfection of Wisdom Sutras). The main ones are:

1. *Śatasāhasrikā Prajñāpāramitā Sūtra* (Perfection of Wisdom in 100,000 Lines).
2. *Pañcaviṃśatisāhasrikā Prajñāpāramitā Sūtra* (Perfection of Wisdom in 25,000 Lines).
3. *Aṣṭasāhasrika Prajñāpāramitā Sūtra* (Perfection of Wisdom in 8,000 Lines—this is the oldest of the perfection of wisdom sūtras).
4. *Vajracchedikā Prajñāpāramitā Sūtra* (the Diamond or Diamond Cutter Sūtra).
5. *Prajñāpāramitā Hṛdaya Sūtra* (the Heart Sūtra).

These texts deal mainly with the true nature of existence and emptiness (śūnyatā).

**The Ratnakūṭa** (Most Excellent Jewel Sūtras). There are 49 of these, each with the same name. Sometimes they are regarded as one work with 49 chapters. They are concerned primarily with the bodhisattva and the bodhicitta (mind of enlightenment).

**Saddharma Puṇḍarīka Sūtra** (the Lotus of the True Dharma Sūtra). Concerned mainly with the Mahāyāna in general as a vehicle for enlightenment.

**Vimalakīrtinirdeśa Sūtra** (the Explanation of Vimalakīrti). Putting forward the view that the layman can become a bodhisattva and attain to the perfection of wisdom.

**Sukhāvati-vyūha** (the Development of the Pure Land). Extolling the virtues of Amitayus/Amitabha Buddha's Pure Land, where aspirants with faith in Amitayus can be born and from where it is easy to attain nirvāṇa.

**Laṅkāvatāra sūtra** (Descent on Laṅka Sūtra). Noted for its development of the ālaya vijñāna (store consciousness) concept.

**Avataṃsaka Sūtra** (the Flower Garland Sutra), which contains both the *Gaṇḍhavyuha* (development of the perfume)—a text which develops a kind of holographic cosmology; and the *Daśabhūmika* (ten stages)—a text on the ten stages of the bodhisattva's career.

**Parinirvāṇa Sūtra, Śrimālā Sūtra and Ratnagotravibhaga.** Three texts on the tathāgata garbha (Buddha nature) theory.

emphasized an aspect of the Buddha's career that had been somewhat, though not entirely, neglected: his deep compassion. The Buddha sacrificed his own tranquillity at the request of Brahmā in order to teach the dhamma, and this was understood as an act of compassion. He also encouraged the cultivation of compassion through the practice of the Brahmā Vihāra (sublime abodes) meditations.[42] As well as embracing Buddhahood as an ideal the Mahāyānists elevated compassion to the same level as wisdom/insight (paññā/prajñā) in the Buddhist hierarchy of values. Insight into the true nature of things is, as was mentioned above, the foundation stone of liberation from suffering and rebirth, and much of its content had to do with what we might call 'depersonalization'.

The Buddha's teaching on no-self (anattā/anātman) had been elaborated through his division of a person into five major constituent parts (skhandha)[43] and these in turn were analysed into smaller, even more evanescent components called dhammas/dharmas. These dharmas are mere flashes of existence that arise and decay in rapid succession, fuelled by karmic energy. Nothing abiding and substantial is found in any person. Ignorance of our true natures and, in particular, clinging to the notion of self is what produces craving and all the suffering that goes with it. The best way to help suffering beings is, therefore, to teach them the Buddha's wisdom and help them to understand that they are not who they think they are. Mahāyānists accepted this, but they also responded to the needs of the beings who experienced the pains of this world, not least because to put one's own welfare above that of others is to give greater value to one's own self and, thereby, prevent full realization of one's essentially selfless nature. Hence, bodhisattvas transfer merit that they have accumulated to others and even offer their lives if another being can be saved by such an act. The story in the Lotus Sūtra of the prince who sacrificed himself to a hungry tigress so that she could gain the strength to feed her cubs is the perfect illustration of this ideal.

Bodhisattvas were understood to be at different stages of development, and some, like non-returners, were believed to dwell in celestial realms. Perhaps the two most famous are Mañjuśrī, personification of wisdom (prajñā), and Avalokiteśvara, personification of compassion (karuṇā). Pictures of Mañjuśrī usually show him holding a sword (symbolic of the insight that cuts away the veil of ignorance from the mind) and a book (the *Prajñāpāramitā Sūtras*). He also rides on a lion, perhaps because the name given to the preaching of the dharma is a 'lion's roar'. Avalokiteśvara has many arms and an eye in the hand at the end of each. This allows him to see the sufferings of all beings, to which he responds in many and skilful ways. He can, for example, appear as a Buddha, an old beggar, a saint from another religion, a woman or a god. Many Buddhists regard the Dalai Lama as an incarnation of Avalokiteśvara.

These bodhisattvas take on so many different forms because they practise a virtue that is greatly emphasized in Mahāyāna Buddhism: skill-in-means (upāya kauśalya). The dharma is deep and difficult to comprehend, not least because it requires us to abandon attachment to everything we ordinarily think we are and take on a radically new, substanceless identity. People often need to be jolted or tricked into perceiving the world in this new way and so Buddhists seek to be as creative as they can in finding as many ways as possible to do this. Indeed, the entire Buddhist tradition can be seen as a gigantic exercise in upāya kauśalya that is designed to bring as many beings as possible to awakening.

One Mahāyānist teaching that helps us to understand how this can work is that of the three bodies (tri-kāya) of the Buddha. This is another elaboration of teachings that were already present in the suttas.[44] For example, in the Kindred Sayings (*Saṃyutta Nikāya*) the Buddha says, 'What is there in seeing this vile body of mine? He who seeth the dharma, Vakkali, he seeth me; he who seeth me Vakkali, he seeth the dharma. Verily, seeing the dharma, Vakkali, one sees me; seeing me one sees the dharma.'[45] The dharma is thus the Buddha's transcendental body, his true identity. His physical body (rūpa kāya) is simply an expression of the dharma, its skill-in-means as it were. The Mahāyānists called the physical body the nirmāṇa kāya (transformation body) so as to convey this understanding. Between the dharma and nirmāṇa kāyas the Mahāyānists inserted an enjoyment body (sambhoga kāya). This is a kind of radiant or celestial form that the Buddha uses to reveal himself to the bodhisattvas and preach the doctrines found in the Mahāyāna Sūtras.

The two most influential traditions of philosophy in Mahāyāna Buddhism are those of the Mādhyamaka (Middle Position) and the Yogācāra (Yoga Practice). Briefly, the Mādhyamakas, most influential of whom was Nāgārjuna (3rd century CE), challenged the teachings that had emerged in some Abhidharma traditions. In following the Buddha's denial of self to any form of conditioned existence, Abhidharmists, particularly those in the Vaibhāṣika/Sarvāstivāda tradition, analysed all conditioned entities into their component parts (dharmas). Different lists of dharmas were produced by different schools. The Sarvāstivāda, for example, offered a list of 75. Examples would be the six āyatanas (sense organs), the six or eighteen dhātus (elements) and the five skhandhas (components of a person). Entities, they argued, were better described in dharma language than ordinary language because the latter tend to allow misleading metaphysical notions like 'self' and 'substance' to pervade our thinking and help to perpetuate samsaric existence. Dharma language, by contrast, restricts itself to what can be experienced.

One drawback with this kind of analysis, as was mentioned above, is that it tends towards depersonalization and the danger that compassion might be lost. The Mādhyamakas saw another danger too: the danger of simply shifting 'thing' language from selves to dharmas. The Buddha's teaching on dependent origination (pratītya samutpāda) precluded this, claimed the Mādhyamakas. Nothing, they pointed out, not even dharmas, has self-existence or an essential nature (svabhāva). Everything is dependently arisen and interconnected; nothing exists independently of the conditions that surround it. In this analysis, the notions of being (sat) and its synonyms ātman and brahman as found in the Upaniṣads are seen to be misguided and to lead to bondage rather than release.

The terms employed by the Mādhyamakas to convey these teachings were also used by the Buddha himself on a number of occasions: śūnya and śūnyatā (empty and emptiness). For example, in *Sutta Nipāta* 1118 the brahman Mogharāja asks the Buddha 'How is any one to look upon the world that the king of death may not see him?' to which the Buddha replies, 'Look upon the world as void (suñña) O Mogharāja, being always thoughtful; having destroyed the view of oneself (as really existing), so one may overcome death; the king of death will not see him who thus regards the world.'[46] Similarly, in the *Saṃyutta Nikāya* the Buddha responds to Ānanda's enquiry about the meaning of the statement 'Void is the world' with the words 'because the world is void of self (atta)... or of what belongs to self... it is said "Void is the world" (suñño lokoti)'.[47] The Mahāyāna teaching about emptiness, then, is essentially a reiteration of the Buddha's emphasis on the dependently arisen nature of all phenomena. In terms of this analysis, the 'things' that we experience are mental constructs (vikalpa) and ultimately illusory (māyā). From the Mādhyamaka perspective, what we ordinarily call 'truth' is not, in fact, accurate. It is only conventionally true (samvṛtti satya) whereas the dharma of the Buddhas is actually true (paramārtha satya).

It was the Yogācāra school that sought to explain the processes by which we mistake our mental constructs for reality and set out the meditational strategy for overcoming this tendency. The principal teachers of the Yogācāra school were Maitryanātha, Asaṅga and Vasubandhu. The first of these may be a mythical or visionary figure (the sambhoga kāya of the bodhisattva Maitreya) who revealed a series of metrical commentaries on the *Māhāyana Sūtras* called alaṅkāra (adornments) to Asaṅga. Vasubandhu is reputed to have been the younger brother of Asaṅga and is widely recognized as one of the greatest scholar-yogis of the Buddhist tradition.

Exploring the Yogācāra tradition can be a rather confusing experience for a student as its two main offshoots interpreted Vasubandhu's teachings differently. One of these, headed by Sthiramati, interpreted Vasubandhu as essentially elaborating the kind of teaching that we find evidence for in both early Buddhism and early Mahāyāna. The other, headed by Dharmapāla, understood Vasubandhu to be teaching a kind of idealism—the doctrine that the stuff of the world is made of mind, is mind-stuff. This latter interpretation, probably because it became the dominant one in China and Japan, was adopted by most Western scholars until the 1960s.[48] Since then, scholars such as Thomas Kochumuttom (1982), Walpola Rahula (1978) and Yoshifumi Ueda (1967) have argued for an interpretation of Yogācāra texts that follows the line taken by Sthiramati rather than that adopted by Dharmapāla, and I accept that interpretation.

The Yogācāra masters teach that the whole of saṃsāric experience is mentally constructed (vikalpa). It is an imagination of the unreal (abhūta parikalpa); it is a mere representation of consciousness (vijñapti mātra) or a representation of mind (citta mātra) or mere representation (prajñapti mātra). This is not, as many have claimed, a teaching that the stuff of the world is mind-stuff. Rather, it is a teaching that all our 'experiences' of the world are mind-made. In modern parlance, it is a teaching that what we call experience is a simulation created by our brains out of information that comes from both our senses and from our past experiences. The simulation (our mind map) is *not* the territory (the world) that it represents.

The Yogācāra masters, like the Buddha, use this as a springboard to develop their soteriological teaching. Fundamental to this is an analysis of the nature of ignorance (avidyā). The fundamental ignorance, which must be uprooted if one wishes to escape from rebirth, is that which divides the world into subject–object, self–other, grasper–grasped, knower–knowable. This is the crucial unreal imagining (abhūta parikalpa) because it affects every perception, every experience. As Kochumuttom puts it,

> the effect of the superimposed distinction between graspable and grasper is so far reaching that it makes the whole universe appear (abhāsa) in a way much different from what it really is. Consequently, the entire cosmos as it appears is rightly called a mental construction (parikalpita), and is, therefore, described as mere representation of consciousness (vijñapti-mātra).[49]

The awakened ones have realized this and uprooted the fundamental ignorance of self-belief, of the self–other (ātman–dharma) distinction and see the world as it really is (yathā-bhūta). Whereas the ordinary person's knowledge is vikalpa (conceptual, mentally constructed) rather than direct, the awakened person's knowledge is nirvikalpa (non-conceptual). It is devoid (śūnya) of thought constructions; it is no-mind (acitta). Fundamental to the attainment of such awakening is the process of aśraya parāvṛtti (the revolution of the foundation) or ālaya parāvṛtti (the revolution of the storehouse). These are transformations in what the Yogācāra teachers call the storehouse consciousness (ālaya vijñāna).

Although not totally absent from earlier Buddhist writings, this teaching about the ālaya vijñāna was most fully developed by Asaṅga. In his *Abhidharmasamuccaya* he divides the vijñāna skhandha (fifth of the five skhandhas, components of the person) into three parts: citta, manas and vijñāna. He writes,

> What is the definition of the aggregate of consciousness *(vijñānaskandha)*? It is mind *(citta)*, mental organ *(manas)* and also consciousness *(vijñāna)*.
>
> And there what is mind *(citta)*? It is *ālaya-vijñāna* (store-consciousness) containing all seeds *(sarvbījaka)*, impregnated with the traces (impressions: *vāsanāparibhāvita)* of aggregates *(skandha)*, elements *(dhātu)* and spheres *(āyatana)* ...

> What is mental organ *(manas)*? It is the object of *ālayavijñāna*, always having the nature of self-notion (self-conceit, *manyanātmaka)* associated with four defilements: viz., the false idea of self *(ātmadṛṣṭi)*, self-love *(ātmasneha)*, the conceit of 'I-am' *(asmimāna)* and ignorance *(avidyā)*...
>
> What is consciousness *(vijñāna)*? It consists of the six groups of consciousness *(ṣaḍ vijñānakāyāḥ) viz.*, visual consciousness *(cakṣur vijñāna)*, auditory *(śrotra)*, olfactory *(ghrāṇa)*, gustatory *(jihvā)*, tactile *(kāya)* and mental consciousness *(manovijñāna)*...[50]

The ālaya vijnana 'perfumes' the other vijñānas whilst they constantly replenish it. Thus it is the ālaya vijñāna that perpetuates saṃsāric experience as all the seeds (bīja) within it are conditioned by the subject–object distinction. As they manifest in awareness or experience they colour it with that distinction. Thus, Asaṅga states in his *Compendium of the Mahāyāna* (*Mahāyāna Saṃgraha*) that the Buddha preached the dharma for the destruction of the ālaya.[51] His view is very much in keeping with the meanings of a number of terms in the Pāli texts that are generally regarded as synonyms for nirvāṇa: ālaya-samugghata (the uprooting of the ālaya) and analāya (no-ālaya). Thus, when the Buddha attained enlightenment he is reported to have said

> Through worldly round of many births
> I ran my course unceasingly,
> Seeking the maker of the house:
> Painful is birth again and again.
> House-builder! I behold thee now,
> Again a house that shalt not build;
> All thy rafters are broken now,
> The ridge-pole also is destroyed;
> My mind, its elements dissolved,
> The end of cravings has attained.[52]

The tool for accomplishing such dissolution of the mind is the noble eightfold path (or one of its variants such as the practice of the six or ten perfections) and, in particular, the right concentration that, through penetrating insight (vipassanā/vipaśyanā), bestows right knowledge. This is an insight into the nature of the ālaya vijñāna and the pervasive and delusory character of the sense of self and the subject–object distinction. Such an insight destroys the āsavas/āsravas and frees one from the grip of karma and the round of rebirth.

In terms of our model of soteriology, for Buddhism, like Jainism and the teachers of the Upaniṣads, the fundamental problem facing human beings is that of karma and its effects: suffering and rebirth. The methods employed can be understood primarily in terms of renunciation, moral conduct and meditation. The adoption of these leads to the acquisition of knowledge about the true nature of existence, which has the effect of liberating the practitioner from karma and rebirth. The path to liberation is thus one of works, though if one adopts Peter Masefield's line of interpretation then something akin to other power seems to be involved or even be crucial. Also like Jainism and the Upaniṣads, Buddhism is predominantly a cool-structured tradition. The differences between the three lie more in their metaphysical claims than their practices, though there are obvious differences here too. The Upaniṣads and Jainism postulate the existence of a self (ātman or jīva), though the former tends to be understood as single whereas the latter are multiple. Also the ātman creates the universe out of itself and the jīvas do not. They are of a different order of existence from the material world of ajīva. The Buddhists deny the existence of anything that could be called a self, though nirvāṇa, the unconditioned, is closer to the idea of an essentially inactive jīva than it is to that of the Upaniṣadic ātman, which not only creates the universe but also controls beings from within as an inner controller (antaryāmin).

## Chapter 4
## THE EPICS AND THE *BHAGAVAD GĪTĀ*

The *Mahābhārata* and *Rāmāyaṇa* are two great epic poems, India's equivalent of the *Iliad* and the *Odyssey*, though much longer. The former took shape over a period of about 800 years, from approximately 400 BCE to 400 CE, whilst the latter was compiled in the period between 200 BCE and 200 CE. In terms of setting, however, the dating is reversed as the *Rāmāyaṇa* is located in a time before the events that are related in the *Mahābhārata*, events that scholars tend to place somewhere between the eighth and ninth centuries CE. As J.A.B. Van Buitenen points out, in the *Rāmāyaṇa* '...rules of conduct are still being formulated by practice, not quoted from immemorial custom'.[1]

In ancient India, most noble families had bards who would sing the praises of ancestral heroes and pass on the exploits of their own lords to the next generation of bards. Many of these bards, as can be seen from their Sanskrit name, sūta, were charioteers. In this role they were able to document the deeds of the nobles whose praises they sang. The cores of the two epics are heroic bardic poems. The texts that we now possess have been both expanded and edited. The *Mahābhārata*, according to V.S. Sukthankar, was about 24,000 verses long, whilst the present version is around 100,000 verses.[2] The *Rāmāyaṇa*, which has an identifiable author, Vālmīki, currently has around 25,000 couplets and is divided into seven chapters, the first and last of which are generally thought by scholars to be later additions. The expansion of the *Mahābhārata*, in Sukthankar's view, was not a haphazard but a coordinated affair undertaken by a brāhman family called Bhṛgu. So we can expect, and do in fact find, that much of the current version of the *Mahābhārata* is concerned with themes that are of greater interest to priestly groups (brāhmans) than to the warrior nobility (kṣatriyas).[3]

Little in the *Rāmāyaṇa* has to do with yoga directly, though it has retrospective value for later practitioners of bhakti yoga (the discipline of spiritual devotion), mainly through the symbolism of Hanumān (the general of the monkey army who expresses deep devotion to Prince Rāma, who, in chapters one and seven, is presented as an incarnation of the god Viṣṇu). In the *Mahābhārata*, two sections are of considerable significance for yoga: sections 13-40 of the sixth book (the Bhīṣma parvan) known as the *Bhagavad Gītā* (Song of the Blessed One), and book twelve (the *Śānti Parvan*).

## THE *BHAGAVAD GĪTĀ*

The version of the *Gītā* that we have today is unlikely to be the original. Śaṅkara (8th century CE), the earliest known commentator, makes no reference to the first 57 stanzas of the present version (1.1–2.10). More recently, a number of scholars have argued that there was probably a briefer work that was revised at some point, probably, in my view, during the Bhṛgu redaction process.[4] Most radical of such suggestions is that of Phulgenda Sinha, who locates the core of the work in the first three chapters. For him, only eleven verses from chapter one, forty-two from chapter two and thirty-one from chapter three are original. The remaining 616 verses of the present version he regards as later interpolation.[5] R.N. Minor, whose commentary is to be commended to all serious students of the *Gītā*, dates the present version around 150 BCE.

My own comments on the text will be based on the *Gītā* as we now have it, though my conclusions support the idea that the work contains within it a number of conflicting doctrines. If the text was composed by a single author, then he was clearly seeking to weave a coherent teaching out of materials that are fundamentally incompatible. Most significant of these incompatibilities is the ontological one. Kṛṣṇa seeks to synthesize Sāṃkhya-Yoga, which is either dualistic or pluralistic, with Vedāntic monism, and, as I argued in the Introduction, monism, dualism and pluralism are mutually exclusive.

During the early epic period a new kind of religion appeared on the spiritual landscape of northern India, the religion of the bhāgavatas—those who worshipped the bhagavat, the blessed or adorable one. In the earliest references we have to bhāgavata religion, the bhagavat was known by the name Vasudeva, who was possibly a warrior king of the Vṛṣṇi tribe. Kṛṣṇa, the personification of the bhagavat in the *Bhagavad Gītā,* is the son of Vasudeva and Devakī, king and queen of the Vṛṣṇis.

The setting for the *Gītā* is a battlefield, on which two branches of a noble family are waiting for the conflict to begin. Arjuna, one of the five sons of king Pāṇḍu, is the person whose signal will cause the battle to commence. At this crucial moment, Arjuna turns to his charioteer Kṛṣṇa and bids him to halt so that he might look upon his enemies. In the opposing ranks he sees various members of his family and the teachers and advisors of his youth, a sight that troubles him. In that moment, Arjuna, the great bowman, reputedly the son of Indra, god of war, is thrown into turmoil. Can the course of action upon which he is about to embark really be the right one? He turns to Kṛṣṇa and expresses his doubts thus:

> ... we should not slay
> Dhṛtarāṣṭra's men, our own kinsfolk.
> For how, having slain our kinsfolk,
> Could we be happy, Mādhava?
>
> Even if they do not see,
> Because their intelligence is destroyed by greed,
> The sin caused by destruction of family,
> And the crime involved in injury to a friend,
>
> How should we not know enough
> To turn back from this wickedness,
> The sin caused by destruction of family
> Perceiving, O Janārdana?
>
> Upon the destruction of the family, perish
> The immemorial holy laws of the family;
> When the laws have perished, the whole family
> Lawlessness overwhelms also.
>
> Because of the prevalence of lawlessness, Kṛṣṇa,
> The women of the family are corrupted;
> When the women are corrupted, O Vṛṣṇi-clansman,
> Mixture of caste ensues.

Mixture (of caste) leads to naught but hell
For the destroyers of the family and for the family;
For their ancestors fall (to hell),
Because the rites of (giving) food and water are interrupted.

By these sins of family-destroyers,
(Sins) which produce caste-mixture,
The caste laws are destroyed,
And the eternal family laws.

When the family laws are destroyed,
Janārdana, then for men
Dwelling in hell certainly
Ensues: so we have heard (from the Holy Word).

Ah woe! 'Twas a great wickedness
That we had resolved to commit,
In that, through greed for the joys of kingship,
We undertook to slay our kinsfolk.

If me unresisting,
Weaponless, with weapons in their hands
Dhṛtarāṣṭra's men should slay in battle,
That would be a safer course for me.

Thus speaking Arjuna in the battle
Sat down in the box of the car,
Letting fall his bow and arrows,
His heart smitten with grief.* (*BG* 1.37-47)[6]

In response to this Kṛṣṇa offers the teaching that constitutes the bulk of the *Bhagavad Gītā*. Kṛṣṇa's aim is obviously to persuade Arjuna to fight, and ultimately he succeeds in this, though Arjuna proves to be remarkably resistant. Indeed, the original Arjuna–Kṛṣṇa dialogue might well have concentrated on this point. As we have it, however, the *Gītā* contains much more and its ultimate message is one of universal relevance, at least to members of Hindu society. It is worth noting, before considering Kṛṣṇa's teaching, that Arjuna's frame of reference for understanding his situation is essentially that

* Mādava and Janārdana are two of Kṛṣṇa's titles; Dhṛtarāṣṭra is the elder brother of Pāṇḍu and hence Arjuna's uncle.

of Vedic religion. There is no mention of karma as a cosmic moral principle, nor of rebirth as a destiny. It is as though Arjuna had never encountered the Upaniṣads nor any of the śramanic teachings.

Kṛṣṇa's initial response to Arjuna's dilemma is very much focused on the aim of getting him to fight. To this end, he introduces in chapter two the teachings of Sāṃkhya-Yoga and karma–yoga. Interspersed with the former are exhortations that warriors of any age would recognize:

Whence to thee this faintheartedness
In peril has come,
Offensive to the noble, not leading to heaven,
Inglorious, O Arjuna

Yield not to unmanliness, son of Pṛthā;*
It is not meet for thee.
Petty weakness of heart
Rejecting, arise, scorcher of the foe! (2.2-3)

Likewise having regard for thine own (caste) duty
Thou shouldst not tremble;
For another, better thing than a fight required of duty
Exists for a warrior.

Presented by mere luck,
An open door of heaven –
Happy the warriors, son of Pṛthā,
That get such a fight!

Now if thou this duty-required
Conflict wilt not perform,
Then thine own duty and glory
Abandoning, thou shalt get thee evil.

Disgrace, too, will creatures
Speak of thee, without end;
And for one that has been esteemed, disgrace
Is worse than death.

* Pṛthā is another name for Kuntī, Arjuna's mother.

That thou hast abstained from battle thru fear
The (warriors) of great chariots will think of thee;
And of whom thou wast highly regarded,
Thou shalt come to be held lightly.

And many sayings that should not be said
Thy ill-wishers will say of thee,
Speaking ill of thy capacity:
What, pray, is more grievous than that?

Either slain thou shalt gain heaven,
Or conquering thou shalt enjoy the earth.
Therefore arise, son of Kuntī,
Unto battle, making firm resolve. (2.31-37)

Interwoven with these passages is a metaphysical rationale for Arjuna to fight, and if we think of Arjuna's mindset as essentially Vedic then this metaphysic is something completely new. It has much in common with the philosophies of Sāṃkhya and Yoga that will receive definitive formulation in the post-epic period in the *Sāṃkhya Kārikā* of Īśvarakṛṣṇa and the *Yoga Sūtra* of Patañjali. Kṛṣṇa's version of these teachings is, however, subtly different from that found in either of these texts. Throughout the *Gītā* Kṛṣṇa employs the compound term Sāṃkhya-Yoga, indicating that they are essentially two aspects of the same teaching. Indeed, in 5.4-5 he explicitly states that the wise understand that Sāṃkhya and Yoga are not separate:

Of reason-method [Sāṃkhya] and discipline [Yoga] as separate, fools
Speak, not the wise;
Resorting to even one of them, completely
Man wins the fruit of both

What place is gained by the followers of reason-method,
That is reached also by the followers of discipline (-method).
That reason-method and discipline are one
Who sees, he truly sees.

The place gained by followers of Kṛṣṇa's Sāṃkhya-Yoga is, however, different from that gained by followers of Īśvarakṛṣṇa's *Sāṃkhya Kārikā* and Patañjali's *Yoga Sūtra*. For the followers of these traditions the final goal is kaivalya (isolation or aloneness), the separation of an individual self (puruṣa) from nature (prakṛti) and, it should be noted, from every other individual self too, a conception that has close parallels with Jainism, where the jīvas seek separation (kaivalya) from ajīva. By contrast, for Kṛṣṇa the self of the follower of Sāṃkhya-Yoga becomes one with the self of all beings (5.7).[7] That self, unlike the ātman of the Upaniṣads, is not responsible for the creation of the universe; nor does it act as an inner controller (antaryāmin). Like the puruṣa in the *Sāṃkhya Kārikā* and the jīva in Jainism, the self is not an actor or an agent at all. It is simply an observer. All action is performed by nature (prakṛti) (5.13-14). About that self, Kṛṣṇa says:

> Who believes him a slayer,
> And who thinks him slain,
> Both these understand not:
> He slays not, is not slain.
>
> He is not born, nor does he ever die;
> Nor, having come to be, will he ever more come not to be.
> Unborn, eternal, everlasting, this ancient one
> Is not slain when the body is slain.
>
> Who knows as indestructible and eternal
> This unborn, imperishable one,
> That man, son of Pṛthā, how
> Can he slay or cause to slay—whom?
>
> As leaving aside worn-out garments
> A man takes other, new ones,
> So leaving aside worn-out bodies
> To other, new ones goes the embodied (soul).
>
> Swords cut him not,
> Fire burns him not,
> Water wets him not,
> Wind dries him not.
>
> Not to be cut is he, not to be burnt is he,
> Not to be wet nor yet dried;

Eternal, omnipresent, fixed,
Immovable, everlasting is he.

Unmanifest he, unthinkable he,
Unchangeable he is declared to be;
Therefore knowing him thus
Thou shouldst not mourn him.

(3.19-25)[8]

The appropriate mental attitude for one who has this knowledge is one of indifference (sama), i.e. treating everything the same (2.38, 48, 55ff.). This is discipline (yoga). For Kṛṣṇa, however, this attitude does not need to be coupled, as it tends to be in the śramanic traditions, with renunciation of the world. Rather, indifference is to be carried into action. Hence Arjuna is urged to perform actions whilst abiding in this attitude. By doing this he will avoid the fruit or consequences of his actions, for consequences, we are told, only attach to actions that are performed out of a desire for a particular outcome. As 4.20 puts it, one who abandons attachment to the fruits of action does nothing whatsoever (in karmic terms) even when acting. This is the new discipline of karma yoga, and, according to Kṛṣṇa, it is superior to other methods.

So Kṛṣṇa accepts that Sāṃkhya-Yoga can lead to freedom from the effects of action, self-knowledge and liberation from rebirth, but he does not consider them to be the most effective means available. 13.24 and 12.12 express his view succinctly:

> Some by meditation (dhyāna) come to behold the self (ātman) in the self by the self; others by the reason-method (sāṃkhya), and others by the discipline of action (karma-yoga).

However,

> Knowledge (jñāna) is better than practice (abhyāsa), and meditation (dhyāna) is superior to knowledge, and abandonment of the fruit of actions (karma-phala-tyāga) is better than meditation; from abandonment (comes) peace immediately.[9]

Moreover, he does not accept that all traditions possess the keys to release. In 2.46, Kṛṣṇa says,

> As much profit as there is in a water tank when on all sides there is a flood of water, no more is there in all the Vedas for a brahmin who (truly) understands.

In other words, the Vedas are as much use as a water tank in a flood, that is, no use at all. Then, in verses such as 3.5 and 14.19 he says,

> No-one, even for a moment, remains without performing actions, for he is made to perform action willy-nilly, everyone is by the strands that spring from material nature (prakṛti).

> No agent other than the Strands (guṇa)
> When the beholder (soul) perceives,
> And knows the higher-than-the-Strands,
> He goes to My estate.

In other words, the Jain aim of coming to a point where one ceases to act at all is doomed to failure, for nature (prakṛti) is constantly acting. The Vedic path and the Jain path are, therefore, according to Kṛṣṇa, dead ends.

By contrast, Sāṃkhya and Yoga can lead to release, though Kṛṣṇa's versions of these methods are different from those found in the *Śānti Parvan* of the *Mahābhārata*, the *Sāṃkhya Kārikā* of Īśvarakṛṣṇa and the *Yoga Sūtra* of Patañjali. The most significant change he makes to Sāṃkhya teaching is that he presents it as theistic. Instead of there just being two types of existant: spirit (puruṣa) and nature (prakṛti), in Kṛṣṇa's teaching there are three: spirit, nature and god. God controls the first two, though they seem to exist in their own right as each is described as beginningless (13.19). The *Gītā* is, however, somewhat confusing on this point as Kṛṣṇa claims that both puruṣa and prakṛti are part of him (Kṛṣṇa = prakṛti: 6.30; 7.12; Kṛṣṇa = puruṣa: 13.1-2). God, it would seem, always has had and always will have puruṣa and prakṛti as aspects of his being. This is how the thirteenth-century Vedānta philosopher Rāmānuja interpreted the *Gītā* and this interpretation provided the foundation for the ontology that he attributed to the entire Vedānta canon of Upaniṣads, *Bhagavad Gītā* and Brahmā/Vedānta Sūtra that is collectively known as the triple foundation (Prasthānatraya). That ontology he called viśiṣṭādvaita (qualified non-dualism), a label that accurately conveys the position adopted by Kṛṣṇa in the *Gītā*.

The most significant change he makes to yoga is that the ultimate focus of the yogin's meditation is not the self (puruṣa) but god (Kṛṣṇa). Patañjali does advocate a practice called īśvara-praṇidhāna (contemplation on the lord), but Patañjali's lord is simply a puruṣa who has never been involved with prakṛti. Kṛṣṇa, on the other hand, is god in the fullest sense: creator and controller of the world. In 6.10-15 he says:

Let the disciplined man ever discipline
Himself, abiding in a secret place,
Solitary, restraining his thoughts and soul,
Free from aspirations and without possessions.

In a clean place establishing
A steady seat for himself,
That is neither too high nor too low,
Covered with a cloth, a skin, and kuśa-grass,

There fixing the thought-organ on a single object,
Restraining the activity of his mind and senses,
Sitting on the seat, let him practise
Discipline unto self-purification.

Even body, head, and neck
Holding motionless, (keeping himself) steady,
Gazing at the tip of his own nose,
And not looking in any direction,

With tranquil soul, rid of fear,
Abiding in the vow of chastity,
Controlling the mind, his thoughts on Me,
Let him sit disciplined, absorbed in Me.

Thus ever disciplining himself,
The man of discipline, with controlled mind,
To peace that culminates in nirvāṇa,
And rests in Me, attains.

Until the second half of v.14 this could be taken for straightforward renunciate yoga practice. The final lines of these verses make it clear, however, that Kṛṣṇa is both the ultimate focus of meditation and the ultimate destiny for the meditator. Here, 'nirvāṇa' could mean what the Buddhists mean by it, though it seems more likely to me that it is being used to indicate the cessation of all desire and rebirth. Indeed, even if Kṛṣṇa is explicitly seeking to claim that this practice yields the same achievement (and higher) as Buddhist meditation, his notion of nirvāṇa is radically different from the Buddhist one. Thus, both Sāṃkhya and Yoga are presented as leading to liberation through access to a knowledge of god, who is the universal soul in all beings, though these essentially renunciant methods are inferior to karma yoga.

We should note, however, that the discipline of action cannot be applied to just any old action. There are constraints on the activities of the karma-yogin. In 3.35, Kṛṣṇa tells Arjuna, somewhat abruptly, that actions falling within the sphere of other men's duties are dangerous and that it is better to act in accordance with the requirements of one's own duty, even if such action is imperfect, than to undertake actions that lie within the sphere of another's duty, even if they are well performed. This message is reiterated in 16.23-24 and in 18.41-48. The second of these informs us that all humans possess a svabhāva (literally 'own-being'; 'inherent nature'—Edgerton; 'the nature of things as they are'—Zaehner). This nature is determined by the guṇas (the three constituents of prakṛti). Śaṅkara, according to Zaehner, explains that 'Brāhmans originate from Goodness [sattva guṇa], princes (and warriors) from Passion [rajas guṇa] mixed with Goodness, peasants and artisans from Passion mixed with Darkness [tamas guṇa], serfs from Darkness with a small admixture of Passion.'[10] A person's nature determines the kind of spirituality to which he or she is attracted:

> Men of Goodness worship the gods,
> Men of Passion sprites and ogres,
> To ghosts and the hordes of goblins others,
> The folk of Darkness, pay worship.
>
> (17.2)

This inherent nature also expresses itself through action. So,

> Calm, (self-) control, austerities, purity,
> Patience, and uprightness,
> Theoretical and practical knowledge, and religious faith,
> Are the natural-born actions of brāhmans.

Heroism, majesty, firmness, skill,
And not fleeing in battle also,
Generosity, and lordly nature,
Are the natural-born actions of warriors.

Agriculture, cattle-tending, and commerce
Are the natural-born actions of artisans;
Action that consists of service
Is likewise natural-born to a serf.

(18.42-44)

Engaging in actions that fall within the sphere of another person's duty is not, then, just something that is socially objectional, it runs counter to one's fundamental constitution. What is more, it goes against the will of god—since god himself created the four-caste system (catur-varṇa) (4.13).[11] Karma yoga is thus the performance of one's natural duty in an attitude of indifference. It is not, however, the highest form of spiritual practice. That status is reserved for what most commentators on the *Gītā* call 'bhakti yoga', the discipline of devotion, though Kṛṣṇa does not employ this term himself.[12] Indeed, my reading of the text is that bhakti is meant to complement karma yoga rather than being an alternative to it. So Kṛṣṇa says in 9.27-28,

Whatever thou doest, whatever thou eatest,
Whatever thou offerest in oblation or givest,
Whatever austerity thou performest, son of Kuntī,
That do as an offering to Me.

Thus from what have good and evil fruits
Thou shalt be freed, (namely) from the bonds of action;
Thy soul disciplined in the discipline of renunciation (saṃnyāsa yoga),
Freed, thou shalt go to Me.

This, I take it, refers to actions performed within the sphere of one's own duty. Although Kṛṣṇa does not comment on the matter, it would be perverse to think, in the light of his emphasis on the importance of remaining within the sphere of one's allocated duty, that actions performed outside of this sphere would be acceptable.

The supremacy of bhakti is indicated in a number of verses, e.g. 11.52-54 and 12.6-7:

> This form (viśva-rūpa, universal form) that is right hard to see,
> Which thou hast seen of Mine,
> Of this form even the gods
> Constantly long for the sight.
>
> Not by the Vedas nor by austerity,
> Nor by gifts or acts of worship,
> Can I be seen in such a guise,
> As thou hast seen me.
>
> But by unswerving devotion can
> I in such a guise, Arjuna,
> Be known and seen in very truth,
> And entered into, scorcher of the foe.
>
> (11.52-54)

At the beginning of book 12 Kṛṣṇa tells Arjuna that those yogins who 'attend on' (paryupāsate) the 'inexpressible (anirdeśya), unmanifest (avyakta), imperishable (akṣara)' also reach him, though it is hard for them to do.[13] On the other hand,

> those who, absorbed in me, resign all their acts to me and contemplatively attend on me with exclusive yoga [ananya yoga], soon find in me their savior from the ocean that is the run-around of deaths, Pārtha, for their minds are conducted to enter into me.[14]

Moreover, not only is this path less arduous than meditating on the unmanifest imperishable, it is also available to those who, in Hindu society, would never get the opportunity to practise such meditation: vaiśyas, śūdras and women. So Kṛṣṇa states in 9.31-32,

> No devotee of Mine is lost.
>
> For if they take refuge in Me, son of Pṛthā,
> Even those who may be of base origin,
> Women, men of the artisan caste, and serfs too,
> Even they go to the highest goal.

Thus the *Gītā* rejects some of the old paths, accepts others (albeit in a modified form), but holds none so effective as the ones it introduces for the first time: karma yoga and bhakti. These new paths offer not only what is claimed to be a more effective route to liberation from rebirth but also a radically different notion of how karma works. The Jain view is essentially that all acts have karmic consequences, though acts that harm other beings have more severe consequences than those which do not. The Buddhists accept this but place more emphasis on the role of intentionality. All acts have three key elements: intention, action and consequence(s). Jains emphasize the second, Buddhists the first. Arjuna, as we see from 1.29-46, thinks in terms of the third. Part of Kṛṣṇa's aim in the *Gītā* is to shift Arjuna away from his consequentialist approach to karma and ethics towards one which has intention and action as central. In this regard, Kṛṣṇa's understanding of karma comes quite close to that of the Buddhists: karmic fruits arise primarily out of a person's intention or motivation. However, in Buddhism and also Jainism right intention is essentially non-violent (ahiṃsā). By contrast, for Kṛṣṇa right intention is either or both of intending to do one's duty without thought for the consequences or outcomes and intending to act as an expression of devotion to god.

A crucial question here is that of how one knows which acts are within the scope of one's duty and which fall outside of it. For Arjuna, and for all members of traditional Hindu society, this is not too problematic for by the time that the *Gītā* was composed detailed guidelines on such matters were available in texts known as dharma śāstras. In 16.23-24 Kṛṣṇa explicitly instructs Arjuna to let the śāstras be his guide on all matters of what to do and what not to do. These texts were not part of the śruti literature, i.e. the Veda, though they were highly authoritative and, like the *Gītā* itself, regarded as smṛti (tradition, that which is remembered). Indeed, they were extensions of what from very early times had been regarded as the third category of the Vedic corpus: the sūtras. In this scheme, the Veda is divided into three parts: Saṃhitā (the four Vedas); Brāhmaṇa (including Āraṇyakas and Upaniṣads) and Sūtra. The first two were deemed to be śruti (revelation), the last smṛti (tradition). Often, these Vedic sūtras are called kalpa (fitting or proper) sūtras. They are themselves further subdivided into three groups:

1. śrauta sūtras—concerned with the procedures at the śrauta (public) sacrifices;

2. gṛhya sūtras—concerned with domestic rituals such as initiation (upanāyana) and marriage;
3. dharma sūtras—concerned mainly with social behaviour.

The collective name for numbers two and three is smārta sūtras (texts dealing with tradition), and for anyone seeking an understanding of Hindu concepts of dharma as duty they are fundamental. As Thomas J. Hopkins puts it,

> The Dharma Sūtras were one of the most important developments in the entire brāhmanical tradition... [they] broke new ground in establishing Brahmanical rules for the social as well as ritual activities of every member of society. Consistent standards of *dharma* were assigned to all men, making explicit the relevance of Brahmanical goals and values for all aspects of life.[15]

In setting out these standards of dharma the sūtras built upon older texts such as *RV* 10.90, the *Puruṣa Sūkta,* which describes the origins of the four varṇa system:

> When they divided [primal] Man,
> Into how many parts did they divide him?
> What was his mouth? What his arms?
> What are his thighs called? What his feet?
>
> The Brahman was his mouth,
> The arms were made the Prince,
> His thighs the common people,
> And from his feet the serf was born.[16]

The sūtras in turn were expanded and elaborated in more comprehensive treatises known as dharma śāstras. Most famous and influential of these was the *Mānava Dharma Śāstra* (the Laws of *Manu*), which was composed at more or less the same time as the *Bhagavad Gītā*. In *Manu* 1.87-91, *Puruṣa Sūkta* 11-12 (above) is elaborated as follows:

> in order to protect this universe He, the most resplendent one, assigned separate (duties and) occupations to those who sprang from his mouth, arms, thighs and feet.

> To Brāhmaṇas he assigned teaching and studying (the Veda), sacrificing for their own benefit and for others, giving and accepting (of alms). The Kṣatriya commanded to protect the people, to bestow gifts, to offer sacrifices, to study (the Veda), and to abstain from attaching himself to sensual pleasures.
>
> The Vaiśya to tend to cattle, to bestow gifts, to offer sacrifices, to study (the Veda), to trade, to lend money, and to cultivate land.
>
> One occupation only the lord prescribed to the Śūdra, to serve meekly even these (other) three castes.[17]

But the specification does not stop there. For example, the names that the different varṇas can choose for their children are circumscribed by *Manu*, as are the times at which different varṇa groups can initiate their male children and even the material out of which the sacred thread is to be made. Women are instructed to be subservient to men at all stages of their lives: in childhood to their fathers, in adulthood to their husbands and in old age to their eldest sons.[18] The psychological effect of these constraints must have been (and probably still are) profound. Consider *Manu*'s instructions on naming:

> Let (the first part) of a Brāhmaṇa's name (denote) something auspicious, a Kṣatriya's be connected with power, and a Vaiśya's with wealth, but a Śūdra's (express something) contemptible.
>
> (The second part of) a Brāhmaṇa's name shall be (a word) implying happiness, of a Kṣatriya (a word) implying protection, of a Vaiśya (a term) expressive of thriving, and of a Śūdra (an expression) denoting service.[19]

Names constitute a significant element to our identities, and we use them most days. The question 'Where are you going O auspicious one?' has a very different effect on a person from 'Where are you going O contemptible one?' Likewise, the feelings that accompany a self-introduction such as 'I am Benign Bliss' will be quite different from those that accompany 'I am Miserable Bogwasher.'

In short, texts like *Manu* not only specified what people had to do but also employed techniques of psychological conditioning to mould their personalities to suit their roles in society. For an Indian living within the kind of framework set by these dharma texts, knowing one's duty and its boundaries would hardly be a problem. And there are clear benefits to this 'Do, don't think' approach to life. I remember a Buddhist monk once explaining to a group of students that the rules and regulations of the Vinaya were a liberation rather than a burden because they took care of all the little decisions that had to be made in the course of every day and so left the monk free for meditation. Kṛṣṇa is saying something similar to Arjuna and to all Hindus: stop being a decision maker, for that is a barrier to knowing god and becoming free from rebirth. The best course to follow is to do what you are told by the lawbooks (for that came from god in the first place and is in accord with your intrinsic nature) and want to do what you are told (for that is how you can express devotion to god).

This is not the entire story, however, for in the *Bhagavad Gītā* Kṛṣṇa tells Arjuna that human choice on these matters is, in fact, illusory. The reality is that god is in control of everything. He determines who is going to live and die, and when; and he controls each and every individual from within. So he says:

> Even without thee (thy action), all shall cease to exist,
> The warriors that are drawn up in the opposing ranks.
>
> Therefore arise thou, win glory,
> Conquer thine enemies and enjoy prospered kingship;
> By Me Myself they have already been slain long ago;
> Be thou the mere instrument, left-handed archer!
>
> Droṇa and Bhīṣma and Jayadratha,
> Karṇa too, and the other warrior-heroes as well,
> Do thou slay, (since) they are already slain by Me; do not hesitate!
> Fight! Thou shalt conquer thy rivals in battle. (11.32-34)

And

> If clinging to egotism
> Thou thinkest 'I will not fight!',
> Vain is this thy resolve;
> (Thine own) material nature will coerce thee.

Son of Kunti, by thine own natural
Action held fast,
What thru delusion thou seekest not to do,
That thou shalt do even against thy will.

Of all beings, the Lord
In the heart abides, Arjuna,
Causing all beings to turn around
As if fixed in a machine, by his magic power.

(18.59-61)[20]

With these statements Kṛṣṇa makes it clear that karma yoga and bhakti are simply vehicles for coming to accept what is inevitable anyway. Autonomous decision making is a delusion that is rooted in a misguided self-centredness. This view has significant implications for ethics. A widely held view among moral philosophers is that 'ought implies can'. In other words, if we say that someone ought to behave in a certain way we assume that they are able to behave in that way; we assume that they have a choice. Where there is no choice there is no morality. Kṛṣṇa's determinism removes morality from human affairs. So it is not simply the case that the ethics of the *Gītā* are different from those of the śramanic traditions, in that they vary from one social group to another (what is right for a person from one caste is wrong for a person from another) rather than being applicable to all people. The *Gītā* reveals that (or claims that) the very idea of morality is just one more self-centred delusion. We have no more control over whether to do right or wrong than Arjuna has over whether he will fight or not.

In terms of our model of soteriology, the fundamental problem facing human beings seems to be that of karma and its effects: suffering and rebirth. We have seen, however, that it is really god's plans for the universe. Moreover, that problem is insoluble in terms of anything that humans can do themselves. Only god can release beings from rebirth and suffering. The means of salvation are thus entirely dependent on other power, though a concession is made to effort in the recognition that those who follow the Sāṃkhya-Yoga way can, with difficulty, reach Kṛṣṇa. The ontology is monistic overall, but with the somewhat peculiar feature of a single totality having three beginingless and eternal divisions within it. In Rawlinson's scheme the teachings of the *Gītā* are an interesting mixture of hot and cool. Hot because surrendering to god's will is essentially emotional in character; cool because the attitude of indifference that underpins karma yoga is emotionally neutral. They would also seem to be structured, because although the path is not one of distinctive practices such as those found in the Buddhist and Jain schemes it is exquisitely structured through the requirements of the dharma texts, which, of course, makes it extremely difficult for any non-Hindu to live according to Kṛṣṇa's teaching.

## THE *ŚĀNTI PARVAN*

Book 12 of the *Mahābhārata*, the *Śānti Parvan*, is divided into two sections, each of which is also referred to as a parva (chapter). They are the *Rāja-dharma-anuśāsana* (instruction on kingly duty) *Parvan* and the *Mokṣadharma* (emancipation and duty) *Parvan*. Most of the material on yoga is to be found in the second of these, which begins at 12.176.[21] Writers on yoga rarely refer to it, however, and the reason for this is easy to discern. The material is unsystematic and heavily modified or redacted. E.W. Hopkins places the entire *Śānti Parvan* in what he calls the psuedo-epic, that which has been added on to the original heroic story.[22] As was noted above, about three-quarters of the epic falls into this category, which modern scholars generally agree to be the work of the brāhman clan of Bhṛgu. A prominent feature of Bhṛgu redaction is that they do not simply add new material to the epic core, they also rework that material to make it conform to the message they wanted to propagate. With regard to yoga, I take this to be assimilating it into a Veda-compatible world view.

One consequence of this reworking is that the expositions of the different philosophical views become incoherent and often impenetrable. As Hopkins comments, 'Either the text is rewritten and interpolated or it is allowed to stand and another section is prefixed or added of the same content differently treated.'[23] As a result, even short passages can contain contradictory statements. Hopkins provides a number of examples, e.g.

1. 12.301 ('an exposition of yoga twisted into sectarian brāhmanism'), where the Sāṃkhya system is first said to be faultless (v.4) and later claimed to have faults as well as virtues (v.13);

2. 12.241-47, where we are told that emancipation (mokṣa) may be gained by women and low-caste men if they practise yoga *and* that yoga should only be taught to snātakas (males of the twice-born varṇas: brāhman, kṣatriya and vaiśya).

Because the texts on yoga within the *Mokṣadharma Parvan* are all affected by such redactive distortions, my procedure here will be first of all to present an outline of the issues that the redactors are seeking to resolve, and then to summarize and comment upon a number of passages that offer reasonably extensive treatments of yoga. Not everyone will be in agreement with such an approach or with my interpretation of the material. Nevertheless, this approach will provide a relatively clear account that readers can employ as a guide during their own researches or as a hypothesis to be challenged and, if possible, falsified.

In 12.350 it is claimed that there are four philosophies (jñānam), namely the Sāṃkhya-Yoga, the Vedāraṇyaka, the Pañcarātra and the Paśupata. The last two are concerned with the gods Viṣṇu and Śiva respectively and dependent for most of their directly philosophical teachings on the first two.[24] Vedāraṇyaka refers to the Vedic corpus of Saṃhitā, Brāhmaṇa, Āraṇyaka and Upaniṣad.[25] Sāṃkhya-Yoga refers primarily to the system of Kapila, the ancient and supreme seer, 'the only founder of a philosophical system known to the epic'.[26] Although Sāṃkhya and Yoga are frequently said to be one practice (ekacāryau),[27] they are sometimes distinguished from each other,[28] though it is far from easy to determine the exact teachings to which these terms refer. As Hopkins points out, there is a fundamental difference between the ancient yoga that is referred to in a number of short stories and the later yoga that is based on 'an elaborate course of breathings and mental confinement in bodily postures'.[29] The former is essentially severe asceticism, e.g. standing still on one leg until birds are comfortable resting in the yogin's matted locks.[30] The practitioner of such austerities is usually called a muni rather than a yogin and seeks to obtain his magical powers through tapas (tapo-bala) rather than yoga meditation (yoga-bala).[31] It is, as Hopkins describes it, Vedic asceticism.

The yoga that is associated with Sāṃkhya and regarded as the supreme source of power is primarily the later form, though even that remains quite ascetic in character. The doctrines of Sāṃkhya/Sāṃkhya-Yoga are presented in terms of three broad variations. The first, which is rarely mentioned, and even then only briefly, offers a teaching that has much in common with what is found in the later *Yoga Sūtra* of Patañjali and the *Sāṃkhya Kārikā* of Īśvarakṛṣṇa: there are two fundamentally different kinds of being: 1) prakṛti (the creative), which is the unitary ground of all physical, emotional and mental existence—though she is insentient, and 2) puruṣa (person), of which there are many. Puruṣa possesses just one defining feature: sentience or awareness.[32] Creation (and bondage) occur when puruṣa(s) becomes aware of and attentive to prakrti. She 'dances' the creation for him. Emancipation occurs when he disengages from her and returns to being self-absorbed, the state of aloneness (kevalatva).

As was noted above, with few exceptions the dominant orientation of Vedic-Vedāntic teaching was towards monism. So the claims of Sāṃkhyayogins that prakṛti is one and puruṣas many must have been troublesome to the redactors. Moreover, those who held this view are claimed to rely on knowledge alone (no ritual, no grace, no social duties) for release and to practise compassion towards all creatures, both of which conflict with Vedic teaching, though they are in essential agreement with Buddhism and, to a lesser extent, Jainism.[33] We may also note that in the dialogue between Kapila and the orthodox brāhman Syumarasmi, which is heavily redacted to make Kapila rather like an Upaniṣadic teacher, that ancient sage makes a number of claims that are antagonistic towards Vedic teaching, e.g. animal sacrifices are wrong; harmlessness is the way to emancipation; purity of heart, the practice of contemplation and renunciation of the world are the marks of a true brāhmana.[34]

The second variation, which is referred to more frequently, accepts the division between prakṛti and puruṣa but maintains that there is only one puruṣa. Interestingly, the principal teachers of this doctrine are brāhmans who endorse Vedic tradition and refer to Vedic deities in the course of their expositions.[35] Also interesting is the fact that none of these one-puruṣa versions of Sāṃkhya-Yoga developed into a viable school or had much impact on post-epic Hindu philosophy. To my mind, this is because such versions were synthetic compromises that sought to bridge the gap between monistic Vedānta thought and the dualistic pluralism of Sāṃkhya-Yoga.

The third variant of Sāṃkhya-Yoga found in the *Śānti Parvan* is broadly Vedāntic in character. One of the best examples of this is to be found in 12.246-48, where Vyāsa offers a teaching based substantially on that of the *Kaṭha Upaniṣad*. The yogin is like a charioteer who controls the senses, etc. in order to go beyond prakṛti to a realization, not of puruṣa but of brahman—which is the highest goal. In Hopkins's view, this material, along with that found in 12.194 and 286, 'are three different versions of an older Sāṃkhya tract, which is worked over into Brāhmanism'.[36] The same may well be true of the *Kaṭha Upaniṣad* itself.

A consideration of these three versions of Samkhya-Yoga against the backdrop of Bhṛgu redaction and the emergence of the pseudo-epic suggests, to me at least, that the issues being addressed are those that are raised by the challenge of heterodoxy. Buddhism and Jainism offer world views that are radically different from those of the Vedic tradition. The Vedas are predominantly this-worldly in orientation; the heterodox traditions are other-worldly.[37] The Vedas look to continued existence after death in the company of ancestors and gods; the heterodox traditions conceive post-mortem existence in terms of perpetual rebirth (saṃsāra). The Vedas promote and defend caste hierarchy and the necessity of performing caste duties (varṇadharma); the heterodox challenge hierarchies based on birth and reject varṇadharma as the highest value in favour of the pursuit of mokṣa. The Upaniṣads steer a middle course between these orientations. Sometimes they have the air of the heterodox about them, as in *MundU* 1.2.7-10.

7. Unsafe boats, however, are these sacrificial forms, the eighteen, in which is expressed the lower work. The fools who approve that as the better, go again to old age and death.
8. Those abiding in the midst of ignorance, self-wise, thinking themselves learned, hard smitten, go around deluded, like blind men led by one who is himself blind.
9. Manifoldly living in ignorance, they think to themselves, childishly: 'We have accomplished our aim!' Since doers of deeds (karmin) do not understand, because of passion (rāga), therefore, when their worlds are exhausted, they sink down wretched.
10. Thinking sacrifice and merit is the chiefest thing, Naught better do they know—deluded! Having had enjoyment on the top of the heaven won by good works, they re-enter this world, or a lower.

At other times they seek a synthesis between Vedic and heterodox ideas, as in *CU* 8.5.

1. Now, what people call 'sacrifice' *(yajña)* is really the chaste life of a student of sacred knowledge *(brahmacarya)*; only through the chaste life of a student of sacred knowledge does he who is a knower *(ya jñātṛ)* find that [world]. Now, what people call 'what has been sacrificed' *(iṣṭa)* is really the chaste life of a student of sacred knowledge, for only after having searched *(iṣṭva)* with the chaste life of a student of sacred knowledge does one find the Soul (Ātman).
2. Now, what people call 'the protracted sacrifice' *(sattrā-yaṇa)* is really the chaste life of a student of sacred knowledge, for only through the chaste life of a student of sacred knowledge does one find the protection *(trāṇa)* of the real *(sat)* Soul (Ātman). Now, what people call 'silent asceticism' *(mauna)* is really the chaste life of a student of sacred knowledge, for only in finding the Soul through the chaste life of a student of sacred knowledge does one [really] think *(manute)*.
3. Now, what people call 'a course of fasting' *(an-āṣakāyana)* is really the chaste life of a student of sacred knowledge, for the Soul (Ātman) which one finds through the chaste life of a student of sacred knowledge perishes not *(na naśyati)*. Now, what people call 'betaking oneself to hermit life in the forest' *(araṇyāyana)* is really the chaste life of a student of sacred knowledge. Verily, the two seas in the Brahma-world, in the third heaven from here, are *Ara* and *Nya*. There is the lake Airaṃmadīya ('Affording Refreshment and Ecstasy'); there, the fig-tree Somasavana ('the Soma-yielding'); there, Brahma's citadel, Aparājitā ('the Unconquered'), the golden hall of the Lord *(prabhu)*.
4. But only they who find those two seas, Ara and Ṇya, in the Brahma-world through the chaste life of a student of sacred knowledge—only they possess that Brahma-world. In all the worlds they possess unlimited freedom.[38]

In the post-epic period Buddhism and Jainism continued to exist as independent systems, though they could not entirely escape the influence of other ideologies, particularly those associated with Śāktism and tantra. Other śramanic traditions such as Sāṃkhya, Yoga and Vaiśeṣika were assimilated into Brāhmanism, though, interestingly, were able to retain a number of non-Vedic features that betray their non-Vedic origins. Brāhmanism itself was able to impose its social philosophy on Indian society and was, therefore, in a position to allow philosophical diversity that did not challenge its social vision. In this way the renunciant traditions complemented brāhmanical social orthodoxy, for they encouraged those who were discontent to abandon society rather than change it.

The three teachers who offer most by way of explanatory comment on the nature of yoga in the *Śānti Parvan* are Bhīṣma, Yajñavalkya and Vyāsa.[39] Moreover, despite evidence of considerable redaction in all the sections where such comments are found, there are significant common threads in or even a common core to their teachings about yoga.

**For Bhīṣma**, the core qualities of a yogin are freedom from attachment, harmlessness and compassion for all creatures. The yogin should regard everything with an equal eye and cast off the five faults of attachment (rāga), heedlessness (moha), affection (sneha), lust (kāma) and wrath (krodha). He should live 'in places free from the companionship of wives and children, without others with whom disputes may arise and favourable to perfect tranquillity of heart' (12.301). He should eat abstemiously, avoiding meat, oil and butter.

The yogin's practice is twofold: 'Brahmacarya [celibacy] and abstention from injury are said to constitute the yoga of the body, while restraining mind and speech properly are said to constitute the yoga of the mind' (12.217). The yogin meditates in silence, undisturbed by his senses (his abstemious diet reduces their influence) and with focused mind.

> There such a person, restraining speech, sits like a piece of wood, crushing all the senses, and with mind undividedly united by the aid of meditation... He has no perception of sound through the ear; no perception of touch through the skin; no perception of form through the eye; no perception of taste through the tongue. He has no perception also of scents through the organ of smell. Immersed in *yoga,* he would abandon all things, rapt in meditation.
>
> (12.195)

By means of his yoga meditation (dhyāna yoga), which involves dhāraṇā and samādhi, the yogin abides in his original soul state and gains discrimination (vicāra), knowledge (viveka) and the power to avoid evil (vitarka). He destroys sins, 'casting off both birth and death, and happiness and sorrow' (12.301). With his yoga power he is 'capable of scorching the entire universe like the sun that rises at the time of the universal dissolution'; he can 'enter into ... the very lords of creation, the rishis, the deities, and the great beings in the universe';[40] neither Yama nor death can touch him; he can create thousands of bodies and wander the earth in them.

There is little here that would conflict with Patañjali's system (see Chapter 6), especially since, as Hopkins points out, the five triṣṭubh stanzas that form the final section of 301 have been added later 'to offset the whole teaching preceding, which is that the soul gets isolation, not absorption into Brahma'.[41] Here then, yoga is presented as a renunciant practice with a śramanic flavour that emphasizes the importance of withdrawing from society, the relinquishing of sense experience and the abandoning of emotions. It advocates the cultivation of speech restraint, inward-mindedness and absorption in the self. By this means the yogin can gain freedom from rebirth (vimokṣa).

**For Yajñavalkya**, Sāṃkhya and Yoga ordain the same practices and are both held to be capable of leading to liberation. They are to be treated as one and the same. Yogins follow an eight-limbed practice and gain eight kinds of powers. They control the vital breaths and the senses. He distinguishes two kinds of yoga: with attributes and without attributes. The first involves concentrating the mind and regulating the breath; the second involves concentrating the mind and subjugating the senses. He then introduces a progressive sequence whereby the yogin comes to contemplate the immutable, eternal, unchangeable, indivisible, deathless, everlasting, infinite pure puruṣa who is brahma—a Vedic version of Sāṃkhya-Yoga, as might have been inferred from the mention of the vital breaths (prāṇa), which have no place in classical Sāṃkhya or Yoga.[42]

Yajñavalkya's description of the samādhi experience has much in common with that offered by Bhiṣma in 12.195.5-9:

> The person in samādhi, the wise say, looks like the fixed and upward flame of a lamp that is full of oil and that burns in a breezeless spot. He is like a rock which is incapable of being moved in the slightest degree by ever a heavy downpour from the clouds. He is incapable of being moved by the din of conches and drums, or by songs or the sound of hundreds of musical instruments beat or blown together. Even this is the indication of one in samādhi.
>
> (12.317.19-21)

**For Vyāsa**, whose comments appear to be the most heavily redacted of the three, a yogin should seek a solitary life, eat abstemiously, regard everything with an equal eye, be neither jubilant on acquiring things nor anxious on losing them, behave equally and with friendliness towards all creatures, be free from attachment and pride, be free from the influence of opposites (pleasure–pain, heat–cold, etc.), speak truthfully, restrain speech, acts and thoughts, be free from lust, be free from grief, be patient, be celibate, be without malice or envy, be firm and steady in all vows and observances, and overcome the five impediments of desire (kāma), wrath (krodha), cupidity (lobha), fear (bhaya) and sleep (svapna).

In terms of activity, Vyāsa provides two lists of yogic practices, which are, however, far from being self-explanatory. The first specifies 12 requirements of yoga: place, acts, affection, objects, means, destruction, certainty, eyes, food, suppression, mind and survey (12.236).[43] The second offers ten ways to enhance energy and destroy sins: meditation, study, gift, truth, modesty, simplicity, forgiveness, purity of body, purity of conduct and subjugation of the senses (12.240). Other statements recommend uniting the senses with the mind, fixing the gaze inwards, restraining the senses in the heart and practising the seven kinds of dhāraṇā. By such practice he gains control over the elements and acquires thereby powers to create all kinds of creatures, cause the earth to tremble, disappear at will, drink up rivers, lakes and oceans, and become so radiant that he cannot be seen.

Despite the many minor differences and often extensive redactions, the comments of these teachers all present us with a reasonably consistent picture of the nature and practice of yoga as understood in the late epic period. It is practised by renunciants. It is grounded on non-violence, compassion, abstemiousness, celibacy, truth-speaking and sensual restraint. It involves the cultivation of detachment and an attitude of indifference along with an inward mental focus which yields both knowledge and supernormal powers. All of these characteristics are found in the later *Yoga Sūtras* of Patañjali but within a philosophical context that makes little or no reference to Vedic-Vedāntic teaching. Here then, we may have some of the source material that Patañjali gathered when compiling his own text.

With regard to our soteriology scheme, these yogas seek to eradicate the effects of karma and enable the practitioner to gain freedom from rebirth, though the acquisition of supernormal powers also plays a central role and may, originally, have been a primary concern. All present us with yoga as an essentially self-power path, though there is considerable variation in the ontologies, ranging from monism through dualism (one prakṛti, one puruṣa) to pluralism (one prakṛti, many puruṣas). Knowledge is gained through the practice of meditation. In Rawlinson's scheme, all these forms of yoga fall into the 'cool' category, though they seem to have both a structured and progressive character (distinct stages or levels) and an unstructured one (via indifference and detachment—vairāgya).

# Chapter 5
# THE ORTHODOX PHILOSOPHICAL SYSTEMS

In the later epic period northern India was in a state of political and religious fragmentation. Across much of the north west, kingdoms ruled by the descendants of the Greeks who arrived with Alexander (called Yavanas, a term that came to refer to 'all the annoying outsiders of the western borderlands'[1]) denied the authority of the Vedas and were organized according to Greek-derived rather than brāhmanical codes. Moreover, heterodox traditions such as Buddhism and Jainism had also established a foothold in these areas. All this changed with the establishment of the Gupta Empire in 320 CE. Much as Constantine did with Christianity, the Gupta rulers gave brāhmans the job of creating ideological unity within their domain.

The brāhmanical approach to this task was primarily twofold. On the one hand, they demanded conformity to the social regulations that found expression in the dharma śāstras; on the other, they embraced a variety of creeds and philosophies into a grand synthesis that was supported by an elaborate mythology, as found in the Purāṇas.[2] Living within the codes or outside of them as a renunciant were both acceptable to brāhmanical regulators. Challenging them was not. This period is often presented as a golden or classical age of Hinduism by brāhmanically-inclined authors. Such a judgement would not, however, win universal acceptance, especially amongst the various minorities whose freedoms were curtailed by brāhmanical ideology. As noted above, Alexander was known as the great by his admirers but as the barbarian by the Persians, whose empire he destroyed. Likewise, the Gupta world was 'golden' in the eyes of the brāhmans and their admirers but distinctly 'brassy' from the perspective of those who found themselves oppressed.

Even rulers had to conform to the ideology they had promoted. As Hein points out, 'Kings in the classical age became the enforcers, not the makers, of law, the heads of limited states whose function was the perpetuation of tradition.'[3]

For all members of brāhmanical society, and we must include the renunciants here for their basic needs were catered for in the brāhmanical codes, a variety of devices were employed to ameliorate the often stifling restrictions imposed on the population by the dharma texts. Pilgrimages were promoted, overtly for religious reasons, though they served a valuable function of providing holidays and temporary relief from the strict confines of life within the caste system. Likewise, festivals such as Dīvalī were used to promote a common Hindu identity, whilst others, such as Holi, acted as pressure valves that provided periodic release from the pervasive straitjacket of dharma. No longer did people have to be called to accept the dharma of the śāstras; that was a given. Accordingly, the character of religion began to change. The Kṛṣṇa of the *Bhagavad Gītā* remains a revered figure, but attention and celebration shift to the exploits of his younger years when he, and by implication those who celebrate those events, were free, momentarily, from what Hein calls the 'structure of steel' that was brāhmanical dharma.

The pursuit of release from rebirth also received increased regulation. Although some dharma texts, such as the *Yajñavalkya Smṛti*, allowed the transition from studentship to renunciation—missing out on householdership and forest dwelling—as had been advocated by Buddhists and Jains, the dominant view was expressed by *Manu*: renunciation is to be undertaken only after one's social obligations have been fulfilled. Zimmer quotes a story from the *Mārkāṇḍeya Purāṇa* that is as fine a piece of religious propaganda as I have encountered anywhere.[4] One of its aims is to present Viṣṇu as the supreme deity, and it succeeds in this admirably. Another is to promote the brāhmanical view of renunciation, and this too is accomplished with finesse. Viśvakarman (all-maker), the Indian Haephestus/Vulcan, is asked by the king of the (Vedic) gods, Indra, to build him a palace. Viśvakarman does this and Indra is pleased, though not completely satisfied. He therefore asks Viśvakarman to extend it. The extension is built, but again Indra is not satisfied and requests a further extension. The pattern repeats and Viśvakarman wearies of his task, so he goes to the highest heaven to ask Viṣṇu for help. The rest of the story is about Viṣṇu's response and, in brāhmanical terms, successful outcome for all concerned.

Briefly, a strange child turns up at Indra's palace and is received by the god, who expresses curiosity at the child's unusual smile. The child begs Indra's forgiveness for his rudeness, it was just that he had realized that no previous Indra had had such a wonderful palace. This comment perplexes Indra, who, as the Vedas present him, is the immortal king of the immortals. Other Indras, what kind of disturbing lunacy was this? We have, in this comment by the child, the clash between traditional Vedic cosmology and the karma-saṃsāra-mokṣa view. The child then draws attention to a parade of ants that is making its way across the courtyard. Every one of them had, in some previous incarnation, been an Indra—though none of them had had such a wonderful palace. Before Indra can respond to this mind-boggling revelation another guest appears: an old, hairy ascetic who has an unusual circular bald patch in the middle of his chest. When asked about this by Indra he says that he is an ascetic who wanders the world without possessions because he has realized that his death is immanent and he wishes to meet it unburdened by desires. The bald patch, he says, has developed because one of his chest hairs falls out every time an Indra dies and, as is plain to see, he has lost around half of the hairs on his chest. Once again, Indra's mind is overwhelmed by the vastness of this perspective and the shift in values that it initiates.

The upshot is that Indra decides to renounce the world. He informs his wife and begins to prepare himself for the life of a saṃnyāsin. His wife, however, does not simply accept his decision. Rather, she seeks out Bṛhaspati, the custodian of brāhmanical values, and asks for his help. In response to the queen's request, Bṛhaspati goes to Indra and congratulates him on his acquisition of wisdom and his decision to renounce the world. He just wants to check, he says, whether Indra has made all the appropriate preparations, for it would be pointless to take such an important step and then find that one was hampered by a burden of unfulfilled duties. The best course of action, explains Bṛhaspati, is to discharge all one's duties and then renounce the world. This gives Indra a new perspective that allows him to retain the wisdom of the karma-saṃsāra-mokṣa view whilst also following a course of action more suited to his current nature. Once again, Indra is swayed by the guidance of a religious teacher and he changes his plans, deciding to remain king—though the allure of extending his palace has lost its sheen. Now he will be a dutiful rather than an indulgent king, and at some time in the future will renounce the world and seek liberation. This is *Manu*'s version of the varṇā-aśrama-dharma in the form of a story that simultaneously exalts Viṣṇu.

Alongside the development of the Purāṇas there is a parallel systematization of philosophical teachings. The Buddhists and Jains were impossible to incorporate into the new brāhmanical synthesis and were, therefore, labelled as heterodox (na-astika), i.e. denying the authority of the Vedas. Other schools, however, were less clearly un-Vedic and could be incorporated even when their teachings had more in common with Buddhism and Jainism than with the philosophies based on the Vedic corpus. Most prominent among these were the Sāṃkhya and Yoga schools, which found a place in the scheme that came to be known as the six orthodox viewpoints (astika darśana). The assumption behind this scheme was that these philosophical schools (darśana) were essentially in agreement with each other, an assumption that has confused many a Western student since an unbiased reading quickly reveals that they are not. Theoretically at least, all the darśanas accept three primary sources or bases of knowledge (pramāna): perception (pratyakṣa); inference (anumāna) and testimony (śabda), though they vary considerably in the emphasis they put on each.

The six darśanas are:

1. Mīmāṃsā (exegesis—sometimes called Purva Mīmāṃsā because it is concerned with the exegesis (mīmāṃsā) of the earlier (purva) portion of the Veda, i.e. the Saṃhitās and the Brāhmaṇas);
2. Vedānta (Veda's end—sometimes called Uttara Mīmāṃsā because it is concerned with the exegesis of the later (uttara) portion of the Veda, i.e. the Āraṇyakas and Upaniṣads);
3. Sāṃkhya (enumeration or distinction);
4. Yoga (integration);
5. Nyāya (going back, i.e. logic and argumentation);
6. Vaiśeṣika (difference).

Each of these has a root text that is regarded as foundational and on which later scholars wrote commentaries. These are:

1. The *Mīmāṃsā Sūtras* of Jaimini;
2. The *Vedānta Sūtras* of Bādarāyaṇa;
3. The *Sāṃkhya Kārikās* of Īśvarakṛṣṇa;
4. The *Yoga Sūtras* of Patañjali;

5. The *Nyāya Sūtras* of Gautama;
6. The *Vaiśeṣika Sūtras* of Kaṇāda.

Sūtras are brief expressions of a point, aphorisms or half-sentences; kārikās are short verses. Of these six, only three are of real significance in the development of yoga: Sāṃkhya, Yoga and Vedānta. I shall, therefore, only offer the briefest outline of the other three.

## NYĀYA-VAIŚEṢIKA

These systems were originally independent of each other but became synthesized around the tenth century CE. Nyāya was primarily a school of logic and many of its methods were adopted by other schools. Vaiśeṣika is a system of metaphysical pluralism. In this scheme, there are nine fundamental substances (dravya) in the universe. These are irreducible to each other but combine in various ways to create the complexity that we experience. The dravyas are:

1. earth;
2. water;
3. fire;
4. air;
5. ether (ākāśa);
6. time;
7. space (diś);
8. self (ātman);
9. mind (manas).

Selves in this system are numerous and, although theoretically omnipresent, they limit themselves to the size of the body they are inhabiting. This teaching has obvious affinities with that of the Jains.

The *Vaiśeṣika Sūtras* are difficult to date, though they must have been compiled before the fifth century CE because a commentary on them by one Praśāstapāda was composed at that time. Likewise, although it is difficult to date the *Nyāya Sūtras* with any precision a commentary on them was written sometime around 400 CE so they must have been compiled before then. The work that is regarded as the classic synthesis of the two sets of teachings dates from around the beginning of the thirteenth century CE. It was composed in East Bengal and called the *Tattva-Cintāmaṇi* ('Thought Gem of the Reals').[5]

## MĪMĀṂSĀ

Unlike Nyāya-Vaiśeṣika, Mīmāṃsā is not an independent system of philosophy but a school of exegesis. Its primary function is to interpret the early portions of the Veda, namely the Saṃhitās and the Brāhmaṇas. Its primary concern is with producing guidance on the performance of duty (dharma). In the earliest phases of its development, Mīmāṃsā seems to have accepted only the three traditional goals of life (artha): wealth, pleasure and duty, and the three stages of life (āśrama): student, householder and forest-dweller. The later Mīmāṃsā does, however, go beyond the early Veda in its acceptance of mokṣa as the ultimate goal and saṃnyāsa as a fourth stage.

The primary text of the Mīmāṃsā school is the *Mīmāṃsā Sūtra* of Jaimini, which was probably composed around 200 CE. It is the largest of all primary darśana texts, containing over two-and-a-half thousand sūtras. The school split into two branches during the seventh century CE under Prabhākara and Kumārila Bhaṭṭa.

In terms of its teachings, the Mīmāṃsā seems to have been influenced by Nyāya and Vaiśeṣika—which suggests that their teachings were in existence prior to 200 CE. Like Nyāya-Vaiśeṣika, Sāṃkhya and Yoga, the Mīmāṃsā admits a plurality of selves that are both eternal and omnipresent. As in Nyāya-Vaiśeṣika, these selves are mutable, subject to change. The dravyas of Nyāya-Vaiśeṣika are accepted and supplemented with a few others. However, instead of liberation resulting in a complete separation of the self from the other dravyas, the Mīmāṃsā understanding is that interaction with the other dravyas continues though the self comprehends that they are different from it.

The way to gain emancipation according to Mīmāṃsā is twofold:

1. identify a reliable source of knowledge on which to base one's practice. For the Mīmāṃsākas this is the Veda. Then employ the correct method of interpretation for extracting its teachings on dharma;
2. follow that dharma.

For the Mīmāṃsākas, the dharma can only be known through the Veda; perception and inference are secondary. This is because, in their view, the Veda is eternal. It is apauruṣeya, an eternal revelation in sound that was not composed by any being, neither human nor god. This is an interesting development that has subtly influenced forms of yoga that employ mantras (chanted formulae), as the idea seems to be widely held that such mantras tap into some kind of eternal vibration that can yield knowledge of the universe and the place of human beings within it. In the final analysis, the approach of the Mīmāṃsākas to liberation is essentially that advocated in the *Bhagavad Gītā*: do your duty in a spirit of indifference.

## SĀṂKHYA

The earliest references to the system of Sāṃkhya indicate that it existed in a number of forms. There is thus considerable controversy in scholarly circles about the early history of Sāṃkhya. Unlike the Vedānta, it does not trace its origin back to the Veda but to the sage Kapila (the tawny-clad one). Likewise, some of its key terms have no Vedic background. On the other hand, many writers do attempt to trace the Sāṃkhya system back to Vedic literature.

When authors write about the existence of early or proto-Sāṃkhya traditions they are referring to pre-*Kārikā* accounts of existence which, in structure or terminology, overlap in some way with that found in the *Sāṃkhya Kārikā*. One thorough survey of such speculations is that of Larson (1979), whose approach makes it clear that he would like to locate the origins of the Sāṃkhya system in the pre-Upaniṣadic Vedic tradition. However, after surveying the evidence the most he can say is,

> the Sāṃkhya in any of its forms is not present in those early speculations. Yet it is *possible* to point to certain trends of thought which *might* have later *been assimilated* into Sāṃkhya. To point to such trends is not to make the claim that these trends can be precisely traced into later Sāṃkhya. The claim is only that certain trends provide *a context* from which later Sāṃkhya *may* have arisen.[6]

Not until we reach the *Kaṭha* and, later, the *Maitrī* and *Śvetāśvatara Upaniṣads* does the existence of embryonic Sāṃkhya or of Sāṃkhyan influence on the Vedic tradition become self-evident. There are clear parallels between the *Kārikās* and the earliest of these Upaniṣads, the *Kaṭha*, in terms of the description of the self (ātman) (*KU* 2.18-25) and in terms of the relation between self and body and the constituents of the person (*KU* 3.3-12 and 6.6-9) and I would suggest that here we have the earliest clear indication of the existence of Sāṃkhya-like analyses in Indian literature.

Some writers, however, identify such analyses in earlier Upaniṣads, most notably the *Chāndogya*. *CU* 6 contains an account of how the one being (sat) evolved from itself in the beginning, three forms (rūpa): fire or light (tejas), water (apa) and earth (anna). From these everything else was produced. Larson thinks it 'quite likely' that the Sāṃkhya of the *Kārikās* could have developed out of such speculations[7] and William Beidler thinks it clearly lays the foundation for the development of the Sāṃkhyan guṇa theory.[8] When the text of *CU* 6 is examined, however, the similarities between it and the *Kārikā* account of evolution are few and far between. The last evolutes in the *Kārikā* scheme are the mahābhūtas: ether (ākāśa), air (vāyu), fire or light (tejas), water (apa) and earth (pṛthivī). In the *Chandogya Upaniṣad* account the first evolutes of the one being are the three 'forms' (rūpa) of tejas, apa and anna (= pṛthivī). Whatever exists, according to Uddālaka, is merely a modification of one of the forms, 'the reality is just "the three forms"'.

From these three forms emerge the subtle faculties of speech (vāc), breath (prāṇa) and mind (manas), which evolves from earth. Thus, in this *Chandogya Upaniṣad* account the mental evolves from the physical. In the *Kārikā* the reverse is the case. Mind (manas) evolves from ahaṃkāra, which in its tamasic manifestation, produces the tanmātras (sense faculties) from which, in turn, emerge the mahābhūtas, the last three of which are the same as the three 'forms' of *CU* 6. That the former should be a prototype of the latter is hardly credible. In fact, the only thing in common between the *Chandogya Upaniṣad* and *Kārikā* accounts would seem to be that the 'forms' of the one being are three in number as are the qualities (guṇa) of prakṛti.

But even if it is accepted that the *Katha Upaniṣad* passages constitute the earliest references to Sāṃkhya thought in Indian literature there still remains the vexed question of whether the compilers of the *Kaṭha Upaniṣad* were developing or just borrowing these Sāṃkhya concepts. Not until the period of the later prose Upaniṣads and the great epic, the *Mahābhārata*, do we find specific references to the existence of a school designated as Sāṃkhya.

Larson suggests that the first recorded mention of 'Sāṃkhya' in the literature of India is to be found in the *Śvetāśvatara Upaniṣad*, *SU* 6.13.1. In fact, the reference is to Sāṃkhya-Yoga, the common term employed in the *Mahābhārata* to denote the system of Kapila.

Moreover, the claim itself is controversial since the date of the *Śvetāśvatara* is actually a matter of some dispute. Hume's chronology of the Upaniṣads follows Deussen's with regard to all the principal Upaniṣads except the *Śvetāśvatara,* which he places in Deussen's third group along with the *Praśna,* the *Maitrī* and the *Māṇḍūkya.* K.B.R. Rao goes even further. He argues that the *Śvetāśvatara Upaniṣad* succeeds rather than precedes the various formulations of Sāṃkhya in the *Mahābhārata.*[9]

Rao's view receives some indirect support from the observations of two other scholars: E.W. Hopkins and J.A.B. Van Buitenen. The former argues that both the *Kaṭha* and *Maitrī Upaniṣads* (which contain undisputed 'Sāṃkhya' material) 'were certainly copied by the epic poets'.[10] With regard to the *Śvetāśvatara,* however, all he can say is, 'This may be loosely copied, but, except for one parallel, the mutual passages are common to this and other sources.'[11] There is thus little evidence from the *Mahābhārata* to support the claim that the compilation of the *Śvetāśvatara Upaniṣad* was carried out in a period anterior to that of the epic.

When commenting on the relationship between Vedic and epic material in general, Van Buitenen points out that the notions of a 'Vedic age' and an 'epic age', with their suggestions of chronological continuity, are perhaps misleading. He suggests that the substitution of the term 'milieu' for 'age' may be a closer approximation to the true state of affairs since 'chronological priority of Vedic to post-Vedic notions is not necessarily a fact'.[12] This in turn goes some way towards supporting Grierson's claim that the developments of the Vedic tradition took place primarily in the 'midland' (madhyadesa), the area around and to the north of Delhi, whilst less brāhmanically influenced systems such as Sāṃkhya and Pañcarātra developed in the 'outland', mainly to the east of Delhi.[13]

Grierson's answer to the question posed earlier about whether 'Sāṃkhya' was developed by Upaniṣadic teachers or borrowed by them would thus be strongly in favour of the latter alternative, an option also favoured by a number of more recent scholars.[14] The evidence of the *Mahābhārata* can also be seen to support such a view since most of the references to Sāṃkhya suggests that it was a well-established system, though perhaps not always uniform in its manifestations. In fact, as Hopkins points out, the system of Kapila 'is *repeatedly* declared to be the oldest'.[15]

In the Mokṣadharma section of *Mahābhārata* 12 a number of teachers are quoted as offering instruction about some form of

Sāṃkhya. They are Pañcaśikha, Bhīṣma, Vyāsa, Yajñavalkya, Vaśiṣṭha, Asita Devala, Sulabhā and Vaiśampāyana. None of these teachers offers exactly the same version of Sāṃkhya teaching as the others and all differ in one way or another from that presented in the *Sāṃkhya Kārikā*. Nevertheless, features which differentiate the classical Sāṃkhya of the *Kārikā* from the teaching of the Upaniṣads: the plurality and separateness of the puruṣas and the lack of a god figure, are in evidence in some epic versions of Samkhya, a fact which indicates that the system of Īśvarakṛṣṇa is not some deviation from a genuine theistic and possibly monistic Sāṃkhya which developed out of the teaching of the Upaniṣads but one which stands in an ancient and well-established tradition of thought. Most epic descriptions of Sāṃkhya are not provided by actual Sāṃkhya teachers but are reports of what Sāṃkhyans believe. In fact, Yajñavalkya distinguishes between those Sāṃkhyans, whom he calls 'yatis', who regard puruṣa 'as existing by himself without a second, immutable, unmanifest (in the form of cause), unstable, and manifest (in the form of effects)', i.e. an Upaniṣadic form of Sāṃkhya, and those who 'depend on knowledge only (for their emancipation) and the practice of compassion for all creatures [and who] say that it is prakriti which is one but purushas are many'.[16]

King Janaka, disciple of Pañcaśikha, makes a similar distinction between those who claim that knowledge is the only means of emancipation and those, called yatis, who argue that actions are the means.[17] In 12.308, Vaśiṣṭha, too, uses the term yati to denote those Sāṃkhyans who believe in the singularity of puruṣa, and in 12.351 Vaiśampāyana goes further, stating boldly that the followers of Sāṃkhya and Yoga do not accept that there is just one puruṣa in the universe.[18] Implicit in such a claim is the argument that those who do accept the singularity of puruṣa are not followers of Sāṃkhya or Yoga. We may also note that it is the Sāṃkhyans who maintain the plurality of puruṣas who practise compassion for all creatures. This clearly links them with Kapila, the recognized founder of Samkhya, who, in 12.269.9, criticizes the Vedic tradition's adherence to animal sacrifice.[19]

Some schools of Sāṃkhya during the epic period also appear to have been atheistic. Chakravarti perhaps goes too far when he claims that the *Mahābhārata* 'is always found to represent the atheistic school of Sāṃkhya',[20] but that the epic knows an atheistic form of Sāṃkhya is clear from 12.301, where Bhīṣma contrasts the followers of Sāṃkhya with those of Yoga. The latter hold that unless a person accepts a lord (īśvara) they cannot attain liberation; the former, however, are said to hold that a person 'by acquiring true knowledge of all ends, becomes disassociated from all worldly objects, and, after departing from this body, it is plain, becomes emancipated...'[21] In other words, god (īśvara) is not necessary for emancipation.

Unfortunately, the epic nowhere provides anything like a detailed account of the Sāṃkhyans who practise compassion towards all creatures, who teach that puruṣas are many and that a person does not need god to attain liberation. Only versions of the other kind of Sāṃkhya are presented at any length. One noticeable detail about these 'one-puruṣa' schools is that they generally subscribe in some way or other to Vedic values, world view and terminology. For example, Vaśiṣṭha, one who knows both Sāṃkhya and Veda, incorporates Hiraṇyagarbha, Virāj and Viṣṇu into his exposition of Sāṃkhya. He also describes the ones who experience 'the supreme soul' as 'high-souled Brāhmanas endued with intelligence and wisdom and conversant with the Vedas'.[22] The Vedas, for their part, are authoritative and eternal.[23] Likewise, Asita Devala is called a brāhmaṇa and maintains that his teachings are compatible with both śruti and reason. For him, emancipation is the attainment of brahma. Bhīṣma too, although attempting to be a neutral expositor, presents a rather Vedic view of Sāṃkhya. Yama and Prajāpati find a place in his version and liberation is the merging of the jīva-soul with the supreme soul through the help of Nārāyaṇa.

Pañcaśikha is even more noteworthy in this respect, for he incorporates Vedic terminology into his teaching, regards the Vedas as sources of right knowledge which guide people along the true path, is conversant with Upaniṣadic teachings such as the five sheaths of the *Taittirīya Upaniṣad* and holds that emancipation is the attainment of brahma. He is also described as 'the foremost of all persons conversant with the Vedas' and he teaches his disciple, King Janaka, that one does not have to renounce kingdom or householder life in order to win emancipation, for 'If men leading the domestic mode of life be endued with Yama and Niyama, they become the equal of Sannyasins.'[24]

That some teachers doubted the authenticity of Pañcaśikha's Sāṃkhya is clear from the Janaka-Sulabhā dialogue in 12.321. There, the latter instructs the former, in what Roy regards as the doctrines of the atheistic Sāṃkhya.[25] She informs him that whilst he might have moved a little beyond conventional domestic life he has not attained emancipation but is stuck between the two, pretending to have reached the goal.[26]

The picture that emerges from a consideration of Sāṃkhya material in the Upaniṣads and the *Mahābhārata* is that there were two broad currents of Sāṃkhyan thought co-existing and competing in the pre-Gupta period. One was identifiably brāhmanical in character, teaching the existence of a single universal soul (puruṣa), though not necessarily a monistic ontology. This current emphasized the importance of the Veda and of dharma, and offered the possibility of gaining emancipation without having to renounce the world. Vedic deities are prominent in the schemes of this current. The other current has many of the features associated with śramanic traditions: an emphasis on non-violence (ahiṃsā), the importance of renunciation, atheism and a pluralistic ontology. To my mind, Sāṃkhya teaching is more congruent and internally cohesive in its renouncer forms, and the attribution of its creation to Kapila, a critic of Vedic sacrifices, clearly points to a situation in which an originally śramanic form of Sāṃkhya was appropriated by brāhmanical teachers in the course of developing their own philosophies. The fact that this process can be traced as far back as the *Kaṭha Upaniṣad* bears testimony to the claims found in the epic that Sāṃkhya was the oldest of all the philosophical systems. Moreover, this interpretation is supported by the very significant fact that the root text of the Sāṃkhya darśana, the *Sāṃkhya Kārikā*, presents us with what is clearly a renouncer version of the teaching rather than a brāhmanical one.

The *Sāṃkhya Kārikā* of Īśvarakṛṣṇa has been accepted as the normative statement of the school since the time of its composition (5th century CE), though it is likely that earlier systematic formulations of Sāṃkhya did exist but are now lost. One reason for thinking along these lines is that there are a number of outline versions of Sāṃkhya teaching in the *Mahābhārata* (see Chapter 4 above). Another is that whilst the other five orthodox (astika) darśanas have sūtra collections as their root texts the Sāṃkhya possesses kārikās or aphoristic verses, which are less concise than sūtras. There may, then, have been a sūtra collection upon which the *Kārikā* is based. The text that currently goes under the name of the Sāṃkhya Sūtras is not, however, that early collection. The *Sāṃkhya Sūtras* date from the fourteenth or fifteenth century CE. The *Kārikā* has attracted many commentaries and elaborations and is the work most frequently quoted by Mādhava in his treatment of Sāṃkhya in the

*Sarva-Darśana-Saṃgraha* (14th century CE). It is composed of 73 continuous verses (kārikā).

The principal features of the system represented by Īśvarakṛṣṇa are that the universe exists because of the conjunction (saṃyoga) of two self-existent realities: puruṣa (spirit/awareness) and prakṛti (matter/energy). There are many puruṣas, all identical. In *Kārikā* 19 we are informed that puruṣa is a witness (sākṣitvam), is isolated or alone (kaivalyam), is indifferent (mādhyasthyam), is a spectator (draṣṭṛtvam) and is not an agent or doer (akartṛbhāvam).

Prakṛti, on the other hand, is unitary. It exists in two modes, an unmanifest (avyakta) and a manifest (vyakta). The manifest is not a coming into being of new existence, however, but merely an actualizing at the manifest level that which already existed at the unmanifest one. This is the teaching of satkāryavāda, that the effect or manifestation (vyakta) already exists in the cause (avyakta).

Prakṛti's unfolding is accomplished initially through the manifestation of psychological faculties: intellect (buddhi) and egoity (sense of self) or self-formulation (ahaṃkāra). The latter, in its different modes as conditioned by the qualities (guṇa) of sattva, rajas and tamas, then proceeds to evolve the remaining principles (tattvas) which make up the world of our experience. The order of evolution can be seen from the following table:

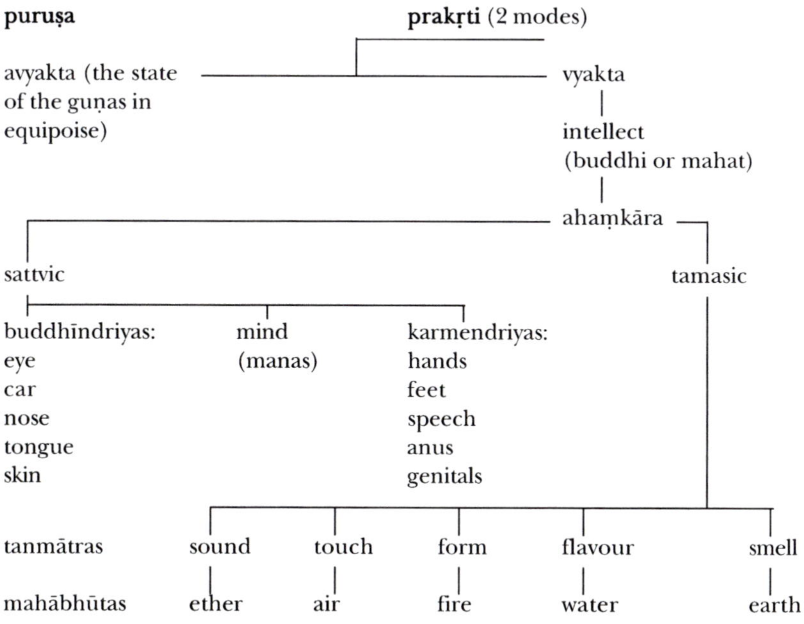

The relationship between the guṇas and tattvas is not very clear in the *Sāṃkhya Kārikā* and Van Buitenen has suggested that they were originally distinct but combined in the classical Sāṃkhya of the *Kārikā*.[27] Rajas, in particular, seems to lack a coherent position in the tattva scheme. When prakṛti is manifest, the experience of the individualized psychic organs as illumined by puruṣa, who has no ontological involvement with the prakṛti, is permeated by suffering, primarily because the vyakta universe is in a constant state of flux. This suffering leads, on the one hand, to a search for pleasure, which does nothing to bring about any kind of ultimate change in the way things are, or for release, which is brought about by discrimination (viveka). When the tattvas are known for what they are, namely aspects of prakṛti, the knower (puruṣa) becomes aware of his own identity as something different from prakṛti. This realization obviates the need for further prakṛtic activity with regard to the particular puruṣa in question. Thus suffering is overcome and the aims of the Sāṃkhya system are realized. However, for those puruṣas not obtaining liberation a periodic rest is provided by prakṛti who, at the end of each aeon, reverses the creative process and returns to the unmanifest state, known in this context as pralaya. After a period (time does not exist in pralaya) the karma of the puruṣas, which was responsible for bringing about the pralaya, becomes expended and a re-manifestation of prakṛti begins.

In essence, the Sāṃkhya system describes the nature of existence by postulating that many identical puruṣas, whose only defining characteristic appears to be that they are conscious, become involved in some way with prakṛti, who is not conscious but subject to modification under stimulus and who responds to the presence of puruṣa by generating the universe in order that puruṣa may realize that the nature of his involvement with prakṛti has no effect upon him whatsoever. In Sāṃkhya, then, there is no need for the postulation of any kind of creator or superintending divinity. It is therefore classed as an atheistic (anaiśvarya) system.

Sāṃkhya is not, however, without its philosophical difficulties. *Kārikā* 63 tells us that prakṛti functions 'for the sake of the release of the puruṣa', and this is problematic if prakṛti is to be regarded as insentient. How could prakṛti desire the release of the puruṣa if she lacks awareness? Sentience would also seem to be a characteristic of prakṛti in *Kārikā* 61 where, when seen by puruṣa, she says 'I have been seen' and 'never again comes into the sight of the puruṣa'. The problem with this is that, according to *Kārikā* 66, prakṛti and puruṣa remain in proximity to each other even though no further creation takes place in response to puruṣa's presence. If this were the case then puruṣa would have to give up his omniscience for an omniscient puruṣa would always have prakṛti in his sight. The idea of creation being for the release of the puruṣa is also problematic on another count. *Kārikā* 62 tells us that no one is bound, no one is released and no one transmigrates. Only prakṛti is bound, transmigrates and is released. If this is so, prakṛti's actions could only be for her own benefit, for puruṣa clearly does not need the creation for anything and is unable to experience either benefit or detriment.

In terms of practice, Sāṃkhya is perhaps best described as advocating a form of jñana yoga. The method for gaining knowledge is to replace one's everyday perceptions and understandings of the world with those outlined in the Sāṃkhya scheme until the point is reached where all modifications of prakṛti are experienced as being other than oneself.

## YOGA

The dating of texts is a perennial problem for those who study Indian spiritual traditions, partly because clear historical markers are rare and partly because many of the texts are composite in nature, often with decades or centuries between their early and later portions. Patañjali's *Yoga Sūtra* is no exception to this and scholars have taken up a variety of positions on the issues of both dating and composition. With regard to dating, two widely differing dates for Patañjali have been proposed. One group of scholars, including S. Dasgupta, R. Garbe and B. Liebich, have argued that the compiler of the *Yoga Sūtra* is probably the same person who wrote a commentary on Pāṇini's Sanskṛit grammar sometime around 200 BCE. Another group, including G. Feuerstein, H. Jacobi, A.B. Keith and J.H. Woods, prefer a dating of around 300 CE, i.e. around the end of the epic period.[28]

Almost every scholar who has examined this text in detail has formed a different opinion about its unity or component parts. As we have it, the text is divided into four chapters or books, 51, 55, 55 and 34 sūtras long respectively. A.B. Keith has argued that the text is a unitary composition.[29] G. Feuerstein agrees with Keith, except for the section on the eight limbs (aṣṭāṅga), which, he suggests, begins at 2.28 and continues to 3.4 or 3.9. Patañjali included the material on the eight limbs because, claims Feuerstein, 'it contained a number of convenient definitions'.[30] By contrast, E. Frauwallner regards the eight limbs section as 'the kernel in the Text'.[31] What he means by 'Text' here is books 2 and 3. Book 1 he regards as an essentially independent work, outlining what he calls 'The Yoga of Suppression'.[32] By implication, Frauwallner treats book 4 as yet another separate component of the text as we have it. In this he has the support of S. Dasgupta who, on the other hand, regards books 1 to 3 as constituting a coherent unity.[33]

One of Frauwallner's main reasons for thinking that book 1 is a self-contained piece is that after setting out the root problem: the self's conformity to the mind's activities and loss of self-awareness, along with the methods for addressing the problem: practice (abhyāsa) and detachment (vairāgya), it seems to end with enlightenment (ṛtaṃbharā-prajñā—literally 'truth-bearing insight') and the self's immersion in itself (sabīja samādhi). In other words, book 1 ends with the experience of liberation.

With regard to the issue of the place of the eight limbs section in the sūtras as a whole, or even just books 2 and 3, an examination of the form of book 2 offers a way of evaluating and adjudicating between the views of Feuerstein and those of Frauwallner. *YS* 2.2 states that the kriya yoga described in 2.1 is 'for the cultivation of concentration and for the attenuation of the hindrances'.[34] The expectation is, then, that these two topics: the cultivation of concentration (samādhi) and the attenuation of the hindrances (kleśa) will form the subject matter of the immediately succeeding sūtras. This is certainly the case for the attenuation of the hindrances, which are dealt with in 2.3-25. The cultivation of concentration is treated in the section on the eight limbs, which, in terms of this analysis, can be taken as commencing at 2.26, not 2.28 as Feuerstein suggests. In other words, the two topics mentioned in 2.2 are addressed in 2.3-25 and 2.26–3.9. Such an interpretation goes against both Feuerstein's and Frauwallner's views. Whilst it may be the case that Patañjali included an already existing formulation of the method for cultivating concentration into his text it was not merely for the sake of a few 'convenient definitions'. Rather, this 'quotation' forms an integral part of the exposition of kriya yoga; without it the treatment would be incomplete. On the other hand, the eight limbs section cannot, as Frauwallner would have it, constitute the kernel of chapters 2 and 3. In terms of 2.2, the account of the hindrances is just as central and integral to these chapters as is that dealing with the eight limbs.

Dasgupta does not accept Frauwallner's division of the text as he regards books 1 to 3 as forming a coherent unit, with book 4 as a later addition. His argument in support of his view goes something like this: at the end of many philosophical and religious works in Sanskṛit we find the word 'iti', meaning 'thus'. It functions in much the same way as 'the end' or 'finis' in European writings. Because of this convention, when we find the word 'iti' at the end of the third book of the *Yoga Sūtras* we would expect the work to come to an end. It does not. Rather, book 3 is followed by book 4, which also ends with 'iti'. Books 1 and 2 do not end with 'iti', so it looks as though book 4 was added later and a sloppy editor (or one who held the first three books in such reverence that he was unwilling to delete even this one small and now unnecessary term) forgot to remove the 'iti'. Dasgupta continues, stating,

> There is also a marked change (due either to its supplementary character or to the manipulation of a foreign hand) in the style of the last chapter as compared with the other three.
>
> The sūtras, 30-34, of the last chapter seem to repeat what has already been said in the second chapter and some of the topics introduced are such that they could well have been dealt with in a more relevant manner in connection with similar discussions in the preceding chapters. The extent of this chapter is also disproportionately small, as it contains only 34 sūtras, whereas the average number of sūtras in the other chapters is between 51 to 55.[35]

One might add, in support of Dasgupta, that in the middle of book 4 we find what seems to be a polemic against a school of Yogācāra Buddhism (see above, pp. 92–95) that taught a form of idealism, i.e. that the material world is actually made of mind. No other chapter contains such a polemic.

Thus, there are at least four ways that one can view the composition of the *Yoga Sūtras* as we now have them:

1. as a unified work (Keith);
2. as a unified work apart from the aṣṭāṅga section (Feuerstein);
3. as a work in two parts: books 1-3 and book 4 (Dasgupta);

4. as an originally concise work consisting of what is now book 1 plus one or more later additions (Frauwallner).

Given this variety, a fifth view of the text as being somewhat crudely stitched together out of existing materials is also plausible. This allows both unity (the same person stitched the whole thing) and diversity (different parts of the text came from different sources).

In outline, the teachings contained in the text as a whole are that the world from which Patañjali and his followers seek to escape is one that is permeated by suffering (duḥkha) (2.15-16). This world has come into existence because of the conjunction (saṃyoga) of two essentially distinct entities, namely prakṛti, that which is seen, and puruṣa, the seer. That conjunction is the cause of ignorance (avidyā), which is the seer losing awareness of its real nature and identifying with the ever-changing manifestations of prakṛti. This ignorance is said by Patañjali to be the fundamental cause of affliction (kleśa) as the body–mind complex with which the bound puruṣa identifies gives rise to further causes of affliction: I-am-ness (asmitā); attachment (rāga); aversion (dvesa), and the will-to-live (abhiniveśa).

The causes of affliction exist in two modes: subtle (sukṣma) and coarse (sthūla). At the subtle level, the kleśas condition the psychological traits (vāsana) and the psychic impressions of former actions (saṃskāra). At the coarse level, they are aroused or active (udara). In this condition they influence the states of consciousness (vṛtti) that are the normal range of experience for most people. The vṛttis are:

1. valid cognition (pramāṇa);
2. misconception (viparyaya);
3. conceptualization (vikalpa);
4. sleep (nidrā);
5. memory (smṛti).

These states of consciousness can be afflicted (kliṣṭa) or non-afflicted (akliṣṭa). The precise nature of this distinction is not elaborated by Patañjali and the traditional commentators offer little by way of insight. A liberated yogin would still, presumably, experience at least some of the vṛttis, and it might be that in such a case the vṛttis would be non-afflicted. 4.7 tells us, for example, that the actions (karma) of the yogin are neither black nor white. However, since the kleśas are only eradicated in the final stages of yogic practice (4.29-30) there is little scope for the akliṣṭa vṛttis. What is clear is that all these states of consciousness are conditioned or affected by the traits (vāsana) and impressions (saṃskāra), which, in turn, are created and modified by the character of ongoing experience. This is the cycle that maintains ignorance and hence saṃsāra. Diagrammatically, it can be represented as follows:

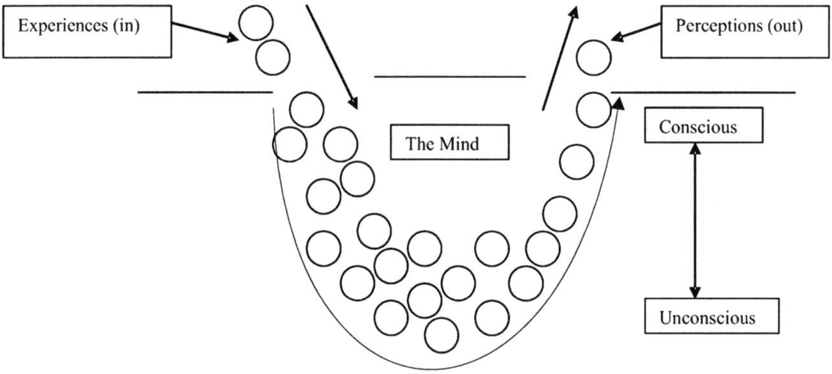


Patañjali's main concern is to set out the elements of the way to escape from this cycle. His initial focus is the vṛttis, since these are what dominate people's awareness and all of them are conditioned by ignorance and the other kleśas. Hence, he states in 1.2 that 'Yoga is the cessation or stilling (nirodha) of the vṛttis.' The way to make the vṛttis still is to cultivate concentration of mind (dhyāna) (*YS* 2.11). The state of dhyāna is thus the state of yoga. Once this is achieved, he tells us in 1.3, the seer abides in its own nature (svarūpa).

All is not quite so simple, however, since, according to 2.11, the vṛttis are merely vehicles for expressing just the coarse aspect of the kleśas. So, although the seer might experience itself in the state of dhyāna such an experience is only temporary.[36] The conjunction between puruṣa and prakṛti still remains. For this to be broken the subtle aspects of the kleśas have also to be eradicated. On this matter, the text makes two statements. 2.10 informs us that the subtle aspects of the kleśas are to be removed through the process of involution (pratiprasava), which, as 4.34 states, is the return of the guṇas to the unmanifest state. This means that the kleśas persist in subtle form right until the moment that puruṣa separates from prakṛti (kaivalya). It is the experience of dharma-megha-samādhi (4.29-30) that brings this about.

Patañjali's path is thus a deeply radical challenge to common sense thinking. He encourages us to stop identifying with *everything* that we have hitherto regarded as our 'self', i.e. our bodies, our minds, our feelings, our memories, much as the Buddha did when he taught that none of the five aggregates of a person (the skhandhas) nor all of them together constituted our self. Patañjali says that we do have a self, but that, unlike our bodies, etc. it is not part of prakṛti. This is why his path involves both practice or meditation (abhyāsa) and detachment (vairāgya). Meditation reveals the nature of things; detachment enables the connection between puruṣa and prakṛti to be broken.

In broad outline then, the *Yoga Sūtras* offer an intelligible soteriology that is quite similar to those developed in other renouncer circles. The problem, suffering, is described, the methods for dealing with it are set out and a notion of what the liberated state is like is offered. In terms of detail, however, parts of the text are less straightforward. So at this point I will address two issues that have been a source of confusion for many students: the nature of the lord (īśvara), and the relationship between the various accounts of samādhi.

## The Role of Īśvara in the *Yoga Sūtras*

To understand the place of īśvara in the soteriological scheme of the *Yoga Sūtras* one needs to have some idea of the cosmological environment in which the salvation or liberation is taking place. That is, we need to know the nature and cause of bondage, the methods suitable for its elimination and the characteristics of the liberated state. On the whole, scholars have tended to regard the cosmology of the *Yoga Sūtras* as being essentially agreement with that of classical Sāṃkhya. Thus, there are two fundamental ontological categories. On the one hand we have prakṛti, sometimes called dṛśya (the seen or objective), grāhya (that which is grasped, perceived, or that which imprisons or is taken in marriage), aliṅga (that which is without characteristics—there referring to prakṛti in her unmanifest state) and pradhāna (the chief). On the other hand is puruṣa, characterized by consciousness. There are many puruṣas, each one identical.

The first transformation of prakṛti is the manifestation of subtle mental categories (buddhi, ahaṃkāra and manas) which act rather like lenses or spectacles and allow the puruṣa to watch the remainder of prakṛti's unfoldment and hence the creation and transformation of the universe. The problem is that puruṣas begin to identify with what they see in prakṛti instead of remembering that what is before them is simply a 3-D, five-sense, all-colour spectacular show, put on for their entertainment. This mistaken identification by puruṣa leads him to think that he is actually bound up with the transformation of prakṛti and hence experiencing a series of 'lives'. This is saṃsāra.[37]

The aim of both Sāṃkhya and Yoga is for the puruṣa to realize his true identity and cease to be involved with prakṛti. This state of non-involvement is called kaivalya (isolation or aloneness).[38] Sāṃkhya's method for gaining such realization is one of reflection and discrimination between what is self and what is not self. In Yoga the technique is to gradually turn the mind away from the world and direct it inwards. Once this process is successful, the buddhi or most subtle aspect of mind no longer acts like a lens to direct puruṣa's attention towards the world but rather functions as a kind of mirror and reflects puruṣa back at himself. When he perceives his own nature he is freed from the illusion of thinking that he is a part of prakṛti.[39]

In his *The Philosophy of Classical Yoga* Georg Feuerstein has challenged the idea that Sāṃkhya and Yoga are two sides of the same coin.[40] Despite its seemingly radical nature, however, this claim is not nearly as strong as it sounds. When we examine his argument closely he is not claiming that the two systems have virtually nothing in common but merely that some scholars have gone too far in their claims that Yoga is simply a sub-school of Sāṃkhya. In this he is absolutely right, and Indian tradition obviously agrees with him since it classes Sāṃkhya and Yoga as two darśanas, not one. In Feuerstein's view the two principal differences between these systems are firstly that Yoga puts the emphasis on practical meditational techniques whereas Sāṃkhya stresses intellectual discrimination. Secondly Yoga is often said to be theistic whilst Sāṃkhya is atheistic. The question is, 'what does theism mean in this context?'

Ten sūtras in the *Yoga Sūtras* refer to 'the lord' (īśvara). These are 1.23-29, 2.1, 2.32 and 2.45. In the sūtras preceding 1.23 we are told various ways of gaining a state which could be either absorption (samādhi) or dispassion (vairāgya). Then 1.23 itself says 'īśvara praṇidhānād va', 'or by contemplation on the lord'. In other words, this state, whatever it may be, can be gained by īśvara praṇidhāna, which is usually translated as 'devotion to the lord', although, as I shall argue, 'contemplation on the lord' is probably a more accurate rendering. The remaining nine sūtras are:

1.24 The lord is a special self (puruṣa) untouched by defilement (kleśa), the results of action (karma-vipāka) and the store of mental deposits (āśaya).
1.25 In him the seed of omniscience is unsurpassed.
1.26 He was also the teacher of the former ones because of his non-boundedness by time.
1.27 His sound is the praṇava (the syllable OṂ).
1.28 The recitation of that produces an understanding of its meaning.
1.29 Then comes the attainment of inwardmindedness (pratyak-cetanā) and also the removal of obstacles.
2.1 Asceticism, self-study and īśvara praṇidhāna are kriya yoga.
2.32 Purity, contentment, asceticism, self-study and īśvara praṇidhāna are the disciplines (niyama).
2.45 Through īśvara praṇidhāna comes the attainment of samādhi.

2.1 tells us simply that īśvara praṇidhāna is a part of kriya yoga (active discipline) whilst 2.34 and 2.45 just inform us that it is one of the five disciplines which act as a preparation for the attainment of samādhi, which is probably why most commentators take the state referred to in 1.23 as that of samādhi. The sūtras from book 1 are more explicit about the nature of īśvara. Firstly, we are told that he is a special kind of puruṣa. What makes him special are the facts that he has always been untouched by defilement, action and its consequences and the store of mental deposits. He was also the teacher of former yogins because he, out of all the puruṣas, has never been bound by time. His symbol is OṂ and the recitation of this will enable the reciter to understand the nature of īśvara. Furthermore, he is said to be omniscient.[41]

It is clear that for Patañjali the īśvara can help the yogin in some way, for he was the teacher of former yogins. But exactly how does īśvara help puruṣas which are in bondage? Mircea Eliade explains it in the following way:

> this divine aid is not the effect of a 'desire' or a 'feeling'—for god (īśvara) can have neither desires nor emotions—but of a 'metaphysical sympathy' between īśvara and the puruṣa, a

> sympathy explained by their structural correspondence ... what is involved then, is ... a sympathy metaphysical in nature, connecting two kindred entities.[42]

If Eliade is correct, however, why do most translators of the *Yoga Sūtras* render sūtra 1.23 as 'or by devotion to the lord' rather than 'or by contemplating the lord'? The answer seems to lie in the commentaries. In explaining this sūtra, Vyāsa tells us that because of the yogin's special kind of devotion (bhakti viśeṣa) the īśvara inclines towards (avarjita) and favours (anugṛhṇāti) the yogin. This implies that the īśvara is an *active* self who can move and affect the yogin's situation in a favourable way. Vācaspatimiśra goes a step further. In his explanation of the next sūtra he informs us that īśvara 'possesses pre-eminence in richness of knowledge and of action and of power',[43] thereby suggesting that the īśvara, if not exactly omnipotent, comes pretty close to it.

What we have to decide is whether the attribution of omnipotence to īśvara is in line with Patañjali's understanding or whether it represents a development of the classical yoga tradition away from a Sāṃkhya-like cosmology where, in essence, the īśvara is the same as other puruṣas in favour of a view more akin to that found in the *Bhagavad Gītā*, where the supreme puruṣa (puruṣottama) creates and destroys the cosmos when he wishes and where the events in this world are determined by him (see *BG* ch. 9). Certainly the concept of omnipotence is not foreign to the *Yoga Sūtras* for, as 3.49 informs us,

> Just the vision of the distinction between the purusa and the sattva (brings) omnipotence (sarva bhava adhiṣṭhātṛtva) and omniscience (sarva jñātrtva).

Thus, on the threshold of liberation the yogin becomes, as one of my former students put it, 'master of the universe'. The important question for our purposes is 'does the yogin retain this mastery in the liberated state?'

Nowhere do the *Yoga Sūtras* themselves indicate that the īśvara is omnipotent, although a complete sūtra is devoted to informing us that he is omniscient. Thus, on the basis of the sūtras alone, a reasonable inference would be that the īśvara is not omnipotent and therefore the liberated puruṣa is also not omnipotent, for it seems unlikely that Patañjali wanted his pupils to think that liberated souls were greater than the īśvara. Such a conclusion is reinforced when we consider sūtra 3.50, which tells us that it is through dispassion towards omnipotence and omniscience that liberation is obtained. In some ways, however, this sūtra complicates matters for if īśvara, who is eternally liberated, can be omniscient there seems no good reason to think that an omniscient puruṣa will lose this faculty on attaining liberation. Why then should he be thought to lose his omnipotence? Part of this must lie with the conception of puruṣa itself. Puruṣas are many and identical. Their one characteristic is consciousness and it is quite likely that in Sāṃkhya-Yoga philosophy they are to be regarded as all-pervading.[44] Omniscience is a natural attribute of an all-pervading consciousness. In itself, however, such a puruṣa would seem to possess no means of manipulating the material world. Only by attaching itself to that world could the puruṣa manipulate it. But attachment to and involvement with the world is bondage, which is what the yoga system is trying to eliminate. Hence if omnipotence implies bondage then the īśvara is not omnipotent and neither is the liberated puruṣa. The īśvara cannot be omnipotent because he has never been bound; neither can the liberated puruṣa because he is liberated. Furthermore, a plurality of omnipotent beings is logically absurd, for imagine what would happen if they tried to engage in antagonistic activities.

Thus, the most logically consistent interpretation of the place of īśvara is likely to be more akin to Eliade's view than that of Vyāsa or Vācaspatimiśra. The īśvara of the *Yoga Sūtras* is probably closer in conception to the Jain ford-maker (tīrthaṅkara) than the omnipotent, omniscient god of the *Gītā*. Tīrthaṅkaras are free from involvement with the world and merely serve as examples for those who are on the path to release. Patañjali's intention seems to have been to encourage the yogin to contemplate on īśvara so that he will gradually realize that his own nature is just like that of īśvara. In other words, because īśvara is and always was liberated he provides the ideal focus for the attention of yogins, hence he helps by his *presence and example* and not by interfering with their lives.

It seems, then, that the notion of an 'active' lord probably does not belong to Patañjali's yoga but was introduced by later commentators such as Vyāsa and Vācaspatimiśra. Both these writers were composing their works when devotional religion was on the upsurge in India and it is not unreasonable to assume that they modified the teachings of their own tradition to keep pace with the times. Thus, the similarity between the teaching of the *Yoga Sūtras* and that of the Sāṃkhya system seems to be a strong one, even on the issue of theism. In fact, even though Kṛṣṇa may be referring to different systems when he speaks of Sāṃkhya and Yoga in the *Gītā*, the same relation would seem to hold between both classical and *Gītā* forms of these systems, namely one of similarity bordering on identity, as Kṛṣṇa says in 5.4-5:

> 'Of Sāṃkhya and Yoga as separate, fools speak, not the wise. Resorting to even one of them completely, man wins the fruit of both.
>
> What place is gained by the followers of Sāṃkhya, that is reached also by the followers of Yoga. Whoever sees that Sāṃkhya and Yoga are one, he (truly) sees.'

## Samādhi in the *Yoga Sūtras*

Traditional commentators identify two sections in the first book of the *Yoga Sūtras* where the topic of concentration (samādhi) is addressed: 1.17ff. and 1.41ff. In the first of these, 'concentration' is described as being of two kinds. The first kind is said to be 'linked with objects' (saṃprajñāta); it is characterized by reasoning (vitarka), reflection (vicāra), joy (ānanda) and egoity (asmitā). The second kind relates to karma formations (saṃskāra) only. It 'follows upon that practice which effects the cessation [of fluctuations]',[45] that is, the mind's fluctuations (vṛttis) described in *YS* 1.5-11.

In the second section on concentration: 1.41ff., states of concentration are again said to be of two kinds: with seed (sabīja) and without seed (nirbīja).[46] Concentration with seed is divided into four types called coincidences (samāpatti): with reasoning (savitarka), without/beyond reasoning (nirvitarka), with reflection (savicāra) and without/beyond reflection (nirvicāra). These states appear to be progressive, for 1.47 informs us that inner peace only arises when there is clarity in the non-reflective coincidence (nirvicāra samāpatti).

If these two sections: 1.17ff. and 1.41ff., both deal with the phenomenon of meditative concentration the two accounts should relate in some way. Vyāsa, composer of the oldest extant commentary on the *Yoga Sūtras*, calls the 'concentration' described in 1.17 saṃprajñāta samādhi (the term 'samādhi' does not actually occur in the text) and that described in 1.18 as asaṃprajñāta samādhi (neither term occurring in the text).[47] Traditional commentators such as Vācaspatimiśra and Vijñānabhikṣu then go on to equate saṃprajñāta samādhi with sabīja samādhi and asaṃprajñāta samādhi with nirbīja samādhi. When these equations are mapped out in detail, however, problems begin to emerge. Saṃprajñāta samādhi appears to be a single state with four characteristics: reasoning (vitarka); reflection (vicāra); joy (ānanda) and egoity (asmitā), whereas sabīja samādhi is clearly an umbrella term covering four stages in the progression of concentration: with reasoning (savitarka); without reasoning (nirvitarka); with reflection (savicāra) and without reflection (nirvicāra). In short, the two accounts do not seem to fit together. Each of the principal commentators on the *Yoga Sūtras* 'solves' this problem in a different way.

Vyāsa takes the four characteristics of saṃprajñāta samādhi to be four different kinds or levels of concentration. The lowest level is that of reasoning (vitarka), which has all four characteristics: reasoning, reflection, joy and egoity. Next comes reflection (vicāra) with three characteristics: reflection, joy and egoity. Then comes joy (ānanda) with two characteristics: joy and egoity, and, finally, egoity (asmitā) with itself as the sole characteristic. Vyāsa himself never explores the relationship between these levels of concentration and those set out in 1.41ff., though by means of the analysis described above he certainly lays the foundations and sets the direction for such an exploration. Vācaspatimiśra equates the vitarka state with savitarka samāpatti and the vicāra state with savicāra samāpatti, and each of these is followed by its negation. To the ānanda state is added a nirānanda samāpatti and to the asmitā state a nirasmitā samāpatti. This is quite a neat solution given Vyāsa's interpretation of 1.17, though Vijñānabhikṣu was not enamoured of it. He took the vitarka mentioned in 1.17 to equal the savitarka and nirvitarka samāpattis combined and the vicāra of 1.17 to equal the savicāra and nirvicāra samāpattis combined, whilst ānanda and asmitā are taken to constitute two further levels or stages.

Although possessing a certain aesthetic appeal, explanations of the relationship between the material presented in 1.17ff. and 1.41ff. such as those outlined above strike the reader as rather convoluted and unconvincing. One is left wondering why Patañjali, who offers intelligible explanations of the relations between other key concepts, left these crucial teachings in such an ambiguous form. Had Patañjali really intended to interpose two (Vijñānabhikṣu) or four (Vācaspatimiśra) stages of samādhi between nirvicāra samāpatti and nirbīja samādhi then surely he would have mentioned them at the end of his account of the varieties of samādhi with seed. In fact, it is clear from the text of 1.47ff. that nirvicāra samāpatti is the highest of the forms of concentration with seed for it is in this state that truth-bearing insight arises. That insight has the effect of nullifying the influence of karma formations (saṃskāra) on perception and this, in turn, facilitates the emergence of concentration without seed (nirbīja samādhi). In this account there is no room for an ānanda samādhi or an asmitā samādhi. It is clear that Patañjali never intended there to be.

Again, a consideration of the way Patañjali presents his teachings suggests an alternative way of proceeding. In the earlier discussion of the place of the eight limbs section in the text as a whole, an examination of the expectations arising out of sūtra 2.2 led to an enquiry into the overall structure of book 2. Interestingly, although Patañjali presents the two themes of that chapter: cultivating concentration and attenuating the hindrances, in that order, his actual treatment of these topics proceeds in reverse. His treatment of the hindrances commences immediately at 2.3 whilst the issue of concentration is not addressed until 2.26. It may well be the case that Patañjali adopted the same procedure in his exposition of practice (abhyāsa) and detachment (vairāgya).

These two concepts are introduced in sūtra 1.12, which states that the restriction of the mind's fluctuations (vṛtti) is attained through practice and detachment. Then each concept is described in two sūtras. 1.13-14 deal with practice; 1.15-16 with detachment. 1.15 and 1.16 each describe one type of detachment. The lower detachment is that relating to 'seen and revealed objects' (1.15); the higher is that relating to the fundamental constituents of existence (guṇa) (1.16). This higher detachment emerges only after the self (puruṣa) has been experienced. There are no unequivocal statements in book 1 of the *Yoga Sūtras* about exactly when the vision of the self takes place but the likelihood is that the truth-bearing insight (ṛtaṃbharāprajñā) mentioned in 1.48 is just such an experience. This is because the primary aim of yoga practice is the eradication of suffering (duḥkha). The root cause of suffering, according to the *Yoga Sūtra*, is the conjunction between two ontologically distinct entities: self or spirit (puruṣa) and nature or matter (prakṛti) (2.17). The primary task of the yogin is thus to eradicate the ignorance of this distinction (2.4-5) which, in turn, will break the conjunction and enable the yogin to experience isolation or aloneness (kaivalya) (2.25). An insight into truth is, then, an experience of the self as being fundamentally different from matter. This truth-bearing insight arises immediately before the attainment of nirbīja samādhi.

If this analysis is accurate, the final stages of the yogin's path according to book 1 of the *Yoga Sūtras* can be described as follows: the yogin cultivates a sense of detachment towards all worldly objects (the lower form) whilst, at the same time, practising mental concentration with an inward focus of attention. At a certain stage in this practice, nirvicāra samāpatti, a vision of the self and its relation to nature is experienced. This experience gives rise to a sense of detachment towards all aspects of nature (the higher form) and facilitates the total absorption of the self in itself (nirbīja samādhi). Such a total absorption is described in book 4 as the isolation or aloneness of the self (kaivalya).

If Patanjali did adopt the same reverse order of treatment in book 1 that he did in book 2 then we would expect the sūtras following 1.16 to deal with detachment (vairāgya) rather than practice (abhyāsa). This, I suggest, is exactly what we find. Sūtras 1.17-28 all deal with the subject of detachment. Thus, the term 'linked with objects' (saṃprajñāta) in 1.17 does not refer to a type or types of concentration, as all traditional commentators have claimed, but to the lower detachment mentioned in 1.15: that relating to seen and revealed objects. This lower detachment has four characteristics: reasoning (vitarka); reflection (vicāra); joy (ānanda) and egoity (asmitā). 1.18 can then be taken to refer to the higher detachment (para vairāgya) mentioned in 1.16. This relates to karma formations (saṃskāra) only since at this point the attention of the yogin is completely inwardly focused. The mind (citta), which is formed from the sattva guṇa,[48] tainted by the karma formations (saṃskāra) and illumined by the self, dominates the yogin's awareness. Detachment towards the mind itself is what enables the yogin to achieve nirbīja samādhi, but this detachment can only arise, as 1.18 informs us, on the basis of 'that practice which effects the cessation [of fluctuations]',[49] i.e. the practice of concentration.[50]

The most significant consequence of talking 1.17-18 as dealing with the subject of detachment is that the 'problem' of the relationship between the accounts of concentration in 1.17ff. and 1.41ff. is dissolved. Patañjali's treatment of concentration in book 1 becomes restricted to 1.41ff. and, in the process, coherent and illuminating. A second consequence is that we now have a much more clear and detailed description of the nature of detachment as understood by Patañjali than was previously the case. In the traditional view, although practice and detachment are presented as a kind of dual foundation for the achievement of the state of liberation (kaivalya), only practice, the cultivation of concentration, is described in any depth. If, on the other hand, one accepts the interpretation argued above, 1.17 and 1.18 provide additional information on the two types of detachment. Both traditional and modern commentators have recognized that the subject matter of 1.17 and 1.18 is discussed further in 1.19. This discussion continues, in fact, until 1.31, for 1.32 introduces the teaching of practice on a single item (eka tattvābhyāsa), i.e. it returns to the other concept mentioned in 1.12, practice (abhyāsa). The likelihood is, then, that sūtras 1.19-31 deal with detachment rather than concentration.

Thus, 1.19 can now be understood as stating that the bodiless ones who have merged into nature only have the lower detachment because they have not shed the desire for further existence. 1.20, therefore, deals not with the concentration of 'the others' but with the detachment of 'the others'. These 'others' are those who have attained the superior form of detachment, which is preceded by faith (śraddhā), energy (vīrya), recollection (smṛti), concentration (samādhi) and insight (prajñā). That is, it follows the insight into the nature of the self described in 1.48 and 3.49. Such an interpretation fits perfectly with the description of the higher detachment in 1.16 where it is said to arise after the yogin has experienced the self. 1.21 and 22 can then be taken to refer to the proximity of yogins to the superior detachment rather than to the superior concentration and 1.23-29 to deal with the yogin attaining the superior detachment by modelling himself on the lord (īśvara). The lord is the perfect example of a being without any kind of attachment for the realm of nature. It is thus detachment and not concentration that leads to the eradication of the obstacles (1.29–30). In this scheme of interpretation, practice and detachment can both be seen to contribute to the yogin's progress in distinct yet essentially equal and complementary ways. This strategy for resolving these issues will not, of course find favour with many interpreters of the *Yoga Sūtras.* Nevertheless, I would argue that even if my own solution proves to be untenable those of Vyāsa and other traditional commentators, not to mention a number of modern scholars, are equally problematic and require further scrutiny.

What the foregoing analysis reveals in general terms is that the parts of book 1 which ought to have a coherent relationship to each other do so, but not in the way that traditional commentators have construed it. The comparison of book 1's teachings with those of the other three has not been attempted here for that would require too detailed and extensive an enquiry. One or two clues have been forthcoming, however. The pattern of listing two topics in one order and then expounding them in detail in the reverse order—well exemplified in book 2—can, in the light of the analysis presented above, be seen to operate in book 1 also. This suggests the same hand at work in both books, though whether it is the hand of an author or a redactor must be left undetermined. Moreover, the account of concentration and detachment in book 1 now fits easily with the account of concentration at the end of the eight limbs section and with the description of the final stages of the path at the end of book 3. In short, whilst it may be the case that book 1, books 2 and 3 and the eight limbs section were originally separate it looks as though they have been brought together and edited rather than being crudely juxtaposed.

The *Yoga Sūtras* of Patañjali form one of the most important Hindu texts on the nature of yoga. Yet, as it has been traditionally interpreted, it is, at root, unintelligible. This is not to claim that the broad orientation of the text cannot be understood, nor that portions of it do not provide clear and detailed expositions of particular concepts or experiences. It is, rather, to claim that, taken from the perspective of tradition, the text of the *Yoga Sūtras* does not yield a coherent teaching. The relationships between different parts are often obscure and, on occasions, statements in one part seem to conflict with those in another. One reason for this, as suggested above, may be that since the principal commentators on the sūtras were not members of Patañjali's own lineage, traditional interpretations are, in places, at variance with Patañjali's own intentions and ultimately the cause of the incoherence. Western exegesis has, unfortunately, been overly influenced by such traditional interpretations and consequently failed to render the text intelligible to the Western reader. It may be that such a task is impossible because the teachings of the sūtras as presently constituted are unintelligible, though my own view is that they are intelligible if interpreted with the assumption that Patañjali set out to present us with a coherent teaching in mind.

## VEDĀNTA

The Vedānta tradition is primarily concerned with constructing an interpretation of the Upaniṣads, which, as noted above, constitute the end portion of the Veda (Veda-anta). By the time when newly compiled Upaniṣads could no longer be clearly linked with one or other of the Vedic schools (śākhā),[51] which was probably sometime during the period when the great epics were being composed,[52] it became evident that there was considerable disagreement among Vedāntins about both central issues and technical details of Upaniṣadic teaching.[53] As Thibaut surmises,

> The followers of the different Vedic śākhās no doubt recognized already at an early period the truth that, while conflicting statements regarding the details of sacrifice can be got over by the assumption of a vikalpa, i.e. an optional proceeding, it is not so with regard to such topics as the nature of brahman, the relation to it of the human soul, the origin of the physical universe, and the like.[54]

As a consequence of this recognition the adherents of the Vedānta tradition, who regarded the Upaniṣads as revelation (śruti) and hence divinely inspired and inerrant, began to formulate interpretations of Upaniṣadic teachings which would demonstrate that they offered a single coherent doctrine. The oldest surviving example of such a work is the *Brahmasūtra* attributed to Bādarāyaṇa.[55] There are many different views about the authorship and composition of this text. Some scholars, such as Dasgupta[56] and Pandey[57] assume a single author whose name was Bādarāyaṇa. Others, such as Radhakrishnan,[58] avoid any definitive statement on the matter, whilst yet others argue that the work was compiled by a later editor[59] or team of editors.[60] Similar attitudes can be discerned with regard to the unity of the text. Dasgupta and Pandey regard[61] it as unitary whereas Nakamura[62] and Mayeda[63] regard it as composite, having been expanded over some 700 years.

By far the most detailed and convincing studies of these is that of Nakamura. In addition to demonstrating the composite nature of the *Brahmasūtra*, and its compilation over a considerable period of time,[64] he shows that it was probably a product of schools of the Sāmaveda which had a particular association with the *Chāndogya Upaniṣad*. He suggests that in the first phase of their activities synopses of Upaniṣadic teaching were attempted which centred on the *Chāndogya Upaniṣad* and followed its arrangement of topics. Next came a process of enlargement, which incorporated other schools' first phase activities and, thirdly, came a final revision which included refutations of the views of schools other than the Vedānta. Thus, whilst in the later period the *Brahmasūtra* was a text subscribed to by Vedāntins from all Vedic schools it emerged out of a partisan activity which is still evident in the final recension. Despite this, there can be little doubt that the *Brahmasūtra* as we have it is the text that indicates most clearly the general tendency of Vedānta thought during the epic period.

What that tendency was is not easy to determine, however, for whilst the sūtras of other schools such as Nyāya, Vaiśeṣika and Yoga are simply difficult to understand without a commentary, those of the Mīmāṃsā and Vedānta are unintelligible without one.[65] As Thibaut explains,

> The most essential words are habitually dispensed with; nothing is, for instance, more common than the simple omission of the subject or predicate of a sentence. And where here and there a Sūtra occurs whose words construe without anything having to be supplied, the phraseology is so eminently vague and obscure that without the help derived from a commentary we should be unable to make out to what subject the Sūtra refers.[66]

Hence, an essential item for the would-be interpreter of the *Brahmasūtra* is a reliable commentary. The main problems with this for the modern student are that on the one hand, the traditional commentaries all assume the unity and coherence of Upaniṣadic teaching and yet, on the other, few of them agree about the overall purport of the text.

The two most influential of the traditional commentators are Śaṅkara[67] and Rāmānuja.[68] At the time Thibaut wrote his introduction to his Sacred Books of the East translation of Śaṅkara's and Rāmānuja's commentaries on the *Brahmasūtra* these two works were the oldest interpretations of the text available to Western scholarship. Subsequently, however, the commentary of Bhāskara has been discovered and published in the Chowkhamba Sanskrit Series, Banares. Bhāskara interpreted the *Brahmasūtra* from a bhedābheda (difference-non-difference) position, a kind of half-way stage between Śaṅkara's full-blown non-dualism (advaita) or illusionism (māyāvāda) and Rāmānuja's qualified non-dualism (viśiṣṭādvaita), though tending to be philosophically more akin to the latter.[69]

With regard to the division of the text, however, Bhāskara follows Śaṅkara on all but three occasions (3.3.29-30 and 32; 4.2.12 and 4.3.7-16).[70] Rāmānuja's arrangement, on the other hand, differs from Śaṅkara's in a considerable number of cases, though when set against the total number of sūtras (555 in all) even these do not constitute what might be called a sizeable proportion. As Thibaut points out,

> in spite of very numerous discrepancies ... the two commentators [Śaṅkara and Rāmānuja] are at one as to the general drift of the Sūtras and the arrangement of topics. As a rule, the adhikaranas [divisions into topics] discuss one or several Vedic passages bearing upon a certain point of the system, and in the vast majority of cases the two commentators agree as to which are the special texts referred to.[71]

The same appears to be true of Bhāskara's commentary,[72] which Nakamura regards as most accurately interpreting the view of the sūtras.

By the time of Śaṅkara (7th century), theologians in the Vedānta tradition commented not only on the Upaniṣads and the *Brahmasūtra* but also on the *Bhagavad Gītā*. These three became known collectively as the Triple Foundation (Prasthānatraya) of the Vedānta. The Vedānta theologians interpret the Prasthānatraya on the basis of one fundamental presupposition: that all the teachings contained within it are compatible with each other. Indeed, the *Brahmasūtra* itself was composed primarily to demonstrate that despite impressions to the contrary the various Upaniṣads taught essentially the same doctrine. The task of all post-Bādarāyaṇa Vedāntins was to expand this into a coherent interpretation of the Prasthānatraya as a whole, a task that led to the creation of innovative hermeneutical strategies and, ultimately, to versions of Vedānta that were fundamentally incompatible with each other, e.g. Śaṅkara's monistic (advaita) interpretation, Rāmānuja's quasi-monistic (viśiṣṭādvaita) interpretation and Mādhva's dualistic (dvaita) interpretation.

In terms of yoga practice, most of the later Vedānta theologians supported varieties of bhakti as this is the most compatible with brāhmanical social organization. Śaṅkara, however, argued for the primacy of what has been called jñāna yoga and, to a lesser extent, dhyāna yoga. Our understanding of Śaṅkara's views on yoga and liberation depends significantly on which of the many works attributed to him we regard as authentic. My own inclination is to follow Sengaku Mayeda and take Śaṅkara to be the person who composed the commentary (bhāṣya) on the *Brahmasūtra* (*BSBh*) that goes under his name. This commentary can then be used, suggests Mayeda, 'as the yardstick against which to measure the authentic works ascribed to him'.[73] On this basis, he accepts the following as authentic: the commentaries on the *Bṛhadāraṇyaka*, *Chāndogya*, *Aitareya*, *Taittirīya*, *Kena*, *Īśā*, *Kaṭha*, *Muṇḍaka*, *Praśna* and *Māṇḍūkya Upaniṣads*, the commentaries on the *Gaudapādīyakārikā* and the *Adhyātmapaṭala* of *Āpastamba-Dharmasūtra* and, finally, the *Upadeśasāhasrī*, which, he suggests, 'is the only non-commentarial work whose authenticity has been conclusively demonstrated'.[74] He also accepts that a sub-commentary on the *Yoga Sūtras*, the *Yogasūtra-bhāṣya-vivaraṇa*, may be a genuine work of Śaṅkara.[75]

Śaṅkara was a great organizer as well as a prolific scholar. He divided India into four regions and established a monastery (maṭha) in each. In the south he established the Sṛingirimaṭha at Śṛingeri, in the west the Śāradāmaṭha at Dwaraka, in the north the Jyotrimaṭha at Bādarināth and in the east the Govardhanamaṭha at Puri. The monks attached to these mathas are divided into ten groups, the daśanāmi sampradāyas. The Sarasvatī, Bhāratī and Pūrī sampradāyas are attached to the Śṛingerimaṭha, the Tīrtha and Āśrama sampradāyas to the Śāradamaṭha, the Giri, Pārvat and Sāgar sampradāyas to Jyotrimaṭha and the Vānam and Āraṇyan sampradāyas to the Govardhanamaṭha.[76] At the head of each monastery, all of which are flourishing today, is a world-teacher (jagadguru) or Śaṅkarācārya who has responsibility for the spiritual welfare of all the people within the region. This has helped to ensure that advaita teachings have remained influential in India down to modern times despite the sweeping success and tremendous influence of the bhakti traditions.

Śaṅkara's works, particularly the *BSBh*, clearly indicate that he was an advocate of what has come to be known as jñāna yoga. For him, however, all forms of yoga *practice* are preliminary. They prepare the way for liberating insight but do not themselves create it. They work, he claims, 'only at the lower level of truth'.[77] Liberating knowledge is knowledge of the non-dual brahman. It is intuitive (anubhāva) in nature and not dependent on any form of ritual or practice. Brahman, as the one and only reality, is there all the time. Ordinarily, brahman is not experienced because of the illusions that obscure it. Most prominent amongst these are the erroneous identifications we make with our bodies, our senses and our minds. Once these are stripped away, a person realizes that 'My very nature is that of seeing; I am unattached, changeless, motionless, endless.'[78]

Such recognition may arise spontaneously, or whilst meditating on a passage from Vedic revelation (śruti), especially one of the great sayings (mahāvākya) of the Upaniṣads such as 'Thou Art That' (tat tvam asi). In all cases, the insight emerges through the stripping away (apoh) of false identifications, a process known as de-superimposition (apavāda).[79] For Śaṅkara, the best way to remove these illusions is to find a teacher who can recite the sacred verses; then to meditate upon them, and finally to become so completely absorbed in them that the nature of the self and of all illusions is revealed.

Yoga can assist the meditator in this process because, as understood by Śaṅkara, dhyāna, like Upaniṣadic upāsana meditation, works to create 'a uniform train of thought'[80] that prepares the mind for apavāda. However, insofar as yoga texts (referred to as yogasmṛti or yogaśāstra by Śaṅkara to indicate their subordination to the śruti of the Upaniṣads) conflict with the teachings of the Vedānta they are to be ignored. Śruti, he claims in *BSBh* 1.3.28, is like perception (pratyakṣa) whereas smṛti is like inference (anumāna), i.e. inferior. Śruti, therefore, provides the best platform for the acquisition of the trans-perceptual, intuitive insight (anubhāva) into the nature of the self and thus for release from saṃsāra.

In a nutshell, jñāna yoga, insofar as it is an activity at all, involves accepting a particular vision or model of reality as the true one and then re-interpreting all one's experiences in such a manner as they come to be understood in terms of the vision/model rather than phenomenologically, i.e. as they appear. We may also note that Śaṅkara's brahman has a great deal in common with the puruṣa of Sāṃkhya. However, since brahman is the sole existent, prakṛti has to be illusory instead of real, as she is in Sāṃkhya and Yoga. On my reading of the Upaniṣads, ātman/brahman transforms itself (parināma) into the universe, which is, therefore, real in its substance though ephemeral in its manifestations. The images of gold being made into jewellery, clay being made into pots, the web coming out of a spider, hair coming out of the head and sparks from a fire all support this understanding. Śaṅkara's interpretation is, therefore, a distortion of their teaching rather than an elucidation of it.[81]

The problematic nature of Śaṅkara's version of Vedānta theology is also apparent from the fact that many later Vedāntins rejected it. Most prominent amongst these was Rāmānuja (11th century). Rāmānuja was a member of the Śrī Vaiṣṇava movement and a bhakta by nature. The Śrī Vaiṣṇavas were a South Indian sect that was founded in the tenth century by Nāthamuni. Its theology was based on two primary sources: the Pañcarātra Āgamas and the hymns of the Āḷvārs, both of which were on the fringes of brāhmanical orthodoxy. The Pañcarātras were denounced as heterodox in the *Āditya, Agni, Bṛhan-nāradīya, Kurma, Liṅga, Śāmba* and *Vāyu Purāṇas,* though defended in the *Bhāgavata, Garuda, Nāradīya, Padma* and *Varāha Purāṇas.* The Āḷvārs composed their poems in Tamil rather than the sacred brāhmanical language of Sanskrit. Both groups worshipped Kṛṣṇa/Viṣṇu.

In Pañcarātra thought, god, souls and the universe are all ultimately identical, though even in emancipation there remains some kind of division between them. Such division is typical of devotional theologies where god is understood as a higher being to be worshipped rather than one's own inner being to be discovered. The fifteenth-century bhakta Rāmprasāda encapsulates this sentiment in his famous statement, 'I don't want to be god, I want to taste god.' To the Pañcarātrins god is known as Vasudeva, who is always united with his power (śakti), known as Śrī, an idea that is shared by many tantric systems.

The most characteristic feature of Pañcarātra thought is the theory of vyūhas (emanations), each of which manifests two of god's six qualities (guṇa). The six are:

1. jñāna—knowledge or omniscience;
2. aiśvarya—lordship, i.e. activity based on independence; sometimes called icchā (will);
3. śakti—power, primarily the power to create;
4. bala—strength, to sustain all beings without tiring;
5. vīrya—energy, here meaning 'changelessness' or being unaffected by the production of the universe;
6. tejas—splendour.

The three vyūhas are known as Saṃkarṣaṇa, Pradyumna and Aniruddha, the brother, son and grandson respectively of Kṛṣṇa.

They not only introduce a focus for popular devotion, they also allow the Pañcarātrins to incorporate the dualistic Sāṃkhya philosophy into their own monistic ontology. Under Saṃkarṣaṇa's supervision the universe evolves in potential; under Pradyumna there is a separation between perceiver (puruṣa) and perceived (prakṛti), and under Aniruddha a link is created between puruṣa and prakṛti, which initiates the manifestation of the physical universe. Saṃkarṣaṇa is also said to control the revelation of divine knowledge, i.e. the doctrines of religion; Pradyumna controls the practice of religion (it was probably the Pañcarātrins who introduced image worship into Hinduism), whilst Aniruddha controls the effects of religious practice.

These ideas would seem to be a development of a simpler and earlier theology that is found in the *Nārāyaṇīya* section of the *Mahābhārata.* There, Saṃkarṣaṇa is said to represent the individual soul, Pradyumna the mind (manas) and Aniruddha the ego (ahaṃkāra). In other words, it seems that initially the vyūha vocabulary acted as a kind of symbolic language to link the members of Kṛṣṇa's family with the principles of Sāṃkhya philosophy. As the theology developed, Sāṃkhya dualism was converted into a form of monism in which the separation of puruṣa and prakṛti only occurs part way through the process of creation, which is understood as a progressive emanation from a single divine source. In order to maintain the status of Kṛṣṇa's family members, they were detached from the Sāṃkhya principles and relocated closer to the source of creation as the vyūhas.

The other notable feature of Pañcarātra philosophy is the theory of avatāras (descents or incarnations), sometimes called vibhāvas (manifestations). According to some Pañcarātra texts, e.g. the *Lakṣmī Tantra* and the *Viṣvaksena Saṃhitā,* all the avatāras spring from Aniruddha. Others, e.g. the *Padma Tantra,* derive different avatāras from different vyūhas.[82]

In terms of practice, much of the emphasis in Pañcarātra texts is on yoga, the means by which the devotee gains union with Vasudeva, though there are also instructions pertaining to the construction of temples and images, worship using images and guidance on the performance of rituals. In most cases the bhakti yoga described in the texts is based on and similar to that found in the *Bhagavad Gītā,* a kind of dutiful devotion. However, some texts, such as the *Ahirbudhnya Saṃhitā,* claim that surrender (prapatti) to God 'achieves the fruits of all tapas (austerity), sacrifices, pilgrimages and gifts, and attains salvation easily without resorting to any other methods'.[83] This, of course, is the kind of claim that makes orthodox brāhmans nervous, because it essentially eradicates the need for the performance of caste duties, the bedrock of brāhmanical ideology.

This conception of devotion was developed in South India by a group of poet-saints called Āḷvārs (7th–9th centuries). 12 Āḷvār saints were finally recognized:

| | |
|---|---|
| Poykai | Pūtnam or Pūdam |
| Pey | Nammāḷvār |
| Tiruppān | Andāl or Godā (Fem.) |
| Kulaśekhara | Periyāḷvār |
| Tirumaṅgai | Tirumaḷiśai |
| Tirupāṇar | Toṇḍaraḍippodi or Vipranārāyaṇa |

In the tenth century their works were collected together by Nathāmuni to form a compendium of around 4,000 verses called the *Nālāyira Prabandham.* This came to be the main source of inspiration for the South Indian Pañcarātrins, who were known as Śrī Vaiṣṇavas because they worshipped Śrī alongside Nārāyaṇa. The *Prabandham* is sometimes referred to as the Tamil Veda, and like the Sanskrit Veda it has four parts:

1. *Mudalāyiram*—a collection of verses by various Āḷvārs;
2. *Periatirumoyi*—the work of Tirumaṅgai Āḷvār;
3. *Tiruvāymori*—the work of Nammālvar;
4. *Iyarpa*—a further collection of verses by various Āḷvārs.

With Nāthamuni we enter the age of the aṛagiyas or āchāryas. Most influential of these were Nāthamuni himself, Yāmunācārya and Rāmānuja. Unlike the Āḷvārs, the āchāryas felt that Vaiṣṇavas should draw inspiration from the *Prasthānatraya* of the Vedānta as well as from the *Prabandham.* Rāmānuja was probably the most outstanding theologian of his age and it was he who established Śrī Vaiṣṇavism as a legitimate tradition within the Vedānta. He wrote nine works, all in Sanskrit: three commentaries on the *Brahmasūtra* (*Srībhāṣya, Vedāntadīpa* and *Vedāntasāra*); one commentary on the *Bhagavad Gītā*; three prose hymns or gadyas (*Śaraṇāgatigadya, Śrīrangagadya* and *Vaikuṇṭhagadya*); a manual for daily worship (the

*Nityagrantha*), and the *Vedārthasaṃgraha* (a summary of Upaniṣadic teaching).

The theology of Rāmānuja is influenced more by the *Bhagavad Gītā* than by any other text. His ontology is described as Viśiṣṭādvaita (qualified non-dualism) where Brahman, the souls and the universe are one, though distinct. Against Śaṅkara, Rāmānuja maintains that a reality without characteristics (nirguṇa) cannot exist (*BSBh* 1.1.1). Brahman, he claims, always has characteristics and these are the souls and the world. This relationship is analogous to that between an individual soul and its body: brahman is the soul and the souls and universe are the body.

Like the other aṛagiyas, Rāmānuja emphasized the importance of works for the attainment of liberation. After his death, however, the Śrī Vaiṣṇavas divided into two main branches, with this issue at the core of their disagreements. One group, the Teṅgalai, who were led by Pillai Lokācārya, gave more weight to the teachings of the *Prabandham* than those of the *Prasthānatraya* and argued that salvation is entirely dependent on God's grace. Their metaphor for this process was the way a mother cat carries her kitten: in her mouth, the kitten does nothing. The other group, the Veḍagalai, led by Veṇkatanatha, stressed the importance of the *Prasthānatraya* and argued that salvation resulted from a combination of God's grace and human effort. Teṅgalais described this through the analogy of a mother monkey and her baby: the mother carries the baby on her back, but the baby has to hold on or it will fall off. Eventually, brāhmanical social regulations won the day and the Veḍagalai view became dominant. From the twelfth century onwards it became customary for the Śri Vaiṣṇava teachers to write commentaries on the *Prasthānatraya*, a practice that was adopted by nearly all Vaiṣṇava sects. Indeed, all of the four main Vaiṣṇava sects are founded on this principle.

### Vaiṣṇava Sects

1. The Śrī sampradāya (tradition) of Rāmānuja (viśiṣṭādvaita—qualified non-dualism).
2. The Haṃsa (swan) sampradāya of Nimbarka (bhedābheda—difference/non-difference).
3. The Brahma sampradāya of Mādhva (dvaita—dualism).
4. The Rudra sampradāya of Vallabha [or Viṣṇusvamin] (śuddhādvaita—pure non-dualism).

For a sampradāya to be regarded as a distinctive line for the transmission of Vaiṣṇava teaching it has to be established on a recognized line of teachers (paramparā). Rāmānuja traces his line of teachers through Mahāpurṇa, Yāmuna, Rāmamiśra, Puṇḍarīkākaśa, Nāthamuni, Nammāḷvār, Viśvakṣena and Śrī, back to Nārāyaṇa. Nimbarka, a younger contemporary of Rāmānuja,[84] traces his paramparā through Nārada, Kumāra to Haṃsa (swan—the union of Radha and Kṛṣṇa). Mādhva, thirteenth century, claims that he received his teachings directly from Vyāsa (the mythical compiler of the *Mahābhārata* and numerous other texts) whom he met at Badarikā in the Himālayas. Vallabha, fifteenth to sixteenth century, is reputed to have received his teachings from Vïṣṇusvāmin, who received them from Rudra, who received them from Viṣṇu, though this line of transmission has been questioned by some scholars.[85]

## An Outline of the Teachings of Each Sampradāya

1. According to the Śrī sampradāya there are three eternal principles: god (īśvara), souls or consciousness (cit) and material nature (acit). The first of these is independent whilst the other two are dependent. Among souls there are three types: the bound (baddha), the liberated (mukta) and the eternally free (nitya). Five forms of god are acknowledged: 1. parā (the highest, also called Vasudeva or Viṣṇu); 2. vyūha (emanation); 3. vibhāva or avatāra (incarnation); 4. antaryāmin (inner controller); 5. arcā (image).

Theoretically, a devotee begins with the worship of images of god and then progresses through the other forms. That this is a normative or ideal scheme rather than an actually practised one is indicated by the fact that the Āḷvārs themselves went around the countryside singing the praises of images.

2. In Nimbarka's Haṃsa system god is both different from and the same as the souls and the world (hence bedhābheda: bheda = difference + abheda = non-difference). Nimbarka differs from Rāmānuja primarily on the issue of the eternality of souls and the universe. For him these are simply transformations (parināma) of god rather than eternal existants. This is essentially the view found in the early Upaniṣads. Rāmānuja is committed to the eternality of souls and the universe because that is what is found in the *Bhagavad Gītā* (because the *Gītā* works with a modified Sāṃkhya ontology that incorporates a god and is monistic). Although both Nimbarka's and Bhāskara's systems are described as bhedābheda there is a subtle

difference between them. In Nimbarka's view difference-non-difference applies to the relationship between brahman and souls (jīva) in both bondage and liberation. For Bhāskara, on the other hand, it only applies in bondage. At liberation, jīva and brahman become absolutely identical.[86] The primary reason for this difference is probably that, in the manner of most devotees, Nimbarka wished to maintain a difference between the being who is worshipped and the being who does the worshipping. As is so often the case in religious philosophies, matters of temperament and practice influence ontology more than ontology influences temperament and practice, which, of course, calls the truth status of these ontologies into question.

3. Mādhva's Brahma sampradāya interpreted the non-dual teaching of the Upaniṣads on the basis of the metaphor of a king and his subjects: the independent (the king) and the dependent (the subjects). In other words, the non-duality is relational rather than ontological. Mādhva was more radical than any other Vedāntin in his identification of differences and, almost uniquely among Vedāntic theologians, drew extensively on Vaiśeṣika ideas. For him, the primary categories are the independent (svatantra) and the dependent (paratantra). God is the only independent. Dependent souls are of four kinds: liberatated (jīvottama); those capable of being liberated (muktiyogyas); the eternally transmigrating (nityasaṃsāris) and those who are eternally damned (tamoyogyas), e.g. demons.[87] Unlike most other Vedāntins, Mādhva also regarded the material universe as being composed of parts, largely understood in Vaiśeṣika-like terms. However, he did not, like Buddhists such as Nāgasena, accept that parts were all there was. With reference to the chariot analogy in the *Questions of King Miliñda,* Mādhva argues that a pile of parts is no chariot at all, so we need to recognize a category of a whole (amśi) alongside those of the various parts (amśas).[88]

Like Rāmānuja, Mādhva takes bhakti yoga to be complete surrender to god. Love of god destroys ignorance (avidyā) and opens up the possibility of a direct experience of god (aparokṣānūbhuti). It is this experience that liberates the devotee from saṃsāra.

4. Vallabha's Rudra sampradāya subscribes to an ontology known as pure non-dualism (śuddhādvaita). Of all the Vaiṣṇava systems, Vallabha's comes closest to Śaṅkara's in its ontology. The universe is an unreal transformation (avikṛta parināma) of the highest Brahman (= Kṛṣṇa). It is the creation of Kṛṣṇa and would remain even if all souls were liberated. Creation is an expression of Kṛṣṇa's playful-

ness; it is his sport or play (līlā). Hence, liberation is achieved not through jñāna yoga but through the grace of god.

Complete surrender (prapatti) to god in the manner of the cowgirls (gopī) of Vṛndāvana is the best method according to Vallabha. This is the path of grace (puṣṭi mārga) that is open to all. Duties are carried out not as a means to liberation but as an expression of the devotee's love for god. 'One who follows the puṣṭi-mārga aspires to be a gopī and worship the lord with that attitude. In fact, all souls represent the feminine principle and have the Lord as their spiritual husband.'[89] The stories of Kṛṣṇa's adventures at Vṛndāvana are found in the *Bhāgavata Purāṇa,* which Vallabha regards as a fourth prasthāna alongside the Upaniṣads, the *Brahmasūtra* and the *Bhagavad Gītā.* Indeed, in cases of doubt or seeming disagreement the *Bhāgavata* should be taken as offering the decisive view.[90]

Another school that has been important in the development of Vaiṣṇavism, though it does not claim to be an independent sampradāya, is the Gaudīya (Bengal) school of Caitanya (b. 1485). Caitanya's teachers came from Mādhva's Brahma sampradāya, though Caitanya described his ontology as inconceivable difference-non-difference (acintya bhedābheda). Metaphysically, Caitanya is probably closest to Nimbarka, though in terms of practice he is close to Vallabha. Like the Āḷvārs, he went around the countryside singing emotional songs of devotion to Kṛṣṇa, often dressed as a gopī. His path of loving devotion (prema bhakti) is divided into five stages:

1. Śanta—peaceful love;
2. Daśya—devotion of a servant;
3. Sakhya—devotion of friendship;
4. Vātsalya—devotion as to a parent;
5. Mādhurya—devotion as a lover.

The last of these is the highest, and many of Caitanya's songs contain highly erotic elements. Today, the Gaudīya school is represented in the West by the International Society for Kṛṣṇa Consciousness, better known as the Hare-Kṛṣṇa movement.

## THE YOGA UPANIṢADS

The Yoga Upaniṣads and, indeed, other minor Upaniṣads present us with a current of Vedāntic thought and practice that differs considerably from those developed by the mainstream theologians who based their teachings on the prasthānatraya. Contra Śaṅkara, they claim that yoga *is* a means to the highest goal. Contra the devotionalists, they advocate the practice of meditation and the cultivation of a thoroughgoing attitude of indifference to all things of the world, though, it should be said, this is often tempered with a typically tantric and Śaivite claim that ultimately emancipation depends on the grace of the guru. Many of them also reinstate prāṇa as a key cosmological and physiological concept that lies at the heart of the quest for emancipation.[91]

There are two collections of yoga upaniṣads available in English translation: one from V.M. Bedekar and G.B. Palsule, based on Paul Deussen's German translation of 60 Upaniṣads, and one from T.R. Srinivasa Ayyangar, based on the Adyar Library edition of G. Srinivasa Murti. These differ from each other considerably. The Adyar version weaves supplementary material from the commentary of Śrī Upaniṣad Brahmayogin (Rāmacandrendra Sarasvatī) into the text. It is also much longer, probably based (though Ayyangar is not explicit about this) on the Telegu version of these Upaniṣads, which, as Deussen points out, are expanded 'through supplements or additions which are tenfold or twentyfold in their extent'.[92] In the Adyar collection 20 of the 108 Upaniṣads listed in the *Muktikā Upaniṣad* are classified as Yoga Upaniṣads. By contrast, Deussen presents us with a list of eleven, the first ten of which are deemed by him to be earlier than the last, the *Haṃsa Upaniṣad.* When deciding which texts to include in his collection Deussen consulted not only the Muktikā list but also that compiled by pandits under the patronage of Sultan Muhammed Dara Schakoh and translated into Persian in 1656, which contained 50 Upaniṣads; that compiled by Henry Thomas Colebrooke in 1837, containing 52 Upaniṣads and that commented on by one Nārāyaṇa, who lived sometime later than the Vedāntic theologian Śaṅkara (c. 800 CE), which also seems to have contained 52 Upaniṣads.[93] Deussen's eleven are *Brahmavidyā, Kṣurikā, Cūlikā (= Māntrika), Nādabindu, Brahmabindu (= Amṛtabindu), Amṛtabindu (= Amṛtanada), Dhyānabindu, Tejobindu, Yogaśikhā, Yogatattva* and *Haṃsa.* They are all listed in the Muktikā, Colebrooke and Nārāyana collections, and nine of the eleven: *Brahmavidyā, Kṣurikā, Cūlikā (= Māntrika), Brahmabindu (= Amṛtabindu), Amṛtabindu (= Amṛtanada), Dhyānabindu, Tejobindu, Yogaśikhā* and *Yogatattva,* are also in the Persian collection (Oupanekhat).

All of these collections were created after the time of Śaṅkara, and it may be that all the Upaniṣads which receive no mention in his writings (and none of the Yoga Upaniṣads do) were only composed after his death. On the other hand, there may have been Upaniṣads around at the time of Śaṅkara of which he was unaware or which he did not regard as authentic or authoritative. A rough relative chronology might be:

**Oupanekhat Collection**—*Brahmavidyā, Kśurikā, Cūlikā (= Māntrika), Brahmabindu (= Amṛtabindu), Amṛtabindu (= Amṛtanāda), Dhyānabindu, Tejobindu, Yogaśikhā* and *Yogatattva.*

**Colebrooke and Narayana add**—*Nādabindu* and *Haṃsa.*

**Muktikā adds**—*Advayatāraka, Triśikhibrāhmaṇa, Darśana, Pāśupatabrahma, Brahmavidya, Maṇḍalabrāhmaṇa, Mahāvākya, Yogakuṇḍali, Yogacūḍāmani, Varāha* and *Śāṇḍilya.*

We may note that the Adyar collection does not include the *Cūlikā* (= *Māntrika*) in the list of Yoga Upaniṣads even though it is included in the Muktikā list of 108 Upaniṣads. The grand total of Yoga Upaniṣads could thus be taken as 21, those in the Adyar collection plus the *Culikā.*

These Upaniṣads can be divided into two broad groups on the basis of their content. The first comprises nine from Deussen's list (excluding the *Culikā*[94] and the *Haṃsa*) plus the *Pāśupatabrahma* and the *Mahāvākya*; the second is made up of the remaining Upaniṣads in the Adyar collection. Upaniṣads in the first group tend to be Vedic-Vedāntic (mostly advaita) in character and describe forms of yoga based on the Oṃ-sound (Oṃkāra). Those in the second group are tantric. All refer to the manipulation of the kuṇḍalinī śakti (coiled power) and locate the practice of yoga within a body of subtle energy that is described in far more detail than is found in earlier Upaniṣads and which has features not found in those earlier descriptions.

As far as I am aware, no scholar has undertaken a systematic dating of these texts. All could easily be post-Śaṅkara. Nevertheless, there is little by way of content in the Upaniṣads of the first group to indicate a post-Śaṅkara period of composition. Indeed, there are reasons for thinking that their composition might have taken place in a period immediately following the completion of the *Mahābhārata.* In *Mahābhārata* 12.196 Yudhiṣṭhira says to Bhīṣma,

> I wish, O Bhārata, to hear of the fruits that silent reciters of sacred mantras acquire (by their practice). What are the fruits

> that have been indicated for such men? What is that region to which they go after death? ... Is such a man to be regarded as following the ordinances of *Sāṃkhya* or *yoga* or *work* [kriya]? Or is such a man to be regarded as observing the ordinances about (mental) sacrifices?[95]

Bhīṣma replies by stating, somewhat confusingly, that both of the methods for gaining emancipation, namely Yoga and Sāṃkhya ('which is otherwise called Vedānta') are 'both concerned and again unconcerned (with silent recitations)'. The commentator explains this rather perplexing statement by pointing out that 'as long as one does not succeed in beholding one's Soul, one may silently recite the *Praṇava* or the original word *Oṃ*. When, however, one succeeds in beholding one's Soul, then one may give up such recitation.'[96] Bhīṣma explains that the reciter must live in solitude, fix the mind, subdue the senses, maintain the sacred fire, meditate, undertake penance, practise self-restraint, forgiveness, benevolence and abstemiousness in respect of food. He should also withdraw from worldly attachments, remain silent and be tranquil. Through recitation within this discipline

> he casts off his life breaths and then enters into the Brahmic body. Or, if he does not desire to enter into the Brahmic body, he at once goes upwards into the region of Brahma and has never to undergo rebirth. Having become tranquillity's self, and being freed from all kinds of calamity, such a person, by depending upon his own intelligence, succeeds in attaining to that Soul which is pure and immortal and which is without a stain.[97]

The Yoga Upaniṣads of the first group are all compatible with this description and probably represent refinements of this kind of practice in the post-epic period. I include here some brief comments on salient points in each of these Upaniṣads (Deussen's versions).

### *Brahmavidyā* (Deussen's version – 14 verses; Adyar version – 111 verses)

Oṃ (auṃ), the syllable of Brahman, contains, in its three and a half moras, the entire universe. That oṃ resides in the centre of 'the brain-conch'. The suṣumṇā nāḍī passes through it and through the other 72,000 nādī. One who takes the oṃ-sound through that nāḍī and then allows it to fade realizes the highest Brahman.

***Kśurikā* (D – 25 verses; A – 24 verses)**

This Upaniṣad contains a description of a prāṇāyāma practice that involves fixing the mind (manas) in the heart by means of the 12 divisions of the oṃ-sound (see also *Nādabindu* 8-11) and then filling the body with breath (prāṇa) via the nose. The body is then, by means of the oṃ divisions, pervaded by the breath in the order of toes, ankles, calves, knees, thighs, anus, penis and navel ('the location of the breath'), where the yogin finds the suṣumṇā nāḍī surrounded by many others of various colours. By taking the path of the white suṣumṇā nāḍī the yogin directs his prāṇa to the heart, the seat of puruṣa, which has the appearance of a red lotus. From there, the yogin progresses to the neck with both prāṇa and manas, where he severs all contact with name and form, giving himself permanently to yoga. Then he cuts off all prāṇa from the legs and joints before gathering the nāḍīs together in the neck to cut them off from prāṇa. Only suṣumṇā is to be left. Then, using manas and prāṇa, he takes good and bad states (= karma phalas), into the suṣumṇā where they are burned up. The yogin is then freed from future births. Verses 24 and 25 summarize the key elements in this process: 1. prāṇāyāma to move the breath and mind into the suṣumṇā; 2. dhāraṇā to fix on the suṣumṇā alone; 3. abandonment of desire (= vairāgya).

***Nādabindu* (D – 20 verses; A – 51 verses)**

This Upaniṣad links the Vedic puruṣa with the 12 components of the oṃ-sound and points out the benefits of meditating on each of them. With the twelfth meditation the yogin dissolves his mind and sheds all attachment, merging into the bliss of the highest brahman.

***Brahmabindu* (= *Amṛtabindu*) (D – 22 verses; A – 22 verses)**

This Upaniṣad begins with a claim that the manas can be pure or impure—the latter when filled with desire, the former when free from desire. Like the Kśurikā, this Upaniṣad advocates locking the manas in the heart, where it becomes inactive. Then, using oṃ as a vehicle, the yogin enters Brahman and knows the highest bliss.

### *Amṛtabindu* (= *Amṛtanāda*) (D – 38 verses; A – 38 verses)

The yogin who meditates on oṃ throws away his books and sets out for the brahmaloka, accessed through the silence following the anusvāra (the dot or bindu at the end of auṃ in the devanāgarī script). This meditation combines with a sixfold yoga practice akin to that found in *MaitU* 6.18, though the components are presented in a different order: pratyāhāra, dhyāna, prāṇāyāma, dhāraṇa, tarka and samādhi (prāṇāyāma, pratyāhāra, dhyāna, dhāraṇā, tarka and samādhi in the *Maitri*). Verse 17 encourages the yogin to adopt a stable, cross-legged posture such as the lotus (padma), cruciform (svastika) or auspicious (bhadra) postures. Meditation on the 12 components of the oṃ is combined with directing the prāṇa through the various gates or doors that lead to mokṣa. Unlike earlier Upaniṣads, the Amṛtabindu describes the various prāṇas as being coloured: prāṇa—red; apāna—cochineal (scarlet); samāna—milky; vyāna—flame coloured; udāna—pale yellow.

### *Dhyānabindu* (D – 23 verses; A – 106 verses)

The opening verses of this Upaniṣad tell us that the only way to destroy karma is by dhyāna yoga. Also, in common with other Yoga Upaniṣads and much tantric literature, the syllable (akṣara) which is elsewhere used as a synonym for Brahman, e.g. *MundU* 2.1, is presented as merely penultimate. The silence beyond sound is the highest place. Again, using the oṃ-sound in conjunction with control of the prāṇa, the yogin should meditate in order to see the divinity hidden within, and then, with the bindu (= anusvāra), draw the manas from the heart to the forehead, where dwells the ātman. This last would seem to be a new teaching as earlier Upaniṣads tend to locate the ātman, often called 'inner-controller' (antaryāmin), in the secret place of the heart.

### *Tejobindu* (D – 14 verses; A – 6 chapters of 51, 41, 59, 81, 105 and 107 verses respectively)

The highest meditation is difficult to achieve, even for renunciants, for it involves abandoning greed, anger, lust, attachment, egoity, fear, pride, sin, delusion, love and pride in descent. By means of such abandonment the yogin attains Brahman, 'the highest goal of all endeavour'. Essentially, liberation through the cultivation of detachment or indifference (vairāgya).

### *Yogaśikhā* (D – 10 verses; A – 6 chapters of 178, 22, 25, 24, 62 and 79 verses respectively)

This text advocates the adoption of the lotus posture (padmāsana) and, with controlled mind (manas), meditation on oṃ in the heart. Through this practice of yoga the yogin ascends through the suṣumṇā nāḍī to the top of the head, where he sees the highest one and destroys saṃsāra.

### *Yogatattva* (D – 15 verses; A – 142 verses)

Deussen points out that the text of this Upaniṣad is so defective that his translation can only be regarded as an experiment at rendering it intelligible. The opening verse presents us with a claim that becomes increasingly common in the medieval period: that one who listens to and recites the teaching will be freed from all sins. Again, the meditation advocated is on the oṃ-sound, which encompasses the three worlds, the three Vedas, the three times of day, the three [great] gods and the three guṇas. The final stage of meditation, on the anusvāra, takes the yogin to the highest place. Following this description are three verses explaining that the manas is located in the lotus within the space of the heart. The oṃ-sound opens this lotus and reveals the luminous soul. Then come four verses advocating pratyāhāra and prāṇāyāma as a means of taking that soul (the guileless)[98] to a point between the brows and the forehead, the great resting place where manas melts away. This notion of the dissolution of the manas has parallels with Buddhist teachings, especially those associated with the Yogācāra school (see Chapter 3 above).

### *Pāśupatabrahma* (A – 46 verses)

Brahman is the supreme being, self-originated (svayambhū). The oṃ-sound is his essence. A threefold symbolism links Vedic sacrificial ideas with yogic ones. The praṇava (oṃ) is the ferry (tāraka) that carries the yogin across saṃsāra. The overall philosophy is pure advaita: nothing exists but Brahman.

### *Mahāvākya* (A – 12 verses)

Another advaitic text. The sādhyas (pitṛs) are identified with jīvanmuktas. One who realizes the paramātman 'attains oneness with Śrī Mahāviṣṇu'.

Those Upaniṣads that I placed in the second group have a different character from the ones in the first. All are clearly tantric and show the influence of Śāktism (see Chapter 6 below) through reference to the kuṇḍalinī śakti (the coiled power) and the various discs (cakra) or lotuses (padma) through which she passes on her ascent of the suṣumṇā towards a blissful reunion with Śiva in the sahasrāra padma (1,000-petalled lotus) at the top of the head. The yoga based on these concepts does not appear in any text that can be unambiguously dated before the period of the siddhas (accomplished ones/adepts), i.e. between the eighth and twelfth centuries CE, though some of the ideas clearly have their origins in: a) earlier Upaniṣadic notions of prāṇa and nāḍī, and b) Paśupata Śaivism (see Chapter 6 below).[99] Most of these texts, as presented by Ayyangar, are quite long, so my comments on them will be rather cursory, simply noting what, to me, are salient points.

### *Advayatāraka*[100]

This Upaniṣad is notably advaitic in its philosophy ('brahman is saccidananda', v.2; 'jīva and īśvara are but the results of illusion', v.3). Kuṇḍalinī is located halfway between the root support (mūlādhara) and the brahmarandhra (the opening at the top of the head). The aim of the practice, which is likened to a ferry (tāraka), is to become a siddha. This is only possible through the grace of a guru (defined via pseudo-etymology as gu—darkness and ru—dispeller). The guru is greater than all else, v.18.

### *Maṇḍalabrahmana*

Another advaitic text, there is 'no existence apart from brahman' (1.1.2), brahman is saccidānanda (1.2.4). An eightfold yoga with the same headings as Patañjali's is described. It has four yamas and nine niyamas (which include devotion to the guru rather than to the īśvara). Kuṇḍalinī, mūlādhāra, brahmarandhra, ajñācakra and sahasrāra are all mentioned. Siddhāsana is recommended for use with the sanmukhi mūdra. Yoga nidrā (yoga sleep) leads to nirvikalpa samādhi (concept-free absorption), which is also known as unmanī, the volitionless state. Nine cakras are mentioned, the standard six plus tālu, ākāśa and bhrū. Five states of consciousness are mentioned: wakefulness, dream, deep sleep, turīya (the fourth and the highest in the earlier Upaniṣads) and turīyatīta (beyond the fourth).

### *Triśikhibrāhmaṇa*

This Upaniṣad presents Śiva as the source of all. From Śiva comes Brahman (characterized by māyā and sat) followed by the unmanifest (avyakta) and the Sāṃkhya tattvas. Divisions of 12 are prominent in the text; so there are 12 nāḍī, 12 elements and 12 presiding deities. A redefinition of aṣṭāṅgayoga is offered based on the manipulation of vital energies. There are ten yamas and ten niyamas in this scheme, and sixteen postures (āsana) are described: svastika, gomukha, vīra, padma, baddhapadma, kukkuṭa, uttānakūrmaka, dhanura, siṃharūpaka, bhadra, mukta, mayūra, matsya, siddha, paścimatāna, sukha. In the navel region lies the kāṇḍa, which is the source of all the nāḍī. Within it, perched on the prāṇa, abides the jīva. Above it lies the eight-coiled kuṇḍalinī. The suṣumṇā nāḍī has its origin here. It goes upwards to the brahmarandhra and ultimately to brahmaloka. The other nāḍī and nāḍīkā (minor channels) go out from there in ten directions via the iḍā, piṅgalā, gāndhārī, hastjihvā, pūṣā, yaśasvinī, alambusā, śubhā, kauśikī, and, of course, suṣumṇā, which, we are told, is only entered by the prāṇa of yogins. Ten vital airs circulate in the ten nāḍī (v.77): prāṇa, apāna, samāna, udāna, vyāna, nāga, kūrma, kṛkara, devadatta and dhanaṃjaya. This is not found in the early Upaniṣads. Nor does it fit comfortably with the statements that follow about the circulation of these airs in various parts of the body. Moreover, we may note that whilst the two sets of ten might seem to go together they do not. No vital air circulates within the suṣumṇā and it is difficult to reconcile the model of channels spreading out from the kāṇḍa with the locations of the vital airs. For example, the samāna pervades the whole body. Does it circulate along with other airs in the same nāḍī, going with prāṇa to mouth, nose, heart, navel and big toes, with apāna to anus, genitals, thighs and knees, with udāna to all joints, legs and hands, with vyāna to the ears, thighs, hips, ankles, shoulders and throat, etc. etc.? We seem to have two schemes here, which do not fit together under scrutiny. Another interesting mis-combination comes towards the end where the best of yogins is described as one who endeavours to attain kaivalya (aloneness), a dualistic concept, which involves the realization that 'there is no universe beyond one's own ātman, which again is no other than the Brahman'.

### *Darśana*

Again, this text presents a reworked eight-limbed yoga rather than a reworked sixfold one. Each limb is explained in turn and the overall perspective is that of advaita Śaivism. There are ten yamas, ten niyamas and ten prāṇas. Fourteen major and 72,000 minor nāḍī come out of the kāṇḍa, which is located in the navel area. The kuṇḍalinī resides just below it. Śiva rules the suṣumṇā, Hari (Viṣṇu) rules the iḍā, whilst Brahmā rules the piṅgalā. Chapter 6 of *Darśana* offers detailed comments on prāṇāyāma practice.

### *Yogakuṇḍalī*

Breath (prāṇa) and memories/impressions (vāsana) keep the mind active. The means to bring the former (hence both of them) to a standstill are threefold: temperance in food, assuming the proper posture, and arousing the śakti. Considerable detail is provided on the three bandhas: mūla, uḍḍīyāṇa and jālandhara as a means of manipulating prāṇa and apāna for the purpose of awakening and directing the kuṇḍalinī. Significant space is also given over to the kecharī vidyā (knowledge of the ethereal regions). One who utters the kecharī mantra (Hrīṃ, Bhaṃ, Saṃ, Maṃ, Paṃ, Saṃ, Kṣaṃ) 500,000 times a day for 12 days will succeed in the kechari yoga, which destroys wrinkles and grey hair. Alternatively, the brahma door can be opened by the physical method of extending the tongue. To achieve this, the yogin scrapes away the froenum (the skin that anchors the tongue to the lower jaw) over a period of six months.

> In the course of six months the fold of skin (froenum) at the base of the tongue will vanish. The yogin should then bandage the tip of the tongue with a piece of cloth and then should draw it up gradually, after knowing the proper season, time and manner of action. In the course of the next six months, O Muni, by thus daily pulling it up, it will reach the middle of the eyebrows and obliquely up to the crevice of the ear. Being

> moved by stages, it will reach downwards as far as the root of the chin. In the course of the next three years, it will undoubtedly reach the brahmarandhra and stand surrounding it completely. Obliquely it will reach the outer surface of the crest, and stretch downwards up to the crevice of the throat and gradually will burst open the Mahā-vajra door of the cranium.[101]

Complete success will come after 12 years. The standard scheme of six cakras is outlined in this Upaniṣad: mūlādhāra above the anus, svādhiṣṭhāna around the genitals, manipūra near the navel, anāhata near the heart, viśuddhi at the root of the throat and ajñā at the front of the head.

### *Yogacūḍāmaṇi*

The text begins with a list of the six components of yoga—no yama, no niyama. They are: posture (āsana), restraint of breath (prāṇasamrodha), withdrawal (pratyāhāra), concentration (dhāraṇā), meditation (dhyāna) and absorption (samādhi).[102] Ayyangar identifies kuṇḍalinī with the vagina (yoni) in the middle of the four-petalled lotus located between the mūlādhāra and svādhiṣṭhāna cakras. However, the text later states that the kuṇḍalinī abides in eight coils above the knot of the navel (as in the Triśikhibrāhmaṇa, rather than just below it, as in the *Darśana*), so this identification would seem to be an error. The kaṇḍa (source of the nāḍī) is shaped like a bird's egg and located between the genitals and the navel. There are ten major nāḍī and ten vital airs. Iḍā, piṅgalā and suṣumṇā all carry the prāṇa. The jīva is kept in constant motion by the pull of prāṇa then apāna. Benefits from applying the three main bandhas (locks): mūla, jālandhara and uḍḍiyāṇa, are described, not least of which is the restriction of the flow of nectar (the water of nabhas or the ethereal region). The kecharī and yonimudrās prevent the loss of semen, essential for immortality, 'even at the point of entering the vaginal cavity' (one of the few indications in these texts of the actual rather than symbolic applications of the teachings).

### *Varāha*

This Upaniṣad seems clearly composite, with the final chapter (ch. 5) constituting an essentially independent work that offers fairly typical haṭha yoga teaching. The preceding four chapters are largely Advaita Vedānta in orientation: 'only by knowing brahman as saccidānanda does one become immortal'; 'there exists the brahman alone actually, which is absolute consciousness, all-pervading, eternal, full, and which is imperishable bliss and nought else exists', though in parts of the dialogue between Ṛbhu and Viṣṇu the latter mentions that he is different from all tattva groups and distinct from jīva, īśvara and māyā—typical dualistic statements. The rest of the text identifies Viṣṇu with the non-dual Brahman, however. Little in these chapters adds significantly to post-epic Vedāntic lore, apart from mentions of 36 and 96 tattvas. One exception to this can be found at the end of ch. 2, where the grace of the true teacher (sadguru), kuṇḍalinī and the innate (sahaja) are introduced. Chapter five mentions three kinds of yoga: laya, mantra and haṭha, and outlines an eight-limbed yoga with the same constituents as Patañjali's, though they are described differently. As in other Vedāntic haṭha yoga texts, there are ten yamas and ten niyamas. Eleven postures (āsana), ten prāṇas and thirteen nāḍī are also mentioned. The prāṇas are manipulated by a combination of āsana and mantra to raise the kuṇḍalinī. Adepts of this yoga are called siddhas. At the end, four stages of yoga are described: ārambha (functioning internally rather than externally), ghāṭa (when the prāṇa pierces the three knots [granthi] in the suṣumṇā), paricaya (when the prāṇa stands motionless is the suṣumṇā) and niṣpatti (the attainment of samādhi and jīvanmukti).

### *Śāṇḍilya*

This is an Upaniṣad in two chapters, each of which was probably an independent text. The second chapter is essentially an Advaita Vedānta teaching, though it presents yoga, contra Śaṅkara, as a means to the ultimate realization of the ātman. Vedic/Vedāntic terminology is used throughout. There is no mention of subtle physiology. The first chapter begins with an almost standardized Haṭha-Vedāntic reworking of the aṣṭāṅgayoga. There are ten yamas, ten niyamas and eight āsanas (svastika, gomukha, padma, vīra, siṃha, bhadra, mukta and mayūra). Prāṇāyāma is for the purification of the nāḍī. Its three phases: in, out and holding, are equated with the three moras of the oṃ-sound. Much of this chapter is given over to information about prāṇāyāma and related matters. The prāṇa extends beyond the body by 12 digit lengths. The eight-coiled kuṇḍalinī obstructs the entrance to the brahmarandhra. There are 14 major nāḍī, including the suṣumṇā, which is 'attached to the vertebral column, behind the anus'. Ten prāṇas move through the nāḍī and pervade the body. The importance of the mudrās, especially the kecharī, which in its external form requires the lengthening of the tongue, is emphasized for the attainment of immortality.

Between the end of the section on prāṇāyāma and the beginning of that on pratyāhāra, i.e. vv.45-52, is a substantial section on dhāraṇā (concentration) and saṃyāma (extended concentration). Here, dhāraṇā seems to be used to refer to a form of prāṇa manipulation for the eradication of disease and the destruction of sins. Saṃyāma, as in the *Yoga Sūtra,* is directed towards different foci in order to obtain a range of knowledges and powers, such as knowledge of the various realms of existence (loka), knowledge of the past and future, knowledge of others' minds, the power to eradicate hunger and thirst and celestial vision. Five kinds of pratyāhāra and five kinds of dhāraṇā are described, plus two kinds of dhyāna. Samādhi is described as the union of the jīvatman with the paramātman.

## CONCLUSION

In terms of our soteriology scheme, these darśanas present us with a range of mutually exclusive teachings, despite the claims that they are just different perspectives on the same truth. Sāṃkhya, in its darśana form, is a self-power path that promotes the pursuit of liberating knowledge through a kind of jñāna yoga—a reinterpreting of all experience in terms of its explanatory model. Its ontology is dualistic pluralism, where the liberated state differs from the unliberated one in that each individual puruṣa disengages form involvement with the unitary prakṛti. Epistemologically, Sāṃkhya does not rely on revelation, though its 'meditation' is distinctive. Perception and inference are the principal sources of knowledge. In Rawlinson's model it is a cool–structured tradition.

Yoga too is a self-power path, for īśvara is an aid not a saviour. It pursues liberating knowledge by removing everything that obscures it: mental activity, deep-seated dispositions and, ultimately, one's identification with a body–mind complex. Its ontology is essentially that of the Sāṃkhya school. Its information derives, as in Buddhism, from meditational experience. In Rawlinson's model it is a cool–structured tradition.

Within Vedānta, many different and incompatible positions can be identified. Śaṅkara's advaita has no room for grace at the ultimate level of realization—inevitably, because within his monism there is no difference between the bestower of grace and its recipient. Neither is there much room for meditation. In this Advaita Vedānta and Sāṃkhya have much in common. Both advocate what we can loosely call jñāna yoga. They are also similar to each other and to Yoga in terms of experience. As Zaehner points out, 'Monism, in practice, means the isolation of the soul from all that is other than itself.'[103] For Śaṅkara that is māyā (which has no ontological status); for Sāṃkhya and Yoga it is prakṛti. The point is that the immersion of consciousness in the non-dual brahman alone and the immersion of consciousness in puruṣa alone are difficult to distinguish experientially. There are, of course, significant differences too. For Śaṅkara, all experience is subordinated to revelation (śruti), whereas in Sāṃkhya and Yoga revelation has no place at all.

The other main forms of Vedānta are other-power paths, though they differ in their teachings about the relative proportionality of works and grace, and also in their ontologies. Works are given greatest weight in in the Śrī sampradāya and least in the Rudra. Vallabha's śuddhādvaita is clearly monist in its ontology. Theoretically, Mādhva's system is too, though he comes as near to being a pluralist as one can be within the constraints of the Vedāntic scriptures. Indeed, we can discern a fundamental tension at the heart of Vedānta. On the one hand, the ontology of the prasthānatraya is overwhelmingly monistic. On the other, the sentiments of the bhakta crave a separation between the devotee and the object of devotion, between the recipient and the bestower of grace. Epistemologically, the whole of Vedānta rests on revelation (śruti). Anything that conflicts with this is subordinated (and where it conflicts with itself creative hermeneutics are required). Vallabha's solution to the works-grace issue is noteworthy because it manages to assert the supremacy of grace whilst maintaining a commitment to works. In Rawlinson's model, Śaṅkara's system is cool–unstructured. The other, bhakti-oriented, systems are all hot, mainly unstructured, though an emphasis on works, as found in the Śrī sampradāya for example, provides significant elements of structure.

## Chapter 6
# SECTARIAN DEVELOPMENTS: ŚAIVISM, ŚĀKTISM AND TANTRA

The development of yoga philosophy continued outside of Vedānta and Vaiṣṇavism in the various schools of Śaivism and Śāktism, both of which have a more ambivalent relation to brāhmanical orthodoxy than does Vaiṣṇavism. These three traditions and their respective deities dominate, medieval and modern Hinduism. Indeed, Viṣṇu/Kṛṣṇa, Śiva and Devī (= Śakti) constitute the real trimūrti (three forms of god); the Brahmā–Viṣṇu–Śiva version is a brāhmanical invention that has little relevance to the lives of most Hindus. Temples to Brahmā are exceedingly rare.

## ŚAIVISM

The god Śiva (the auspicious one) is a complex composite of deities. He is referred to as Hara (destructive power), Īśāna (the ruler), Maheśvara (great lord), Śambhu (abode of joy) and Rudra (the howler). In his most fearful aspect he is called Bhairava (the terrible). The god Rudra can be traced back to the *Ṛgveda*, where he has two hymns dedicated to him. Unlike most other Vedic gods he has no close relationships with other divinities. Rather, he is something of a loner. His children are the Maruts or Gaṇas (forces of the storm). Sometimes they are called Rudras. The Maruts often help Indra in his battles with demons (non-Vedic peoples?), though Rudra himself never does. Rather, he is the patron of those who live outside Aryan society, which makes him an ideal vehicle for the assimilation of non-Aryan forms of spirituality.

Like the later god Śiva, Rudra has a dark as well as a light side to his nature. The *Yajurveda* distinguishes between his benign and malignant forms.[1] As a god who can send illness and destruction he is feared and has to be appeased, though when such appeasement has occurred words like Śiva (auspicious), Śaṅkara (beneficent) or Śambhu (benign) are used of him. In the *Taittirīya Saṃhitā* he is called lord of cattle or beasts (Paśupati), though he kills as well as protects them. Thus, unlike Viṣṇu, he is never fully regarded as a friend of mankind. There is always a distance between him and his devotees. Also, unlike Viṣṇu, he never incarnates in animal or human form. On the other hand, like Viṣṇu, he was a deity who rose to prominence during the epic and Purāṇic periods whilst other Vedic deities receded into the theological background.

In the *Śvetāśvatara Upaniṣad* Rudra is presented as the great lord (Maheśvara), one of whose names is Śiva. It is this text that lays the foundations for much of later Śaiva theology. The *Śvetāśvatara* teaches that there are three unborn entities:

1. the ruler or lord (īśā);
2. the self or soul (ātman);
3. the stuff of the universe (pradhāna).

The lord is all-knowing, the self is ignorant. However, as 1.10 informs us, 'By meditating on Him, by uniting with Him, by reflecting on His being more and more, there is complete cessation of every illusion.' The possibility of the union of the self with god confuses the ontology here. Are there three existents or just one? This same ambiguity remains throughout much of later Śaiva theology, both in the primary Śaiva scriptures (Āgama) and in the doctrines of the various Śaiva schools. What appears to be an essentially Sāṃkhya plus god ontology seems to have been reworked to make it compatible with Vedāntic monism, much as we find in the *Bhagavad Gītā.*

That the Vedic Rudra is not the only primary source for the full identity of the later god Śiva is indicated by the existence of a number of anomalies in the relationship between Rudra and Śiva. In the first place, Rudra is praised for his red (rohita), reddish (aruṇa) and tawny (tāmra) colour.[2] By contrast, the later Śiva is invariably blue, probably indicating (as in the case of Kṛṣṇa) a dark complexion. A second anomaly is that nowhere in the early literature is Rudra connected with Umā or Pārvatī, daughter of Himālaya, which the later Śiva certainly was. Nor is Rudra connected with the elephant, as Śiva was through his elephant-headed son Ganeśa. A third anomaly has to do with the stories about Dakṣa's sacrifice. In *Mahābhārata* 10.18 and 12.274, and elaborated in the *Kurma Purāṇa* 1.14.4-97, we are told how Dakṣa or Prajāpati held a sacrifice to which Śiva was not invited and no portion of the offering was reserved for him.[3] In response to this slight Śiva destroys the sacrifice and Dakṣa along with it. In commenting on the episode, Sukumari Bhattacharji writes,

> The anomaly is rather striking, for a Vedic god being deprived of his share in the sacrifice is simply inconceivable. Oblations to every member of the Vedic pantheon were obligatory, and Rudra is a Vedic god. Now after enjoying his rightful share of oblation for centuries Śiva is suddenly denied it, and, at least in one version, is quite reconciled to it, saying that it is ordained so. This is a somewhat strange phenomenon. In every version, whether in the gods' sacrifice or in Dakṣa's, he has to fight his way into the sacrifice; and whether at Pārvatī's mortification or at his own initiative has to wreak fearful vengeance on the perpetrator of the sacrifice. Even then it is not clearly mentioned that he does receive his share of the oblation, except in one instance. This fierce hostility cannot be against an old and recognised deity, it can only be turned against an interloper, an upstart. And the epic-Purāṇic Śiva was largely that.[4]

The implication is clear: Śiva was essentially a non-Vedic deity who, in the process of being rendered acceptable to brāhmanical orthodoxy, absorbed the identity of Rudra.

A fourth anomaly is that some central Śaivite symbols are quite un-Vedic in character. Most significant of these is the liṅga (phallus), the centrepiece of many Śaivite temples and most popular iconographic representation of the god. In the *Ṛgveda* (7.21.5; 10.99.3) phallus worshippers, those who have the phallus as their god (śiśna deva) are denigrated. By contrast, many liṅga and liṅga-yoni (phallus-vulva) carvings have been discovered on Indus Valley sites, which suggests a possible link between the Indus civilization and the later god Śiva, as well as presenting a challenge to those who claim that the Indus civilization was the creation of Vedic peoples.

## ŚAIVA SCHOOLS

A variety of Śaiva schools emerged in India from the second century BCE onwards. Many did not survive or had only fleeting influence.[5] The most significant are:

1. Paśupata;
2. Vīra Śaivism;
3. Śaiva Siddhānta;
4. Kaśmir Śaivism.

### The Paśupata

The earliest literary reference to a Śaiva sect is to be found in Patañjali's commentary on the grammar of Pāṇini, where he mentions the Śiva bhagavatas—devotees of Śiva. This was in the second century BCE. Although the Paśupatas are not mentioned by name, the reference is probably to them as they are the oldest of the various Śaiva movements in India. The first specific reference comes in book 12 of the *Mahābhārata* (349.64). There, the Paśupata system is said to have been founded by Śiva Śrikaṇṭha, consort of Umā. Paśupata Śaivism is sometimes referred to as the Lakulīśa, after an important teacher of the sect, though some scholars, e.g. K.C. Pandey, differentiate the early Paśupata from the Lakulīśa version because the latter appears to teach a 'dualism-cum-nondualism' (dvaitādvaita) ontology whereas the former subscribed to a dualistic (dvaita) one. On the basis of epigraphical evidence, Pandey locates Lakulīśa in the second century CE. The Kāpālika and Kālamukha sects are, or were, branches of the Paśupata.[6] Many of the tantric practices that challenge both brāhmanical notions of purity and pollution and Buddhist ideas about the importance of chastity for salvation may well have originated in these circles.

In his commentary on the *Brahmasūtra*, Rāmānuja describes the Kālamukhas as using skulls as drinking vessels, consuming alcohol, going about naked, smearing themselves with the ashes from dead bodies, eating the flesh of dead bodies, engaging in ritualized sexual intercourse and holding that their initiation rite turns men of all castes into brāhmaṇas. The Kāpālakas, so-called because they wear skulls around their necks, share most of the Kālamukha characteristics and are known for their great yogic powers. They taught that 'without renouncing the pleasures derived through the organs of sense, the eight great *siddhis* [powers] may be obtained'.[7] This outlook is typical of what came to be known as 'left-handed' or literalist tantrism in contrast to 'right-handed' or symbolic tantrism. Practitioners of the former incline towards doing what the texts instruct whereas those of the latter prefer to employ imaginative equivalents of those instructions.

Most of our information about the philosophy of the Paśupata sect comes from much later works, primarily the *Sarva-darśana-saṅgraha* of Mādhava (14th century CE) and the *Paśupata Sūtras* with Kauṇḍinya's commentary. Kauṇḍinya is reputed to have lived between the fourth and sixth centuries CE. We learn from these texts that the five fundamental features of the system are:

1. the lord (pati), sometimes called the cause (kāraṇa);
2. the effect (kārya), which has three subclasses:
   - the stuff of the universe (paśa or kalā)
   - the soul (paśu)
   - cognition or knowledge (vidyā);
3. contemplative exercise (yoga);
4. conduct or religious activity (vidhi);
5. the end of suffering (duḥkhānta).

The essence of Paśupata theology is that God is in control; it is his grace that releases souls from suffering. God's grace works through guidance on yoga and vidhi. Paśupata is the only Śaiva system to subscribe to the Sāṃkhya teaching of 25 categories (tattva) of existence. All the others adopt versions of the later 36-category scheme, which functions to transform the dualistic ontology of Sāṃkhya into a monistic one by adding 11 additional categories to the 25 of Sāṃkhya (see below). This is further testimony to the antiquity of the system.

### Vīraśaivas/Liṅgāyats

Vīraśaivas are sometimes referred to as Liṅgāyats because they wear a small liṅga (phallic symbol of Śiva) on their bodies. The reputed founder of the school is one Basava, who lived in the twelfth century CE. This is challenged by K.C. Pandey, who calls attention to the writings of Rājaśekhara (10th century CE) where we are told that the yoga school is also known as Śaiva, that its teachers carry staffs, have matted hair, cover their bodies with ashes, eat bulbs and fruits and wear a consecrated linga on their arms. Some have wives and some do not. The latter are the best. This description is so close to what could be said of the Vīraśaivas that Pandey is inclined to regard Basava as a reformer rather than a founder.

In their teachings, the Vīraśaivas exhibit some orthodox (smārta) views, some typically Śaiva views and some distinctive ones. Ontologically, the system is monistic, the world and souls ultimately resolving themselves into Śiva. The essence of Śiva is often called brahman and is characterized by sat (being), cit (consciousness) and ananda (bliss), just as in Ādvaita Vedānta. Through the movement of Śiva's śakti (power) a duality is set up between Śiva in himself, called Liṅgasthala, and the creation (= souls plus world), called Aṅgasthala. The Liṅgasthala exists on three levels:

1. Bhāvaliṅga—pure, simple, non-dual existence;
2. Prāṇaliṅga—a kind of subtle manifestation only perceivable by the mind (a kind of Śaivite equivalent of the Buddhist Sambhogakāya);
3. Iṣṭaliṅga—the physical liṅga that is worn on the arm or set into a base.

The categories of existence are those of the Sāṃkhya plus 11 higher ones. In this system, a devotee of Śiva is called a bhakta, and liberation is understood as a realization of blissful union (samarasya) with Śiva.

In many ways, the Vīraśaivas can be regarded as operating a rival system to that developed by smārta brāhmans. Like the orthodox, they abstain from meat and alcoholic drink, and they are divided into monks (ācāryas) and householders (pañcamas). They also employ orthodox-style rituals, though they substitute their own content for the brāhmanical material. For example, their initiation ceremony (dikṣa) substitutes a liṅga for the sacred thread; and the orthodox Gāyatrī mantra is exchanged for 'Oṃ namas Śivaya'. Unlike the orthodox, they allow widows to remarry and menstruating women are not regarded as polluting.

## Śaiva Siddhānta

Śaiva Siddhānta means something like 'Śaiva Doctrine', though it came to be used explicitly to refer to the system that developed in the south of India out of the teachings of the poet-saints known as the Nāyanmārs. These saints, 63 in all, lived between the seventh and ninth centuries CE. Most influential amongst them were Appar, Campantar (or Sambandhar), Cuntarar (or Sundarar) and Māṇikkavācakar (author of the famous *Tiruvācakam*).[8] During the tenth and eleventh centuries the poems of the Nāyanmārs were brought together in a collection known as the *Twelve Tirumurai*, which, along with the 28 *Śaiva-Āgamas*, form the basis of the Śaiva Siddhānta. In addition, the system also recognizes the 14 Śaiva Siddhānta śāstras as authoritative. Most famous of these texts is the *Śiva-Jñāna-Bodha* of Meykantar (13th century).

Whilst accepting the division of pati, paśu and paśa, Meykantar emphasizes the unity aspect, thus producing a kind of separation in unity doctrine that bears a marked resemblance to the viśiṣṭādvaita of Rāmānuja. However, unlike Rāmānuja, Meykantar does not regard creation as being the play (līlā) of god; rather, it is for the purpose of liberating souls. Like the other main Śaiva schools (apart from the Paśupata) they accept 36 categories of existence (tattva), and, prefiguring Caitanya, they distinguish between four levels of devotion (bhakti):

1. servant–master;
2. child–parent;
3. friend–friend;
4. lover–lover.

## Kaśmir Śaivism

There are actually three traditions of Śaivism that emerged in Kasmir: the Krama, the Kula and the Pratyabhijñā. All teach a monistic ontology.

### THE KRAMA SYSTEM

The Krama exhibits a number of distinctive features. First there is an emphasis on the attainment of liberation (union with Śiva) by gradual stages. This proceeds through yoga practice which entails *either* the merging of experiences of the external world with those of the internal—promoting the idea that external objects are really mind-made, *or* by seeing the external as a projection of the internal.

Another distinguishing feature is the emphasis on the female energy (śakti) as the most important aspect of the divine, because whereas Śiva is the tranquil, immutable consciousness the śakti is dynamic energy, responsible for creation, destruction and liberation. For this reason it has sometimes been described as a Śākta rather than a Śaiva system.

### THE KULA SYSTEM

Perhaps the most distinctive feature of the Kula system is its stress on the possibility of sudden enlightenment through the bestowal of grace by a spiritual preceptor (guru), who is said to be perfectly united with Śiva. Despite this, Kaulas are not encouraged to cultivate ecstatic devotion but to practise those forms of tantric yoga that seek the awakening of the kuṇḍalini śakti.[9]

### THE PRATYABHIJÑĀ

This is probably the most well known of the Kaśmiri Śaiva schools. It betrays the influence of both Buddhist and Vedāntic teaching alongside its Śaiva doctrines.[10] The reputed founder of the system was Somānanda, with a work called *Śivadṛṣṭi*. Roughly contemporaneous with him was Vasugupta, who 'discovered' another root text of this system, the *Śiva Sūtras*. He may also have been the author of another influential Pratyabhijñā work, the *Spanda Kārikā*, a kind of commentary on the *Śiva Sūtras*. These two works are complementary, the *Śiva Sūtras* emphasizing the consciousness aspect (prakāśa) of the divine, the *Spanda Kārikā* emphasizing the dynamic or creative (vimarśa) one.

Whereas the Krama might be said to concentrate on yoga practice and the Kula on the effects of divine grace, the Pratyabhijñā (literally 'recognition') emphasizes knowledge or discrimination. It thus teaches a kind of jñāna yoga. Here, the aspirant seeks to recognize that everything is one (much as in Advaita Vedānta) and that the universe in all its variety is nothing more than a manifestation (abhyāsa) of the divine consciousness (Śiva). The world is not, therefore, an illusion but a genuine transformation of the divine being, whose essence is consciousness.

# The 36 Tattvas in Kaśmir (Pratyabhijñā) Śaivism

Śiva
|
Śakti
|
Sadāśiva
|
Aiśvara (lordship)
|
Śuddhavidyā (pure knowledge)
|
Māyā (the power of illusion)
|
Kalā (time)
|
Niyati (regulation or destiny)
|
Rāga (attachment)
|
Vidyā (knowledge)
|
Kala (art, the power to create) ──────────────┐
|
**puruṣa**                              **prakṛti** (2 modes)

avyakta (the state                                      vyakta
of the guṇas in     ─────────────────────────          |
equipoise)                                              intellect
                                                        (buddhi or mahat)
                                                        |
┌───────────────────────────────────── ahaṃkāra ─┐
|                                                 |
sattvic                                          tamasic
├──────────────┬──────────────┐
buddhīndriyas:     mind          karmendriyas:
eye               (manas)        hands
car                              feet
nose                             speech
tongue                           anus
skin                             genitals

            ┌────────┬────────┬────────┬────────────┐
tanmātras      sound      touch      form      flavour      smell
            |          |          |          |            |
mahābhūtas     ether      air        fire       water        earth[11]

## ŚĀKTISM

Śāktism is essentially a medieval development.[12] Its roots, however, are much more ancient. The *Mahābhārata* contains a number of passages which indicate that many of the tribal peoples who were eventually absorbed into mainstream Indian culture were worshippers of goddesses. Umā, consort of Śiva, is described as a Kirāta woman (3.38-40). The term 'kirāta' is used to refer to a Himālayan people in particular and to tribal peoples in general. One goddess, who resides in the Vindhya mountains, is said to have been fond of wine and meat (sīdhumāṃsapaśupriyā),[13] the consumption of which became an integral part of many later tantric rituals.

The Durgāstotras of the *Mahābhārata* (4.6; 6.23), according to Bhattacharyya, reveal the process through which numerous local goddesses combined into one in terms of an all embracing female principle. Other slightly later texts (e.g. the *Harivaṃśa*, the *Silappadhkāram* and the *Manimekalai*) mention many goddesses who eventually became aspects or epithets of the great goddess of the Purāṇas and Śāktism. Similar evidence is found in Buddhism and Jainism, where female divinities from tribal cults were incorporated into the mainstream tradition and presented as devotees of the great sages or personifications of spiritual principles. Their parallels within Hinduism are relatively easy to identify, which suggests that all came originally from the same sources.

In Buddhism, the composite goddess Tārā came to be regarded as a primordial female energy, sometimes consort of Avalokiteśvara and also as the personification of perfect wisdom (Prajñāpāramitā). In Vaiṣṇavism, Śrī, Lakṣmī and Sarasvatī, who originally had little by way of particular association with Viṣṇu, came to be regarded as his consort and eventually as an integral part of his being, his śakti (literally 'power'). In Śaivism, perhaps because its roots were similar, the goddess always had a close relationship with the god. Statues of the ardhanārīśvara (the lord who is half woman) begin to appear in the Gupta period (320–400 CE). These sculptures 'have the right half possessing all the iconographic features of Śiva and the left half those of Umā'.[14] In the hymns of some Tamil Nāyanmārs, Śiva and Umā are identified with the prakṛti and puruṣa of Sāṃkhya.

All these developments constitute what Bhattacharyya calls 'dependent śāktism', where the worship of the female principle is channelled through the structures of the mainstream traditions. Not until the Devīmahātmya section of the *Mārkaṇḍeya Purāṇa* does an 'independent śāktism' begin to emerge. One of the invocations in this text presents the superiority of the goddess in no uncertain terms:

> Thou art the cause of all the worlds.
> Though characterised by three qualities [the Sāṃkhya guṇas],
> Even by Hari, Hara [Viṣṇu and Śiva] and other gods thou art incomprehensible.[15]

In Buddhism, Śākta ideas and practices began to appear within the framework of what was called Mantrayāna or Mantranaya. The later tantric Buddhist movements of Vajrayāna, Kālacakrayāna and Sahajayāna developed under these influences, and tantric Buddhist philosophy clearly indicates Śākta influence. The teachings of the two oldest Buddhist tantras, the Guhyasamāja and the Mañjusrimūlakalpa, are that:

> The gods and goddesses are the symbols of the Buddhist conceptions of the four elements and five constituents of being. Earth is represented by the goddess Locana, water by Mamaki, fire by Pandaravasini and air by Tārā while the five constituents of being are represented by the five Dhyāni Buddhas. Creation is due to the śakti or female energy of the Adi-Buddha, and as such the adepts should realise that the female sex is the source of all.[16]

Some of the later Tārā stotras go so far as to present Tārā as the mother of all the Buddhas. This is pure Śāktism. Likewise, in the arena of practice Śākta rites and rituals increase in prominence. The Guhyasamāja and Mañjusrimūlakalpa introduce the use of mudrās (gestures/spells), maṇḍalas (symbolic diagrams), kriyas (rites), cāryas (duties), meat-eating and union with females as part of tantric practice. These are typically Śākta in character and bear little resemblance to what is advocated in early Buddhism.

Within the Hindu tradition, Purāṇas are composed which exhalt the goddess, e.g. the *Devī*, the *Kālikā*, the *Devībhāgavata*, and 108 sites sacred to the goddess are identified. Yoga too was transformed under Śākta influence, particularly among the Siddhas and the Nāths.

## TANTRIC YOGA AND THE TEXTS OF THE NĀTHA YOGIS

In *The Tantric Tradition* A. Bharati writes, 'there is nothing in Buddhist and Hindu tantric philosophy which is not wholly contained in some non-tantric school of either ... it is on the ritualistic or contemplatively methodical side that differences arise.'[17] Thus, what is distinctive about the tantric movement, according to Bharati, is not its doctrines but its development of novel techniques for spiritual transformation. To a large extent this is correct, although, as will be demonstrated below, there are some concepts in tantric yoga which, despite their arising in practical contexts, offer some radical departures from antecedent conceptions of humanity and its place in the universe.

On the philosophical side, tantric schools, both Hindu and Buddhist, tend towards some kind of monistic ontology: the ultimate reality and the changing, phenomenal universe are viewed as one. They thus rejected the dualistic ontology of the classical Sāṃkhya and Yoga schools.

On the other hand, they did not emphasize the pole of the absolute to the detriment of the phenomenal, as did the Advaita Vedānta theologian Śaṅkara. Rather, the tantrics gave equal emphasis to both poles or emphasized the feminine. Thus, in a number of Hindu tantric texts we encounter the statement 'śivaḥ śāktivichīnah śavaḥ' (Śiva is a corpse without Śakti). The supreme realization thus occurs in the merging of the two poles; not in the negation of the phenomenal one. Much of Śaiva and Śākta iconography illustrates this principle.

Another aspect of tantric cosmology shared by most schools is the holographic conception of existence. H.V. Glassenapp explains it thus:

> the notion that the whole universe with the totality of its phenomena forms one single whole, in which even the smallest element has an effect on the largest, because secret threads connect the smallest item with the eternal ground of the world, this is the proper foundation of all tantric philosophy.[18]

In the Buddhist *Avataṃsaka Sūtra* (Flower Garland Sūtra) the same principle is explained by reference to the metaphor of Indra's Net:

> high above in heaven, on the roof of the palace of the God Indra, there hang innumerable ornaments in the form of small crystal marbles. They are interlaced in various patterns forming a great complex network. Because of the reflection of light, not only does each and every one of these marbles reflect the entire cosmos, including the continents and oceans of the human world down below, but at the same time they reflect one another, including all the reflected images in each and every marble without omission.[19]

Here we see the basic properties of a hologram expounded in mythical terms, namely that every part contains the information of the whole. It is this theoretical framework which renders tantric practice (sādhanā) intelligible.

Many Hindu tantrics classify humans into three categories according to the quality (guṇa) predominating in them. People with sattva guṇa predominating are called divine (divya), those with rajas heroic (vīrya), whilst those with tamas are called creaturely (paśu). Each of these classes has a different sādhanā prescribed for them, though some texts, e.g. the *Meru Tantra*, suggest that these three are successive stages through which a person has to pass sequentially.

In general terms, **the practice of the creaturely person** will be based on external forms such as temples and icons.[20] Both temples and maṇḍalas or yantras drawn by individual worshippers are symbols of the entire universe and the worship a symbolic reintegration of that universe. They also symbolize the human body, which is regarded as a microcosmic universe. As Peter Masefield points out, there is a presupposition

> commonly found in many Indian schools from the Vedic period onwards that to speak about the cosmos (adhidaivic) and to speak about the human mind (adhyātmic) are two different ways of speaking about the same thing. For each level of consciousness there is a cosmic counterpart—or for each level of the cosmos there is a corresponding state of consciousness. Neither is in any sense prior. To say that one reaches the Brahmaloka or enters jhāna is to say the same thing but with a different model. Neither is reducible to the other: rather both are equally figurative ways of referring to some elusive neutral phenomenon lying somewhere between the two.[21]

This kind of thinking is found frequently in the early Upaniṣads where the various sensory and vital faculties of the individual are referred to as gods (deva) who have their equivalents in the wider cosmos. Hence, breath (prāṇa) is the individual (adhyātmic) manifestation whilst wind (vāyu) is the cosmic (adhidaivic) one. Similarly, the eye (cakṣus) and the sun (sūrya) represent individual and cosmic manifestations of the same force.

The two main styles of Hindu temple reflect two of the most frequently encountered models of the person. The nāgara temples, found principally in northern India, have a vertical emphasis which echoes the idea that the human being has, within his or her body, access to all the different planes or worlds (loka) that constitute this universe.

With regard to the model of the human being represented in nāgara temples, we find a representation in terms of a vertical structure taken from the idea of cakras (centres of subtle energy located at various points along the spine). Each cakra represents a plane of existence (loka) and its condition reflects a person's access to or attunement with the energies associated with that particular plane.

The other major temple style is the drāviḍa. It is mainly found in South India. The structure of the drāviḍa temple reflects the other influential model of the person in Indian thought: that of the sheaths (kośa). It is an image that goes back to the *Taittirīya Upaniṣad:*

> Verily, other than and within that [body] that consists of the essence of food is the self that consists of the breath. By that this is filled. This verily has the form of a person. According to that one's personal form is this one with the form of a person...
>
> other than and within that one that consists of breath is a self that consists of mind... By that this is filled. This, verily has the form of a person. According to that one's personal form is this one with the form of a person...
>
> other than and within that one that consists of mind is the self that consists of understanding... By that this is filled. This, verily has the form of a person. According to that one's personal form is this one with the form of a person...

> other than and within that one that consists of understanding is a self that consists of bliss... By that this is filled. That one, verily, has the form of a person. According to that one's personal form is this one with the form of a person.[22]
>
> The self consisting of bliss is the real, is whatever there is here. In other words, the self made of bliss (ānandamaya) is the true self and the source of the cosmos.

In this model the spiritual journey is understood not as an ascent from the mūlādhara cakra at the base of the spine to the sahasrāra at the top of the head but as a movement within, each stage being characterized by an awareness of a more subtle aspect of an individual's nature. Just as the experience of the bliss of union when Śakti reunites with Śiva in the sahasrāra is the same for all, so too is the experience of the self made of bliss (ānandamaya ātman). This inner movement is concretized in the series of walled enclosures through which the worshipper has to pass en route to the heart (garbha gṛha) of the drāviḍa temple.

**The most notable of the vīrya sadhanas** is the cakra pūja. The cakra pūja is performed in a circle (cakra) of worshippers, normally an equal number of men and women, which reflects the fundamental polarity of existence. This ritual centres on the partaking of five things that are normally regarded as detrimental to the spiritual life:

1. liquor (madya);
2. meat (māṃsa);
3. fish (matsya);
4. aphrodisiac (mudrā—possibly a kind of parched grain. The word also means a lock or closure or seal/stamp or spell[23]);
5. sexual intercourse (maithuna).

There is some controversy about the nature of this ritual. Some texts suggest the use of symbolic substitutes for these items; others stress the importance of using the actual items on the list. Not surprisingly, it is the last item that has caused the most disagreement. Even in texts where actual sexual intercourse is advocated the male worshipper is often encouraged to use his wife as a partner. Nevertheless, there are a number of texts where the female partner, known as the Śakti or goddess, is referred to as ḍombī (washerwoman), suggesting the involvement of low-caste females rather than wives in the ritual.

For the orthodox, it is important to remember that whatever items are involved in the cakra pūja it is not an orgy. A description of the ritual can be found in Bharati's *The Tantric Tradition* (pp. 244–68). The reason why the ritual is not to be understood in orgiastic terms lies in the fact that so-called 'forbidden' substances and acts are only designated as such by the ignorant, who are trapped in the experience of duality. If existence constitutes just one integrated system, and enlightenment comes through the reintegration of opposites, then particular manifestations of this polarity need to be overcome—such as the opposites of beneficial/detrimental, good/bad, desirable/undesirable and pure/impure.

Such an achievement must involve a genuine perception of all substances and acts as manifestations of the one divine reality. If this is achieved, a significant step on the path to release has been taken; if not, the normal karmic consequences of such acts are what the worshipper reaps. Mircea Eliade, quoting the *Jñānasiddhi*, writes, 'By the same acts that cause some men to burn in hell for thousands of years, the yogin gains eternal salvation.'[24]

The difference in status between the act of the common man and that of the yogin practising the vīra sādhanā comes from the latter's engagement in the rite of 'āropa' (attributing). That is, the worshipper must, through meditative ritual, experience the items being used as manifestations of the goddess herself. Then, as T.J. Hopkins explains it,

> the male worships the female as Devī, performing *pūjā* to her as he would to the Goddess present in an image. Sexual intercourse with his partner is then the culminating act of devotion, the union of the worshipper with the divine power.[25]

This, of course, represents the cleaned-up interpretation of such practice. We have already noted that groups such as the Kālamukhas and Kāpālikas employed many practices of this kind. They also had a reputation for killing people, as did the Thugīs (deceivers), worshippers of Kālī. With regard to Buddhist tantra, David Snellgrove points out that

> There is a tendency nowadays, much promoted by Tibetan lamas who teach in the Western world, to treat references to

> sexual union and to forms of worship carried out with 'impure substances' (referred to usually as the 'five nectars') as symbolic. There is some justification for this but it is only part of the truth ... when modern apologists use the term 'symbolic' as though to suggest that the external practices were never taken in any literal sense, they mislead us.[26]

Buddhists were able to incorporate many of the tantras in a manner similar to that employed by the compilers of the Mahāyāna Sūtras: they had the Buddha teach them in celestial locations, usually on the summit of Mount Meru. Some were more difficult to accommodate, however, particularly those classified as Supreme Yoga Tantras (anuttarayoga-tantra). Often, such tantras are revealed not by the Buddha but by 'a fearful being with the name of Śambara, Vajraḍāka, Heruka, Hevajra or Caṇḍamahāroṣana ("Fierce and Greatly Wrathful")'.[27] These divinities are usually surrounded by female attendants, whose names are indicative of the socially marginal origins of their teachings. Hevajra's attendants thus include Pukkasī (the outcaste), Śavarī (the hill-woman), Caṇḍālī (the half-caste) and Ḍombī (the washerwoman). Others are referred to as 'kāpālinīs', companions of kāpāli-yogins.[28] Many of these names are Śaivite in origin and suggest that the tantras in which they are found were promulgated by Śaivite yogins. Often known as adepts (siddha) or great adepts (mahāsiddha), these yogins were recognized by both Buddhist and Śaivite tantrics. They seem to have originated in north-eastern India sometime between the eighth and twelfth centuries and were assimilated into tantric Buddhism by association with Akṣobhya, the Buddha of the eastern quarter. Moreover, the introductions to many of these tantras are significantly different from those found in other types of Buddhist tantric literature. 'Thus I have heard: at one time the Lord reposed in the vagina of the Lady of the Vajra-sphere—the heart of the Body, Speech and mind of all Buddhas'[29] is, according to Snellgrove, typical of the genre.

Can all this be symbolic language or do these 'left-hand' tantras really advocate a yoga practice rooted in an abandonment of all conventional taboos? Most modern commentators think not and explain many of the seemingly debauched instructions as forms of secret code, twilight language (sandhābhāṣya). They feel that it is important to make tantrism 'respectable'. Snellgrove, however, argues that the enigmatic or twilight language often functions to conceal the real nature of the sacramental objects used in tantric rites from the uninitiated. Flesh, sometimes human, was consumed, as was alcohol, and actual sexual intercourse was engaged in. Moreover, many tantric texts provide enigmatic instructions, in terms of cakras and nāḍī, on meeting sites for different tantric groups.[30] The likelihood is, then, that groups of yogins and yoginīs actually engaged in these tantric yoga rituals with all of their taboo features. Indeed, what better test is there of a person's abandonment of all dualistic perception?

**The sādhanā of the divya** is conducted in isolation, within the sphere of his/her own body and mind. Utilizing the notion that the universe is constructed holographically, the yogin works on his own body, vital energy (prāṇa) and mind to bring about the reintegration of the poles of existence. This entails the practice of haṭha or laya yoga. 'Haṭha' means 'force' and 'laya' means 'dissolution'.

The idea conveyed by the term 'haṭha' is that working on the physical body invigorates and directs or forces the vital energies in the body to awaken the creative power or śakti, who is regarded as being dormant and coiled at the base of the spine.[31] This power is thus often referred to as kuṇḍalinī (the coiled feminine one). The term 'laya' refers to the systematic dissolution of the various planes of existence until the realization of original unity is attained. In the body, these planes are represented by the cakras or lotuses found at various points on or in the subtle channel running the length of the spinal cord, the suṣumṇā nāḍī. The realization of unity occurs when the kuṇḍalinī reaches the 1,000-petalled lotus, the sahasrāra, at the top of the head and is reunited with Śiva.

This subtle physiology of cakras, nāḍīs and kuṇḍalinī represents a distinctive tantric development or concept, though a number of scholars have sought to trace them back to earlier ideas, even as far back as the *Atharvaveda*—so far without gaining agreement from many of their colleagues. There is certainly no mention of this scheme in any śruti text.[32] Whatever the prehistory of these ideas and practices the tantric movement in general (and therefore these ideas too) seems to have surfaced in Indian literature sometime around the fifth or sixth centuries CE or a little later.

The *Haṭha Yoga Pradīpikā* is one of a number of practical yoga manuals associated with a group called the nātha or kānphaṭa yogis. 'Nātha' means 'lord', hence the natha yogis are ideally those who have reached the enlightened state or who are on the path towards it. Kānphaṭa means 'split-eared', a sign of group membership.

The nātha movement started in Bengal, perhaps during the eleventh century CE, though many of their practices are straightforward tantra. The two most famous teachers of the movement were Matsyendranātha (also called Mīnanātha) and Gorakṣanātha (also called Gorakhnāth).[33]

It is clear that right from its inception the nātha movement had close connections with tantric Buddhism—now represented by just the Tibetan tradition and Japanese Shingon. In fact, there is a Bengali tradition that both Matsyendranātha and Gorakṣanātha were Buddhists and the names of both can be found in the Buddhist lists of siddhas (perfected ones).[34]

## Nātha Literature

In *Gorakhnath and the Kānphaṭa Yogīs* G.W. Briggs lists 47 works of the nātha school. Four of these have been translated into English. They are:

1. *The Gorakṣa Śataka.* This work has not been published independently but comprises ch. 14 of Briggs' book. He regards the *Śataka* as a fundamental text of the nātha yogins and dates it in the twelfth or thirteenth century.
2. *The Haṭha Yoga Pradīpikā (HYP).* This work is usually dated around the fifteenth century CE. The author was one Cintāmaṇi, who took the name Svātmarāma when he became a yogi. Quite a number of its verses are borrowed from the *Śataka.* It is also regarded as a work which reconciles haṭha and rāja (Patañjali's) yoga.
3. *The Gheraṇḍa Saṃhitā.* This text is shorter than the *HYP* and borrows from it. In general, its emphasis is more on health and personal hygiene than is the case with the *HYP.*
4. *The Śiva Saṃhitā.* This is the latest of the four texts and is quite Vedāntic in its orientation. That is, it attempts to explain haṭha yoga in terms that the orthodox (smārta) brāhmanical tradition could accept (or one might think of it as yet another example of a brāhmanical takeover). The early nāthas were regarded by the brāhmans as outcastes and their teachings as heterodox—hardly surprising given their Buddhist connections—though during the sixteenth century they were gradually assimilated into the orthodox fold and their teachings amended accordingly.

## The teachings of the *Haṭha Yoga Pradīpikā*

Whilst not the oldest work in its class the *HYP* has the merits of being both systematic, which the earlier works tended not to be, and relatively unaffected by the encroachment of orthodox philosophy. The underlying world view is typically tantric: the aim of the practice is to awaken the dormant kuṇḍalinī and reunite her with Śiva, the absolute plane of existence, in the sahasrāra cakra. The details of the practice can be divided into two sections: preparation and integration.

### PREPARATION

The preparatory activities are mainly those concerned with purifying the nāḍīs, the subtle channels along which the prāṇa or vital energy flows. In its ultimate sense, the prāṇa is simply a modification of the divine consciousness. However, its activities take the mind out into the world of objects by linking it with the senses. In its coarsest form, the prāṇa manifests as the breath. As long as it is active (and it is active so long as respiration is taking place) the mind is also active.

*HYP* 4.21-22 reads:

> By whom the breathing has been controlled, by him the activities of the mind have also been controlled; and conversely, by whom the activities of the mind have been controlled, by him the breathing also has been controlled.
>
> There are two causes of the activities of the mind: (1) vāsana (desires) and (2) prāṇa (respiration/vital energy). Of these, the destruction of the one is the destruction of both.[35]

According to this philosophy, in the state where the mind is active the true nature of consciousness and existence cannot be perceived. Such also is the teaching of the *Yoga Sūtra*. The *HYP*, in common with many tantric texts on yoga, adds the dimension of prāṇa to the scenario. Whereas Patañjali presumably assumes that the mind-control route is all that is needed, the *HYP* approaches the issue via prāṇa control. For this the prāṇa has to be taken from its passage around the body and into the suṣumṇā—an extremely demanding process. For this reason the tantric yogins developed a system of preliminary procedures to produce a state of mental and physical health capable of withstanding the stresses inherent in the advanced processes of prāṇa control—the precursors of modern postural yoga.

In the *HYP* the steps on the yoga path are the same as those in the *Yoga Sūtras*. Other haṭha yoga texts, however, provide a different breakdown. The *Gorakṣa Śataka*, for example, gives only six stages instead of eight, whilst Woodroffe claims that the practice of haṭha yoga is divided into seven parts: the six cleansings (ṣaṭ karmas), postures (āsana), gestures (mudrā), prāṇāyāma, pratyāhāra, dhyāna and samādhi. The ṣaṭ karmas, however, only need to be practised by those with an imbalance of the three humours. In the *HYP* the first two stages of yama and niyama are exclusively for the cleansing of the nāḍīs (1.17-18). The next two, āsana and prāṇayāma, along with their two sub-disciplines of mudrā (gestures) and bandha (locks) help to complete the process of cleansing and also begin to manipulate the prāṇa so as to get it to enter the suṣumṇā nāḍī and arouse the kuṇḍalinī energy. Woodroffe tells us that for the haṭha yogin, pratyāhāra (withdrawal of consciousness from externals), dhāraṇā (concentration), dhyāna (contemplation) and samādhi (absorption) are all merely progressions in prāṇāyama, referring to the length of time that the prāṇa is held in the suṣumṇā nāḍī. Thus, both yogas seek to accomplish the same task of 'citta vṛtti nirodha'—the cessation of the modification of mind (*YS* 1.2). Rāja yoga does this by controlling the mind directly and the prāṇa indirectly, whilst haṭha yoga controls the prāṇa directly and the mind indirectly.

It is clear that yama, niyama and āsana are primarily employed for cleaning the nāḍīs, as are the ṣaṭ karmas. Prāṇāyāma is part of the kuṇḍalinī rousing practice for, as pointed out in the *Gheraṇḍa Saṃhitā* (5.2), purification of the nāḍīs is a prerequisite for prāṇāyama. The *HYP*, however, suggests its use for cleaning out the nāḍīs (2.70), whilst the āsanas, mudrās and bandhas are employed for raising the kuṇḍalinī. What seems to be the case, then, is that yama, niyama and the ṣaṭ karmas are only used for purifying the nāḍīs whilst āsana and prāṇāyāma contribute both to this and to the arousal of kuṇḍalinī. Mantra, mudrā and bandha are accompaniments to the latter two. Mantra is an expression of the śakti in sound, which is only effective, however, when the mind of the sādhaka is 'awakened' (prabuddha) to it. This occurs when the practitioner (sādhaka) becomes aware of the forces and hence the sounds that constitute a particular form. As Woodroffe points out, kuṇḍalinī is both light (jyotrimayi) and mantra (mantramayi) and therefore mantra is used in rousing her.

Mudrās have a close affinity with āsanas and are performed for the same purpose: to gain control over the prāṇa. Bandhas also have the same purpose but are specific in blocking the flow of the vāyus/prāṇas to certain areas and hence forcing them to go to others. It could be argued, however, that all these are merely forms of prāṇāyāma (prāṇa control) which do not employ the direct manipulation of the breath for the attainment of this end. Nevertheless, the most common method of controlling the prāṇa is through the breath and it is this method that is called prāṇāyāma. Because breath and prāṇa are so intimately linked and since breath is probably the clearest manifestation of prāṇic activity at the gross level this is a natural starting point for one who wishes to control prāṇa. Here again we are reminded of the most fundamental correspondence in haṭha yoga: that between the physical and subtle realms. If this did not exist, the efficacy of haṭha yoga in terms of achieving its goal of liberation would be difficult to understand, though its practical benefits at the level of psychophysiology would remain.

Prāṇāyāma based on breathing can be divided into three stages: control of inspiration (puraka), control of retention (kumbhaka) and control of expiration (recaka). Of these three, says Eliade, the most important is the breathing retention, for it is this that actually arouses the kuṇḍalinī. Briggs tells us that in prāṇāyāma practice, inspiration, retention and expiration are required to be in strict ratio to each other. At the first level of practice, inspiration is performed for 12 recitations of the mantra Oṃ, held for 16 and expelled for 10. This practice causes perspiration. The second level requires inspiration for 24 recitations of Oṃ, retention for 32 and expulsion for 20. This causes trembling. For the third and final level of practice inspiration is for 36 recitations, retention for 48 and expulsion for 30; as a result there is a 'raising up' (of kuṇḍalinī). The *HYP* substitutes 'making the breath motionless' for raising up, but the idea is the same, as a study of 2.75–4.10 reveals.

## INTEGRATION

Once the kuṇḍalinī has been aroused and the prāṇa taken into the suṣumṇā the yogin experiences deep concentration and the life processes come to a virtual standstill. Furthermore, as *HYP* 4.12

informs us, in this experience the yogi is free from the effects of karmas. In commenting on this state John Woodroffe writes,

> There is one simple test whether the śakti is actually aroused. When she is aroused intense heat is felt at that spot but when she leaves a particular centre the part so left becomes as cold and apparently lifeless as a corpse. The progress upwards may thus be externally verified by others. When the śakti has reached the sahasrāra the whole body is cold and corpselike; except the top of the skull, where some warmth is felt.[36]

Merely raising the kuṇḍalinī and taking the prāṇas into the suṣumṇā does not constitute liberation, however. First of all, the yogin must be able to hold the prāṇas in the suṣumṇā for as long as he wishes. Woodroffe, quoting a commentary on *HYP* 2.12, states, 'If the prāṇa is retained for a particular time it is called pratyāhāra, if for a longer time it is called dhāraṇā and so on until samādhi is attained, which is equivalent to its retention for the longest period.'[37] This retention, however, is retention of the prāṇas (along with kuṇḍalinī) in the susumna and not merely retention of breath in the lungs. The different stages of concentration referred to in classical yoga are thus regarded as progressions of prāṇāyāma in haṭha yoga.

Nevertheless, stillness of mind and freedom from karmic effects do not constitute liberation; for this the yogin has to raise the kuṇḍalinī (and along with it the prāṇas) to the sahasrāra and be able to hold her there as long as he wills. To do this he must first pierce the cakras, each of which is a barrier to be overcome, especially the granthis (knots), where the power of māyā is particularly strong. Kuṇḍalinī is roused by a combination of āsana, mudrā, bandha, kumbhaka and mantra. For example, the *HYP* says that 'siddhāsana is the opener of the door to salvation' (1.37), and mahāmudrā, in conjunction with jālandhara bandha, is said to make the kuṇḍalinī become 'straight like a stick in the suṣumṇā (3.11). Kumbhaka should be performed in conjunction with the other methods. The mantra 'huṃ haṃsa' is used to rouse her and 'so'haṃ' to bring her down. This latter will only be used by jīvan-muktas, however, for until emancipation is gained the kuṇḍalinī has a natural tendency to return to the mūlādhāra.

At each cakra, a particular bliss is experienced and certain powers are gained. Also the cakras through which kuṇḍalinī passes on her upward journey become laya (dissolved); she recreates them only on her return. By constant practice of the yoga techniques for rousing kuṇḍalinī and uniting the prāṇas the yogin is able to pierce all the cakras and drink the divine nectar exuding from the sahasrāra. This is normally consumed by the digestive fire of samāna vāyu. The kecharī mudrā is expressly designed to prevent this downflow of the nectar and make it available to the yogin. If the yogin is unfortunate enough to die before he has succeeded in raising the kuṇḍalinī to the sahasrāra, his efforts are not in vain because he begins his next life still possessing the benefits he has gained. This makes sense because arousal of the kuṇḍalinī and piercing the cakras evokes a permanent change in the subtle body, and since it is this which transmigrates, the changes transmigrate along with it.

Another important feature of haṭha yoga is what I would call 'the other power' and is embodied in the guru. Initiation or dikṣa is a part of tantric practice which most schools regard as indispensable. S.B. Dasgupta, quoting from the *Kruja-saṃgraha-pañjīka*, tells us that 'The yogin who wishes to obtain the yogihood without proper initiation only darts a blow at the sky with fists and drinks the water of mirage.'[38]

The *HYP* claims that the guidance of the guru is essential (for example, see 1.14 and 2.1), and that the awakening of kuṇḍalinī is accomplished 'through the favour of the guru' (3.2). We also read in 4.9 that 'It is very difficult to get the condition of samādhi without the favour of a true guru.'

Other texts support this claim. For example, the *Gheraṇḍa Saṃhitā* 7.1 tells us that 'The samādhi is a great yoga; it is acquired by great good fortune. It is obtained through the grace and kindness of the guru, and by intense devotion to him.'

In the same vein the *Śiva Saṃhitā* 3.11 says, 'Only the knowledge imparted by a guru, through his lips, is powerful and useful; otherwise it becomes fruitless, weak and very painful.' And again, in 3.14, 'By guru's favour everything good relating to one's self is obtained. So the guru ought to be daily served; else there can be nothing auspicious.' And finally in 4.13, 'When the sleeping goddess kuṇḍalinī is awakened, though the grace of guru, then all the lotuses and the bonds are readily pierced through and through.'

The situation seems to be, then, that dikṣa is an essential prerequisite for effective haṭha yoga practice and that for dikṣa to take place a guru is needed. In defining a guru A. Bharati writes, 'A guru is one who has received dikṣa from one or more gurus, is capable of conferring and has actually conferred dikṣa on another person or persons.'[39]

Here there is a clear indication that dikṣa is necessary for salvation, and that a guru is necessary for dikṣa. If this is the case then liberation is not attainable by one's own efforts alone. Effort may be needed but it is of no use without the help of the guru. It is this position that is expounded in *Saraha's Treasury of Songs*,[40] where 14 of the 112 verses explicitly state the indispensability of the master. For example, in v.33 we read: 'How by meditation should one fondly gain release? And why accept such falsehood? Have confidence in the word of your good master. This is the advice that I Saraha give.'

Some writers, however, would not be prepared to make such a sweeping claim. Mohan Singh, for instance, argues that 'The true guru's aid (word) is indispensable for achieving what the followers of other paths achieve through difficult practices followed by constant self-abnegation and profound contemplation.'[41]

In the same vein Danielou writes, 'Knowledge which at great pains is gained through the patient practice of hatha yoga, may be experienced in a flash by the grace of a true guide.'[42]

Here self-accomplished liberation is accepted as being possible, although it is clear that this is an extremely difficult way and only for persons of great spirit, a view that echoes Kṛṣṇa's teaching in the *Bhagavad Gītā*.

Thus, an outline of this yoga would be as follows: the first thing to do is find a guru who will accept one as a disciple and bestow a formal initiation (probably a mantri dikṣa). Following this, the disciple should practice the haṭha yoga techniques and purify the nāḍīs. Then, at an appropriate time, the guru will enable the sādhaka to awaken the kuṇḍalinī and undertake the practice of laya yoga, which begins when kuṇḍalinī is roused and the prāṇas are taken into suṣumṇā; at this stage concentration proper begins and the sādhaka is able to attain samādhi. Constant laya practice should only be undertaken under the guidance of a guru. However, once the ājñā cakra (between the eyebrows) is reached the yogin is able to receive the direct command (ājñā) of the guru and thereafter carries on independently.

# Chapter 7
# MODERN YOGA

What is 'modern yoga', and how does it relate to 'traditional yoga'? Different writers offer different answers to these questions. DeMichelis uses the term 'modern yoga' to mean 'certain types of yoga that evolved mainly through the interaction of Western individuals interested in Indian Religions, and a number of more or less Westernized Indians over the last 150 years'.[1] She locates its origins in the latter half of the nineteenth century. At that time (1849), in the West, Henry David Thoreau, the American Transcendentalist, expressed a desire to practise yoga and admitted that he sometimes thought of himself as a yogi.[2] The letter that records these sentiments is taken by DeMichelis to be the earliest expression by a Westerner of a wish to practise yoga. A little later, in 1893, Swami Vivekananda spoke at the Chicago Parliament of Religions and was warmly received by Westerners with an interest in Indian spirituality. He stayed in the USA until 1897 and then returned for a brief visit in 1899. It was during this sojourn in the USA that two of his most influential works were published: *Karma Yoga* (1896) and *Rāja Yoga* (1896). The other two works in what became a quartet on yoga, *Jñāna Yoga* and *Bhakti Yoga,* did not, however, go to press until after his death in 1902.

The four forms of yoga outlined in these texts are frequently employed as organizing categories by contemporary writers who are seeking to map out the territory of yoga. Sometimes, one or more additional categories are attached to this fourfold scheme.[3] Initially, Vivekananda followed Keshubchandra Sen, one of the leaders of the Hindu renaissance, in connecting these four kinds of yoga with four kinds of religious person: the yogi or meditator (rāja yoga); the bhakta or devotee (bhakti yoga); the jñāni or philosopher (jñāna yoga), and the shebak or 'active servant of humanity' (karma yoga).[4] Most influential of Vivekananda's four books was *Rāja Yoga*, a text that has guided and confused Western yoga practitioners for over a hundred years. In this work, Vivekananda presents what DeMichelis calls 'three models of yoga': the prāṇa model, the samādhi model and the neo-advaitic model.[5] The first of these is rooted in Vedic ideas about vital energy (prāṇa) that were more or less discarded by medieval schools of Vedānta but resuscitated by tantrics, especially the practitioners of haṭha yoga. The second derives from Patañjali's teaching in the *Yoga Sūtras*, which has little or no place for vital energies, based as it is on non-prāṇic and, I would argue, non-Vedic Sāṃhkya teachings. Rather, the emphasis is on bringing the mind (citta) to a state of stillness—which Vivekananda accepts—so that the self (puruṣa) can perceive its fundamental difference from nature (prakṛti)—which he does not accept. Instead, Vivekananda contextualizes both models within a neo-advaitic framework not dissimilar to that formulated by Śaṅkara in the eighth century. These three models are fundamentally incompatible with each other, and all attempts to combine them that I am acquainted with end up being incoherent, which is one of the main reasons, I suggest, why students often find popular yoga philosophy confusing.

Vivekananda's works were widely disseminated in both India and the West. The ideas contained within them gave renewed confidence to Hindus about the value of their own spiritual heritage and a tantalizing hint to Westerners that the kind of direct spiritual experience so many of them were seeking might be available in practical form in 'ancient' Indian teachings about yoga. Moreover, his ideas may have had a pronounced influence on the founders of India's first two modern yoga centres: Manibhai Haribhai Desai (Sri Yogendra) and J.G. Gune (Swami Kuvalyananda) through their common guru, Paramhamsa Madhavadasji.[6] Sri Yogendra founded the Yoga Institute in 1918/19 and, a little later, in 1934, Swami Kuvalyananda established the Kaivalyadhama Yoga Ashram at Lonavla, mid-way between Bombay and Pune.[7]

The extent of Vivekananda's influence on these teachers is a matter of some dispute. According to Jayadeva Yogendra, 'son of the founder and current head of the Yoga Institute', Madhvadasji had been 'very receptive to the Swami's [Vivekananda's] message'.[8] J.S. Alter sees things rather differently. He claims that although Vivekananda and Sri Aurobindo 'had a profound influence on the intellectual history of modern India', they had little influence on either Yogendra or Kuvalyananda.[9] Whereas Vivekananda and Aurobindo addressed the intellectuals and propagated a spiritual and metaphysical yoga, Kuvalyananda and Yogendra made it available to 'the man in the world',[10] and sought to use it for health improvement. 'Yogendra and Kuvalyananda transformed the practice of yoga into a physiologically based form of physical education and attempted to turn it into a scientifically verifiable form of therapy.'[11] This change in orientation is, for Alter, the defining moment in the emergence of modern yoga. For the first time, the physical, worldly and health-promoting aspects of yoga were given priority over the mental, spiritual and liberation-promoting ones. The proliferation of modern forms of yoga, many developed by Westerners, can be seen to be rooted in this fundamental shift.[12] Moreover, it would be fair to say that in the West and, indeed, in much of modern India, a yoga class is generally understood to be concerned with physical movement, stretching and breathing first and with meditation, philosophy and spirituality only second.

What needs to be realized, however, is that spiritually oriented yoga did not fail to make the journey to the West; it just did so under other names. DeMichelis has constructed a fourfold typology of modern yoga that distinguishes between Modern Psychosomatic Yoga, Modern Denominational Yoga, Modern Postural Yoga and Modern Meditational Yoga, though she does point out that 'Modern Yoga types will and do overlap when observed in the field.'[13] The most important difference, in my view, is that between those forms of practice that are concerned primarily with the body, meditation perhaps being introduced as a practitioner advances, and those that emphasize mental culture, with perhaps some encouragement to undertake physical practices. Hence the really useful distinction is between Modern Postural Yoga (MPY) where the practitioner starts with āsana, etc. and maybe progresses to meditation, and Modern Meditational Yoga (MMY), where the emphasis from the outset is on the kinds of meditational practice that characterized earlier forms of yoga and may not even require any postural practice at all.

Within this simplified division, examples of Modern Postural Yoga traditions would be:

1. The Santa Cruz Yoga Institute
2. Kaivalyadhama at Lonavala
3. Sivananda and his disciples

4. Krishnamacharya-inspired groups such as those established by B.K.S. Iyengar, Pattabhi Jois and T.K.V. Desikachar
5. Dru Yoga
6. Kundalini Yoga (3HO).

Examples of Modern Meditational Yoga would be:

1. Transcendental Meditation (TM)
2. The Brahma Kumaris
3. Divine Light Mission
4. The International Society for Krishna Consciousness (ISKCON)
5. Sahaja Yoga
6. The Radha Soami Satsang (Sant Mat)
7. Various Buddhist groups.

These lists could be expanded considerably, since religious and quasi-religious groups such as these have a tendency to divide into branches as disciples set up their own centres and develop a distinctive version of the teaching, or disciples cannot agree on a successor when a master dies and a number of variants are established by leading figures in the group. Usually, each subdivision will seek to establish a line of transmission (paramparā) that guarantees the legitimacy of the teaching, a practice that goes back at least as far as the Upaniṣads.[14] Sometimes, however, a self-appointed teacher appears on the scene and establishes his (rarely her) own authority, as was the case with Bhagwan Shree Rajneesh (Osho).

To outline the history and teachings of all these groups and other forms of modern yoga would require a book in its own right and is beyond the scope of this chapter. I will, therefore, concentrate my comments on just two traditions of Modern Yoga that are firmly rooted in Indian traditions, encourage their students to engage in meditational practice alongside the postural work, and have had considerable influence on the understanding of yoga in the West. They straddle, therefore, the postural/meditational categories.

## THE TRADITION OF T. KRISHNAMACHARYA

Tirumalai Krishnamacharya (1888–1989) lived a life made extraordinary by the combination of two qualities that are only rarely found in a single person: a profound traditionalism and a radical creativity. Both revealed themselves early in his life and continued to inform it thereafter. As a young man, he studied, in accordance with his family's Śrī Vaiṣṇava heritage, at the Parakala Math in Mysore, where he learned Vedic grammar, Vedānta theology and Logic (nyāya). He was also instructed in āsanas (postures) at the Advaita Vedānta Math at Śringeri by Narasimha Bharati Swamigalavaroo.[15] After three years in Vārāṇasī (Benares), where he deepened his knowledge of the classic brāhmanic curriculum (1906–9), he returned to Mysore in order to study the texts of Śrī Vaiṣṇavism and gain qualifications in the study of the Vedas and of the Mīmāṃsā. In 1914 he returned to Vārāṇasī and enrolled at Queens College. The following year he qualified as an Upadhyāya (teacher). Subsequently, he obtained advanced qualifications in Mīmāṃsā, Nyāya, and the Vedas, as well as astrology and ayurveda.[16] He spoke fluent Sanskrit and a number of other Indian languages. A more traditional education would be hard to find, even in India. He was also scrupulous about observing the traditional brāhmanic rituals and regularly ran chanting groups with brāhman priests.[17] In 1924, after studying with a yogin in the Himālayas for over seven years, he returned to Mysore and was soon employed by the Mahārāja, Nalvadi Krishnaraja Wodeyar, as a yoga teacher. Later, he was given the old gymnastics hall in which to establish a yogaśālā (yoga school).[18]

Krishnamacharya's yoga teaching was not merely traditional, however, for he was also a visionary and an innovator. Whilst just 16 years of age he had a visionary experience of the Śrī Vaiṣṇava ācārya Nāthamuni reciting a text called the *Yogarahasya* (Secrets of Yoga or Essence of Yoga). He committed this to memory, as he did so many traditional texts, and later wrote it down in Telegu script (though the recitation was in Sanskrit). Exactly how long after the vision the written version was produced is not clear from the sources, though we do know that Krishnamacharya taught it to his son, T.K.V. Desikachar, during the years 1963–65.[19] As T.K.V. Desikachar points out, the *Yogarahasya* is an innovatory text, which emphasizes

> the importance of considering the uniqueness of the individual in prescribing practice—including such characteristics as age, sex, body type, and station in life. There is also a great deal of emphasis upon the need for, and the nature of, Yogic practice for pregnant women.[20]

Moreover, it introduces 'previously unknown techniques of *pranayama*', brings āsana and prāṇāyama together rather than developing them sequentially, and introduces, for the first time, the śirsāsana (headstand) and sarvāṅgāsana (shoulderstand) into yoga practice.[21] Dr V. Varadachari, who wrote the Introduction to T.K.V. Desikachar's English translation of the text, is in no doubt that Nāthamuni is the author. Others, including myself, are less confident, for a number of reasons.

In the first place, if this text was really composed by a figure as eminent as Nāthamuni and it contains such radical teachings, how could it not have been preserved? Secondly, many features of the teaching seem more compatible with the idea that Krishnamacharya himself was the author. If this were the case, the status of the text might be diminished in the eyes of many Indian students, though many Westerners would probably take that possibility as further evidence of Krishnamacharya's creative contribution to the development of yoga.

In favour of the view that the *Yogarahasya* was a product of Krishnamacharya's own (probably subconscious) mind is the likelihood, or lack of it, that the spirits of deceased persons exist in a form that enables them to communicate any kind of information (and particularly detailed, innovative information) to another person living hundreds of years after their demise—though this is, of course, a common belief among people of mediumistic persuasion such as 'channellers'.[22] There are also teachings in the *Yogarahasya* that link specifically with Krishnamacharya's own life and times. N.E. Sjoman has argued that 'there is no continuous tradition of [āsana] practice that can be traced back to the texts on yoga',[23] and that therefore many of the āsanas, prāṇāyāmas and principles of movement taught by Krishnamacharya were created by him. Some āsanas he had been taught by Sri Narasimha Bharati Swamigalavaroo of the Advaita Vedanta Math at Sringeri;[24] others, suggests Sjoman, he developed from positions and movements used in exercise halls (vyāyāmaśālā), especially by wrestlers. A text on gymnastic exercises, the *Vyayamadipika*, by S. Bharadwaj,[25] acknowledges the help of Veeranna, Nalvadi Krishnaraja Wodeyar's gymnastics teacher from 1892 to 1901. It describes, in ch. 2, a series of danda exercises which 'appear to be the foundation for Krishnamachariar's vinyāsas'.[26] This text, unlike most earlier Indian works on exercise, stresses its therapeutic rather than its strengthening benefits, a characteristic it shares with Krishnamacharya's teachings on yoga. Another text on wrestling, the *Mallapurāṇa*, describes the śīrṣāsana (headstand), another of Krishnamacharya's innovations in yoga. These references suggest that Krishnamacharya recognized the therapeutic benefits of various wrestling practices and incorporated them into his yoga. Since he could not trace them to an earlier yoga text he incorporated them into the work that he had previously learned via spiritual revelation.

Awareness of these possible sources of influence on Krishnamacharya in no way detracts from his creative genius. All great artists use existing materials to some extent, and Krishnamacharya was doing no more than this, albeit in a manner consistent with the Indian approach to establishing the validity of a teaching: identifying it in earlier established tradition. In the absence of such a tradition the innovator has to work with whatever is available, and if that is a vision-inspired text, then so be it.

Not all of Krishnamacharya's innovations related to practice, however. Some of them were profoundly social and, to the modern eye, perceptively enlightened. As his son T.K.V. Desikachar reflects,

> He dismayed relatives and neighbours by doing the most menial chores, unthinkable for a high-caste Brahmin, such as chopping wood and washing his own clothes... even in the most conservative period in his life, Krishnamacharya had no use for castes.[27]

Here, then, we have the kernel of a truly modern yoga: available to all, regardless of age, sex, nationality and social status; emphasizing health and well-being; grounded in physical practice (āsana, prāṇāyāma, etc.) yet drawing inspiration from ancient yoga texts that focus on meditation and spirituality.

On this basis, Krishnamacharya's students took his yoga to other countries and made it international. They did not, however, simply pass on what they had learned. In the spirit of Krishnamacharya's own approach to the teaching of yoga, which adapted it to the needs of each individual, his internationalist students adapted it according to their own perceptions of what their students needed. B.K.S. Iyengar put greater emphasis on the attainment of perfect posture and holding postures for extended periods of time, eliminating the continuous movement sequences built up through vinyāsas.[28] Pattabhi Jois, in some respects, went in the opposite direction. He grouped the āsanas, along with their vinyāsas, into three series of increasing difficulty. Continuity and fluidity between one movement and the next is central to this approach. Krishnamacharya's own approach has been continued and is still being developed by his son, T.K.V. Desikachar, and his grandson, K. Desikachar, who are based at the Krishnamacharya Healing and Yoga Foundation (formerly the Krishnamacharya Yoga Mandiram), Chennai, India.

According to Gill Lloyd, one of Desikachar's senior teachers in Britain, and co-founder of Yoga Journey, an organization established to make this tradition more widely available in the UK, there are a number of features that make the Krishnamacharya/Desikachar approach to yoga distinctive. First of all, the needs and outlook of the individual student are primary. Most work in this tradition is conducted on a one-to-one basis. Yoga classes are points of contact rather than primary vehicles for teaching, though they do have a value for beginner students. Secondly, all work, whether āsana, prāṇāyāma or mantra (Vedic chanting), is approached in a graduated and sequenced manner (vinyāsa krama). Each key posture is prepared for through the performance of easier postures, and after the key posture has been achieved subsequent postures, including counterposes, gently bring the body back into balance. Students are taught to perform all postures without tension and that they can be modified to meet individual requirements.

The one-to-one approach helps to ensure that a student's sequence contains an appropriate balance between the various key elements that might make up a practice. These are āsana, prāṇāyāma, vedavam (Vedic chanting) and attentional focusing (meditation). For non-religious students Vedic chanting could be omitted altogether and the foci for meditation just parts of the body or images from nature. For the more religious, images from a student's own tradition might be used, e.g. Jesus for a Christian, Buddha for a Buddhist, and so on. T.K.V. Desikachar does not require any particular religious commitment and is not himself formally involved with any religious group, though, as is clear from his writings, he does have a personal spirituality.

For Gill, it is also important that these teachings are rooted in a householder tradition of yoga. To fully support students who are householders, teachers need to understand the nature of householder life and the kinds of challenges it brings. She put it like this:

> Working within a householder tradition is comforting to a Westerner like me, as my teachers have had similar experiences to my own; whereas I wonder whether a teacher from a monastic tradition, however sympathetic, can really identify with a householder's problems and concerns.

Students are also encouraged to study texts on yoga, particularly Patañjali's *Yoga Sūtra*, the *Yogarahasya*, the *Yogayajñavalkya Saṃhitā*[29] and the Upaniṣads of the *Black Yajurveda*.[30] The *Yoga Sūtras* are learned by heart by most of the serious students in this tradition, and other key texts are approached in a similar manner according to the student's inclinations and capacities. In this tradition we have what its practitioners regard as a truly modern yoga with roots that go deep into the history and philosophy of the yogic way of life.

## THE ŚIVĀNANDA TRADITION

Swami Śivānanda entered this world in 1887 and departed from it in 1963. His family lived in Pattamedai, Tamil Nadu and bequeathed to him the name Kuppuswami Iyer. From an early age he showed himself to be accomplished in body and in mind: a good gymnast and a good scholar. After training as a doctor at the Tanjore Medical Institute he accepted an offer to work in Malaya. As this involved travelling over the sea it was deemed to be polluting for brāhmans such as himself. Undeterred by such views, he told his family that those rules did not apply to the modern world, and that such conventions should be subordinated to the requirement for service.[31] At an earlier time he had also drawn criticism from other brāhmans for taking fencing lessons from an untouchable teacher.[32] Now he was crossing the polluting sea. In Malaya, he and his cook ate their meals together and he gained a reputation for treating everyone alike.[33] Here was a young man who was thinking for himself, and here we see the beginnings of his iconoclastic approach to the spiritual life.

It was whilst in Malaya that the young doctor Kuppuswami began reading spiritual books, practising yoga and reflecting on suffering (presented to him every day in the lives of his patients and the local poor). With the aid of a few books, he started to practise the śirsāsana (headstand) and other important yoga postures.[34] Later, he began to study theosophical writings and the work of Swamis Ram Tirtha and Vivekananda. Eventually, in 1923, he returned to India and, by stages, he made his way northwards to Rishikesh. In May of the following year he was initiated into the daśanāmi order of Śaṅkarācārya by Swami Viśvānanda Sarasvatī of the Śringeri Math, the viraja homa rite being performed by Swami Vishnudevananda at the Kailash ashram.[35] The name given him on initiation was Swami Śivānanda. The daśanāmi are a monastic order and require the adoption of a sannyāsi lifestyle. This, Śivānanda felt, was quite appropriate. As he wrote in his autobiography, 'When there is a change of heart there should be a change of the external form also... Only a real sannyāsin can cut off all the connections and ties and completely get rid of attachment.'[36]

For Śivānanda, the cultivation of detachment (vairāgya) was a crucial component of a sannyāsi's spiritual life. Some of the reminders he wrote in his pocket book reveal just how rigorously he applied the advaita (non-dual) philosophy to his everyday life:

1. Serve bhangis (scavangers).
2. Serve rogues.
3. Serve inferiors.
4. Eat from Muhammedan's hands.
5. Remove faecal matter.
6. Clean clothes of sadhus. Take delight.
7. Carry water.[37]

All of these were deemed to be polluting by traditional brāhmanical conventions.

Throughout this period and for most of the rest of his life, Śivānanda practised āsana and prāṇāyāma as well as aerobic activities such as running, again, something that swamis were not expected to do.[38] By the late 1920s the young sannyāsi was beginning to attract disciples of his own. Like himself, he encouraged them to be active and to live a life of service to others rather than one of pure renunciation and contemplation. He also gave his talks and wrote his books in English, once more attracting criticism from the orthodox. Moreover, he sang, danced, led continuous chanting sessions and gave demonstrations of āsanas and prāṇāyāma—all highly unusual for advaitic sannyāsis.[39] Despite his unorthodox behaviour, or perhaps because people saw a genuine freedom in it, he continued to attract students and disciples.

His desire to disseminate his teachings and that of his disciples to be near him led, in the 1930s, to a number of significant institutional developments. First, there was the founding of the Swarg Ashram Sadhu Sangha in 1933; this developed into the Divine Life Trust Society in 1936, which, in 1939, became the Divine Life Society.[40] Membership of the Society was free and open to anyone 'who is eager to have Self-realisation, who practises ahimsa, satyam and brahmacharya'.[41] Secondly, Śivānanda acquired a four-room cottage for him and four of his disciples, Swamis Paramananda, Krishnānanda, Yogi Nārāyan and Swarna Giri. This grew by stages as new disciples came along and built their own cottages on land granted by the Mahārāja of Tehri Garhwal. This formed the nucleus of what eventually became the Śivānanda Ashram and Śivānanda Nāgar (city).

By the early 1940s, Śivānanda was sending his disciples all over India to spread the message of what would come to be known as Integral Yoga. In 1947 he described the devout disciple as

> noble, gentle and soft... He mixes with all, serves all and loves all. He sings the Lord's names. He does kirtan. He is very efficient in doing service. He is an adept in karma yoga... He does japa and meditation. He practises asanas and pranayama, bandhas and mudras. He practises the yoga of synthesis... karma, bhakti, yoga and jnana are inseparable for him. He is a bhakta, yogi and jnani.[42]

Aspirants would go to him for training in kuṇḍalinī yoga and find themselves serving the old and the sick alongside their lessons in āsana, and so on. For Śivānanda, purity of heart came before the awakening of the kuṇḍalinī.[43] At one point, he initiated a laughing competition with Swami Venkatesananda in order to cheer up the ashram residents. He also broke the traditional swami mould for handling money, bowing to other people and wearing an overcoat in winter rather than the conventional woollen blanket—all of which attracted criticism from the orthodox.[44]

Śivānanda's practicality and liberal attitude were not entirely due to his personality, however. They are all consistent expressions of the advaita philosophy to which he subscribed. This can be seen most clearly in his attitude to money: the supply comes from the Source and returns to the Source. Indeed, his generosity frequently created financial crises for the ashram's administrators, some of whom took to calling him 'Swami Givananda'.[45] This indifference to money, rare among the religious—who usually manage to slip some kind of collection box into situations, is nicely illustrated in the story of a burglar who stole a number of the ashram's silver vessels from a room full of sleeping people. When informed about the event, Śivānanda said 'He must be a very clever thief. If he is found, I'll award him the title "Chora Shikamani" (which means an expert in stealing).'[46]

From the 1930s onwards, Śivānanda's teachings started to reach the West, first in Latvia, then Estonia, the Scandanavian countries and eventually throughout Western Europe and beyond. Before the outbreak of the Second World War they were being disseminated as far afield as Mexico, various African countries and the Middle and Far East. After the war Swami Satchidananda was sent to Sri Lanka (formerly Ceylon) and then to the USA; Swami Venkatesananda to Australia and then south Africa; whilst Swami Cidananda travelled widely around the Far East before becoming president of the Divine Life Society, branches of which were established across the world.[47] At home, Śivānanda established the Saraswathi Sanskrit Vidaya in 1944 in order to help students read the Vedāntic scriptures in the original. Linked to this was the establishment of the Yoga Vedānta Forest Acadamy, to prepare students to become sadhus and saints. There, they studied kuṇḍalinī yoga, Vedānta and the six astika darśanas.[48] In 1951 it acquired its own press for the publication of works on yoga and spirituality.

In keeping with his medical background and emphasis on service, Śivānanda established, in 1950, annual eye camps where poor people could be helped with eyesight problems. In 1957, with a benefaction from a wealthy student, a permanent Eye Hospital was opened at Śivānanda Nāgar. When medical people with other specialities arrived Śivānanda would announce Relief Camps, where they could turn their expertise into service for the needy. This, in turn, led to the creation of a health education programme. Books and journals were published, classes were organized and yoga āsanas were taught for their therapeutic and health-giving benefits. For Śivānanda, 'Health is at the basis of all achievement', whether worldly or spiritual.[49] Hence he began, in the 1930s, to publish practical books on yogic exercises. Typical titles are *Yoga in Daily Life, Easy Steps to Yoga, Yoga Asanas* and *Yogic Home Exercises.*

> Till then, asanas, pranayama, etc., had only been dealt with in their yogic aspect as angas (limbs) of Patanjali Maharishi's astanga yoga. Now, thanks to the rational approach set up by Swamiji's books, asanas and allied exercises have come to be accepted as a safe means of getting and keeping good health and a sound, diseaseless physique.[50]

The Divine Life Society's *Śivānanda, Biography of a Modern Sage* contains some interesting photographs of Śivānanda practising āsanas in later life. None of them could be described as a 'perfect posture'. For him, it seems, the doing was more important than the showing.[51]

As his organization expanded, Śivānanda began to bestow sannyāsa initiation on almost everyone who asked for it, whether they were young or old, male or female, Indian or foreign. He even bestowed initiation through the mail. This too was criticized by the traditionalists, not least because many of those new sannyāsins either failed to maintain their vows or took to the householder life. Even these, said Śivānanda, are worthy of veneration.

> For, at least one day they were sannyasins. They had the courage to throw up their hands and say 'I renounce the pleasures of the three worlds.' They had the boldness and daring to stand up against the greatest forces of nature, the forces that maintain this samsara—those of self-preservation and procreation.[52]

For Śivānanda, sannyāsa was not a fixed ideal accessible to just a select few but a goal that could be reached via a number of stages. As Paramhamsa Niranjananda explains, the 'modern' principles of sannyāsa, i.e. those instigated by Śivānanda and his disciples, differ considerably from the traditional rules.

TRADITIONAL

- Sannyāsins should shun karma in order to achieve mokṣa.
- All contact with women is to be avoided to the extent that even looking at, thinking about or talking about women is taboo.
- Eligibility for sannyāsa is restricted to those who are born in the brāhman caste.
- Women are prohibited from entering the order.

MODERN

- The aim of sannyāsa is to discover yourself and to establish your own independence in life.
- Sannyāsa is a way of life which promotes physical, emotional, mental, psychic and spiritual well-being.
- Sannyāsa is not confined to any religious or socio-political identity.
- Sannyāsa life is total involvement in ceaseless service, relinquishing all the fruits of action.
- Sannyāsa does not mean expecting maintenance by the society without contributing anything worthwhile in return, which amounts to living on the allowance provided for the unemployed.
- By devotion to service, meditation and study, the sannyāsin becomes a model and inspiration for others within the society.
- By establishing viveka (discrimination) and vairāgya (detachment), the sannyāsin cultivates tyaga (renunciation), internally as well as externally.
- Without depending on dogmas or doctrines, the sannyāsin attunes him/herself with the spirit within, which is divine.
- As the divinity develops within him/her, the sannyāsin becomes more powerful for the good of others.
- The sannyāsin shows through his life that religion is not mere words; it means spiritual realization, communion with God.
- Only those sannyāsins who attain spiritual realization can communicate it to others. They alone are the beacons of light.[53]

The dissemination of this new vision of sannyāsa was facilitated by the teaching that there are seven varieties of it:

1. *Jigyasu*—for young, unmarried people who are living in the world;
2. *Karma*—for householders;
3. *Gurukul*—intermittent sannyāsa, motivated by the desire to be near to and emulate the guru;
4. *Jnana-Vairagya* (rishi)—for the person who has a natural disinclination to adopt worldly values but who prefers to live in the world rather than in an ashram;

5. *Vairagya*—those who devote their entire life to their personal sadhana (practice) and the dissemination of their guru's teachings;
6. *Paramahamsa*—total dedication to sadhana, usually after many years of service to the guru;
7. *Pakhand*—a false sannyāsa. Such people take on the outward appearance of a sannyāsin but without the inner aspiration. This can occur because of setbacks in life, disappointment in love or some other great loss. Some of these false sannyāsins are just in it for what they can get out of people.[54]

By their fruits shall ye know them! Genuine aspirants can now, therefore, take a sannyāsa initiation that is appropriate for their situation and 'upgrade' it, so to speak, as their life evolves.

In 1956, Swami Satyānanda, perhaps the most well-known of Śivānanda's disciples, was told by his guru to find a mission for himself.[55] Since then he has founded the International Yoga Fellowship (1962), the Bihar School of Yoga (1964), the Śivānanda Math (1984) and the Yoga Research Foundation (1984). More than any other swami, he has been an advocate of admitting women into sannyāsa. Indeed, as Swami Niranjānanda points out, he claimed that

> one of the most important reasons for the success of his work was the introduction of female sannyasis into the movement. He did not mean that men are useless; they have their own place. But in the scheme of creation, he believed that women were superior.[56]

Śivānanda's chief disciples are all initiates into the daśanāmi order and their advaitic philosophy provides them with a common foundation for their teachings. At the same time, Śivānanda's integral approach to the spiritual life allows each of them to develop their own emphasis. Swami Satyānanda put great energy into developing the practice of āsana, prāṇāyāma, etc. and promoted a range of tantric practices. The Bihar school is probably the most haṭha and tantra oriented of all the Śivānanda traditions. By contrast, Swami Oṃkārānanda, who was sent to Europe by Śivānanda and has centres in Austria and Switzerland as well as in Rishikesh, emphasizes bhakti and karma yoga. Haṭha yoga is rarely promoted in his teachings, though many of his Western disciples are, in fact, practising yoga teachers.[57] Where Śivānanda channelled his service through medical work Oṃkārānanda emphasizes community education. For the Bihar school 'The most important karma yoga for the karma sannyasin is teaching yoga... [and] conducting classes on yoga for their community members.'[58] For Oṃkārānanda's students this is an optional extra. The impression I gained when interviewing one of them, Swami Vivekānanda Mā (Val Davies), for this book was of a tradition that holds its members in a loose yet supportive embrace. They are encouraged, as was Satyānanda, to find their own mission in life. They can choose the forms of practice that suit them best and progress to higher levels of sannyāsa commitment at a speed that matches their lifestyle. Guidance and support is available whenever required. Swami Vivekananda Mā has an immediate, local mentor in Swami Satchidānanda Mā (formerly Patricia Wissett-Warner), who introduced her to the tradition, as well as direct access to Oṃkārānanda's ashram, which she can visit at any time.[59]

We see, then, in the traditions of Krishnamacharya and Śivānanda, some radical transformations in the way that yoga is understood and the role it can play in people's lives. Access has been widened, traditional barriers have been eroded (particularly as they relate to social status/caste, gender and country of origin). Yoga is for being in the world as well as taking one out of it. The monastic, renunciant life is still regarded as the ideal in the Śivānanda tradition whilst Krishnamacharya's lineages continue to stress the value of householdership. Despite such differences, both these branches of the yoga tree can be seen to have initiated quite significant changes in the way that yoga is understood and practised. It is these changes that make their yoga teaching truly 'modern'.

# Chapter 8
# SOME REFLECTIONS ON THE PSYCHOLOGY OF YOGA

Reflecting on the manifestations of yoga outlined in the preceding chapters, the student of yogic traditions soon becomes aware of an interesting asymmetry. Yoga meditation, whether grounded in the Buddhist eightfold path, the sixfold yoga of the *Maitrī Upaniṣad*, the eightfold yoga of Patañjali or one of the forms of haṭha yoga, tends to involve the meditator in very similar kinds of activities. On the other hand, the descriptions of human nature and the structure of the cosmos that are based on such experiences are often very different and frequently incompatible with each other. How is it that people who engage in similar practices can arrive at such different positions on these matters? The traditional approach is to look for sources of error in the practices or reasoning of dissenters from one's own view/conviction, much as we saw the Buddha doing in the Introduction to this work. Here, I want to approach the issue in a rather different way.

If we seek the one right view or teaching among incompatible teachings, then when we have found it the others must inevitably be wrong. If the Buddha is right, Patañjali must be wrong; if the nātha yogis are right, the author(s) of the *Maitrī Upaniṣad* must be wrong. Of course all these teachings may be wrong and the truth may actually lie in Christianity, or Islam or Judaism or Zoroastrianism. How could one know? Where would we find the criteria to judge that the monists are right and the pluralists wrong or vice versa? The fact of the matter seems to be that we have no way to access such criteria. This plurality of teachings, each of which claims authority for its views, therefore constitutes a major challenge for anyone who recognizes that each of these traditions contains wisdom within it and is unwilling to follow the fundamentalist in consigning all but one's own to the dustbin of error. For such a person, the following questions will arise at some point: 'What if *all* of these versions of "the truth" are wrong? Does that mean the traditions are valueless?' My own answer is that value need not always entail truth. Indeed, psychologist Shelly Taylor has offered persuasive reasons for thinking that human beings can actually benefit from the construction of what she calls 'positive illusions'. Teachings need not necessarily be 'true' in order to facilitate human flourishing.

In her influential study of mental health, Marie Jahoda argued that it involves more than an absence of mental illness, more than normality and more than a sense of well-being.[1] She also provided an account of the constituents of this 'more', an account which has received substantial support from subsequent researchers. A mentally healthy person exhibits:

> a positive view of the self, the ability to be happy or contented, the ability to care for and about others, the capacity for productive and creative work, and the ability to grow and achieve within the context of a challenging and sometimes threatening environment.[2]

For those involved in mental health promotion the operationalization of these components has been a significant challenge. One problem has been that different researchers define mental health in different ways. In 1993 Daniel Batson and Larry Ventis identified seven broad approaches to mental health in the literature:

1. absence of mental illness;
2. appropriate social behaviour;
3. freedom from worry and guilt;
4. personal competence and control;
5. self-acceptance/self-actualization;
6. personality unification and organization, and
7. open-mindedness and flexibility.

Clearly, any notion of optimum mental health will need to find space for all of these features and offer methods for their realization. The best model that I know of in terms of mapping the territory of optimum functioning has been developed by my wife, Lynn Holly Connolly. She calls it 'The Eight Limbs of Human Flourishing'. Schematically, it can be represented as follows:

1. **Mental and behavioural flexibility** is coping effectively with expected and unexpected changes in life. In particular, it has to do with how well one copes when things run counter to one's expectations. Sometimes this involves being able to accept things; sometimes it involves 'reframing'—attaching meanings to situations that are different from those originally employed to make sense of events.

2. The kernel of **self-belief/self-esteem** is the acceptance of oneself as one is, recognizing that one is a person of value who shares a common humanity with all other human beings.

3. **Enabling beliefs** are ones which empower oneself and others; thoughts and beliefs which facilitate success—both in terms of creating positive mental and emotional states within oneself and in terms of being effective in the world.

4. There are two primary facets to having **purpose and direction in life.** The first is having goals to aim for, things that motivate one to act; being 'future orientated'. The second is having a feeling of

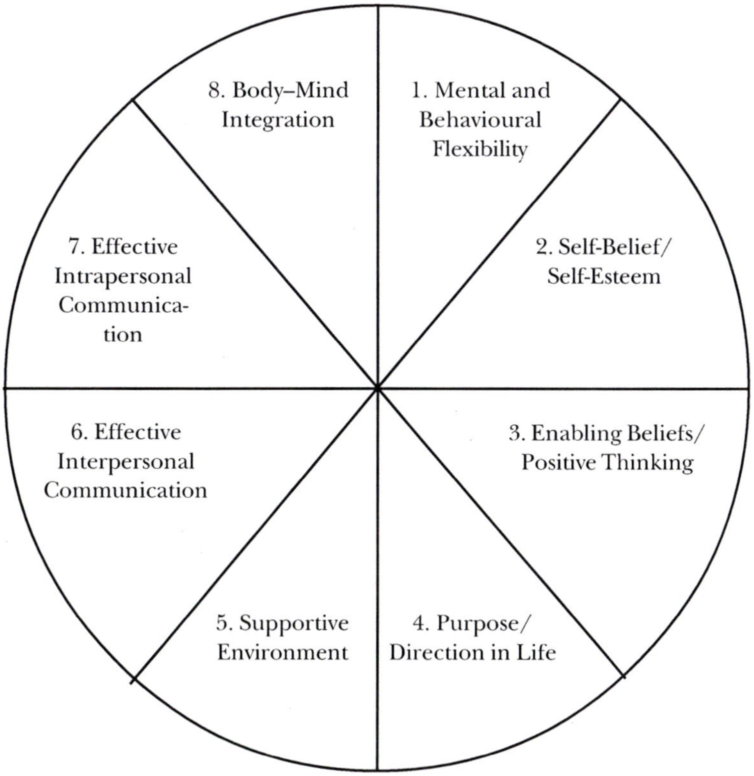

being part of something bigger than oneself, a community, a noble cause or a religion for example.

5. **A supportive environment** is one that we create to meet our needs, obviously varying with the nature of our goals.

6. **Effective interpersonal communication** involves having the ability to communicate congruently with people, that is, being able to convey the same message through all channels: body language, voice quality and words, when it is appropriate to do so. It also involves being receptive to feedback from those with whom one is communicating and having the ability to adapt one's behaviour accordingly.

7. **Effective intrapersonal communication** is essentially what has been called emotional intelligence: learning to understand the messages that our emotions are sending us and managing them effectively.

8. **Body–mind integration** involves being responsive to messages from your body and recognizing that you are your body and your body is you. It also involves knowing how to use your body to change your mental and emotional states.

The beauty of this model is that all of its eight components are learnable and teachable; so, like many yoga teachings, it offers not just a map, it is also a programme for personal development. With regard to yoga, we may note that people who are recognized as spiritually advanced often exhibit many or all of these characteristics.

It is also worth noting that there is no mention of an accurate perception or conception of reality in this model, nor in the summary of Jahoda's account mentioned earlier. Many psychotherapists, particularly those of psychoanalytic persuasion, have argued that this should be a primary aim of therapy and is a significant indicator of mental health. We may also recall that seeing the world as it really is (yathābhutam) lies at the heart of the Buddha's enlightenment experience. Indeed, Jahoda did emphasize this component in her survey and, more recently, so too has Robin Skynner. This probably reflects the influence of his early training in psychodynamic psychotherapy, not least because in the same work where he states that the central idea he can't repeat too often is that 'if we can stay in touch with reality, the truth will heal us',[3] he offers Japanese social organization as an example of one way of promoting mental health. Yet, by his own admission, 'For the Japanese, reality is negotiable... because they value cohesion above any other quality, the Japanese are not interested in finding an accurate view of reality; they want a formula that everyone can agree on.'[4] Reality distortion may, then, have beneficial effects.

Recent research supports this conclusion and points to the need to reject accurate reality testing as a central criterion for mental health. Indeed, the people who seem to have the most accurate understandings of themselves and their situation in the world are depressives.[5] The most mentally healthy actually display a positive talent for self-deception, particularly in terms of flattering perceptions of the self, illusions about the extent of their control over their lives and an unrealistic optimism about the future. This is not to say that the healthy fail to perceive things accurately, for they are quite good at perceiving the nature of both physical and social situations. Rather, it is to note that such perceptions are far less salient for them than for depressives. In other words, the healthiest people seem to be able to operate accurate and illusory conceptions of the world in parallel.

The reason why this ability helps to promote mental health is, according to John Schumaker, that the generally accurate perception of reality made available to us by our developed cognitive abilities (for example, the recognition of the inevitability of death) can be debilitating. Human beings require, therefore, something to counterbalance the sense of powerlessness, meaninglessness and futility that an accurate understanding of our existence can generate. This something, suggests Schumaker, is our capacity for reality distortion. Religion, in his view, is the traditional method employed by cultures to distort reality in a way that is deemed to be beneficial—by the promotion of meanings and values for example. It succeeds in this because of the brain's capacity for dissociation, the capacity to run different programs at different times and even in parallel.[6]

Reality distortion is not, however, always beneficial. Individuals and cultures can create negative illusions almost as easily as they can create positive ones. What is more, illusions seem to be more potent when they are given objective status, when they are taken to be realities. This, I would suggest, is exactly what we find when we examine human conceptions of value, meaning and the sacred. In contrast with the long-standing, dominant tradition of moral objectivism in Western ethical philosophy the main thrust of meta-ethical enquiry in the twentieth century has been to establish that moral principles are invented rather than discovered.[7] Likewise, recent psychological investigations into the attribution of meaning to situations and events suggest that it is constructive rather than perceptual in character[8] and Schumaker's *The Corruption of Reality: A Unified Theory of Religion, Hypnosis and Psychopathology* (1995), presents a strong case for understanding conceptions of the sacred in the same way.

From the pragmatic perspective of assessing their contribution to mental health or human flourishing, value systems, meaning systems and religious systems would all seem to be on a par. They are often attributed with objective status though there are good reasons for thinking that they are all illusions, constructed by human minds with the aim of benefiting human lives. Whether they do so is a matter for well-constructed empirical enquiries to determine. To paraphrase one well-known religious teacher, 'By their fruits shall ye know them.' In advance of such enquiries being undertaken my personal strategy for 'fruit testing' is to ask of any value, meaning or religious system whether it contributes to the development of the eight limbs of human flourishing outlined above.

From this perspective, yoga traditions offer us examples of illusory accounts of reality which have the potential to promote optimum mental health. From the perspective of the meditators, however, things surely seem quite different. The confidence with which yoga practitioners present their accounts of human nature and the cosmos suggests that their experiences have led them to think that those accounts are accurate. How can intelligent people come to believe, on the basis of meditative experience, that inaccurate accounts are, in fact, accurate? And some of them must be inaccurate since they are incompatible with each other. The answer, I would suggest, lies in the nature of trance and the relationship between yogic experience and trance experience.

Given that yoga students and readers of this book know a good deal about yoga and probably a good deal less about trance, I will begin by outlining the nature of trance states and suggest that when properly understood they can be seen to be extremely valuable to human well-being if they are employed skilfully. Then I will draw a number of parallels between states of yogic meditation and states of trance, suggesting that the former are probably best understood as a sub-category of the latter.

Let us begin by considering some popular misconceptions about trance. The image that comes to the minds of many people when the word 'trance' is mentioned is of individuals in a zombie-like state who are not in control of themselves and/or confused. Such individuals are probably thought of as being under the control of some kind of evil hypnotist and being unaware of the external environment to such an extent that they are unable to recognize their friends and family. If I thought about trance in this kind of way, I would think of it as a rather unsavoury subject and certainly not as something that could be highly beneficial for people. That view, however, is a misconception that has been propagated by works of fiction, sensationalistic journalism and the movie industry. Here I shall present a different, more accurate and altogether more attractive picture of trance.

Robin Skynner and John Cleese, in their best-selling book *Life and How to Survive It,* distinguish between what they call 'open mode' and 'closed mode'. These modes are what Skynner calls 'two different ways of relating to the world'. The open mode is essentially a fluid and receptive frame of mind that is not action-oriented. We do not initiate and carry out planned actions in the open mode. Rather, it is a receptive and relaxed condition. Skynner describes it as 'the mode we're in when we open ourselves up to the world, take in new information, and let it change our internal maps'.[9]

By contrast, the closed mode arises when some particular action has to be taken. So, temporarily, we narrow our focus and stop taking in all the information around us.

Access to both modes is necessary if we are going to function effectively in the world for any length of time. However, most of us are less adept at switching from one mode to the other than we could be. Moving from open to closed mode is not too difficult for most people. If a child falls over or a light bulb fails or if the time has come for us to get down to work we slip into closed mode almost automatically, tensing those muscles that will enable us to carry out the appropriate action. Moving the other way can often prove more difficult, however. As John Cleese puts it,

> Once I'm focused and directed, and experiencing the slight but pleasurable anxiety you get when you're 'getting on with things', but also feeling some time pressure, I tend to run on like that for the rest of the day, even if I really need to stop and take a wider view of what I'm doing...[10]

Most of Skynner and Cleese's discussion is about the role of humour in shifting us out of the closed mode and into the open one, but they do make one or two comments that are significant for anyone with an interest in trance. Skynner says that the postural changes associated with emotions like awe and wonder can shift us from closed to open mode, as can the experiences of bewilderment and confusion, 'if we can avoid reacting to them with anxiety'.[11] Of course, evoking emotions or creating confusion (both, incidentally, classic ways of inducing a trance state) are *indirect* ways of influencing changes in posture and muscle tension. One can also approach these *directly*, through physical activities such as bouncing on a trampoline, swimming or doing yoga.

Hypnotherapist Stephen Gilligan makes similar remarks about the nature of trance. He distinguishes between what he calls conscious and unconscious processing or the conscious and the unconscious mind. The conscious mind, he suggests, is lineal in orientation and is the domain of roles, sensory-motor cybernetic loops, goal-achieving plans, scripts, strategies, structures and rationality. It is a manager or a regulator and is primarily conservative rather than generative in nature. It can allow ideas emerging from the unconscious to be implemented in behaviour or it can veto them. This power of veto enables the conscious mind to ensure that implemented ideas conform to the frame or map of the world with which it is operating. The conscious mind, says Gilligan, arises from and is maintained by muscular tension patterns, and it is usually accompanied by discontinuous, arrhythmic movements. It lacks the kind of holistic quality of the unconscious mind because conscious attention is highly selective, directed as it is to only frame-relevant stimuli. It does, nevertheless, perform a number of important functions. It 'can be thought of as a blackboard available to all the various subsystems of the brain'.[12] It is thus a link between these subsystems and, as such, has an integrating function—particularly through memory which, as Peter Brown puts it, is 'the matrix of personal identity'.[13] It works, according to Gilligan, by 'structuring information into action frames or programs (mental sets) and sequencing and computing conceptual relationships'.[14] It is also highly sensitive to context, that is, it is realistic.

These benefits come at a price, however. Because conscious processing involves a dissociation from broader-based unconscious processing, people can become more or less permanently disconnected from a wide range of life-enhancing resources. Reconnection with such resources thus requires some kind of inhibition or displacement of conscious processes, and this is exactly what trance states are: frames of mind where conscious processes are displaced. In trance states (from the Latin *transitus*—a passage, and *transire*—to pass over) attention is not selective; asymmetrical patterns of muscular tension are reduced, and arrhythmic movements tend to become more fluid. Clearly, Skynner's open and closed modes are not exactly synonyms for unconscious and conscious processing, but they are close enough for us to recognize that both Skynner and Gilligan are writing about similar and related states. If, then, it is the case, as it seems to be, that trance states facilitate a shift from conscious to unconscious processing or from closed to open mode, and that such shifts, whilst highly beneficial at the appropriate time, are often difficult for people to make, we should think of them not as something detrimental to be feared but as a highly valuable resource. Indeed, many of the world's cultures have regarded them in that way. In the West, however, they have been treated with distrust—perhaps because much of our acquaintance with trance states comes through the medium of hypnosis, particularly stage hypnosis and the fictional character of Svengali; though the Christian Church probably had an important part to play as well.

One of the difficulties that immediately confronts the student of trance states is that they are so diverse in their manifestations and so varied in the means of their induction. These two factors, manifestation and induction, are quite closely related. The method of inducing a trance state significantly influences the kind of trance experience that a person will have. For example, if a trance is induced by the use of suggestions for comfort and relaxation then the trance will be accompanied by bodily relaxation and the subjective experience of being comfortable. Because these kinds of suggestions are commonly employed by hypnotherapists to induce trance, some authors have gone so far as to suggest that relaxation is a defining characteristic of trance.[15] It isn't. Suggestions for movement and rhythmic muscular tensing can be just as effective in producing trance states as suggestions for relaxation—and we know that they are trance states because researchers have found that people in states induced by suggestions for both relaxation and tension can manifest the traditional hypnotic phenomena such as analgesia, hallucination and amnesia, and also pass easily from one state to the other. Thus, the kind of trance produced by bodily immobilization and the kind produced by rhythmic movement such as the whirling of the dervishes will have different characteristics but they can both be identified as trance states because they both facilitate the elicitation of phenomena that are extremely difficult to create out of trance and because each can easily be converted into the other. In short, many of the characteristics that are commonly associated with trance are actually products of the method of induction that is employed.

This way of understanding trance states has significant implications for our understanding of Altered States of Consciousness (ASCs). In particular, the kinds of ideas promoted by writers such as the psychiatrist Roland Fischer from the late 1960s to the late 1980s that ASCs can be arranged on a continuum with mystical rapture at one end, yogic samadhi at the other and ordinary consciousness in between will have to be rejected. Instead, we will need to think of the ASCs that Fischer places on either side of normal consciousness as going together under the heading of 'trance states', all of which are to be contrasted with 'conscious states'. A schematic version of this arrangement might be something like the following:

**Trance States in Relation to Normal Consciousness**

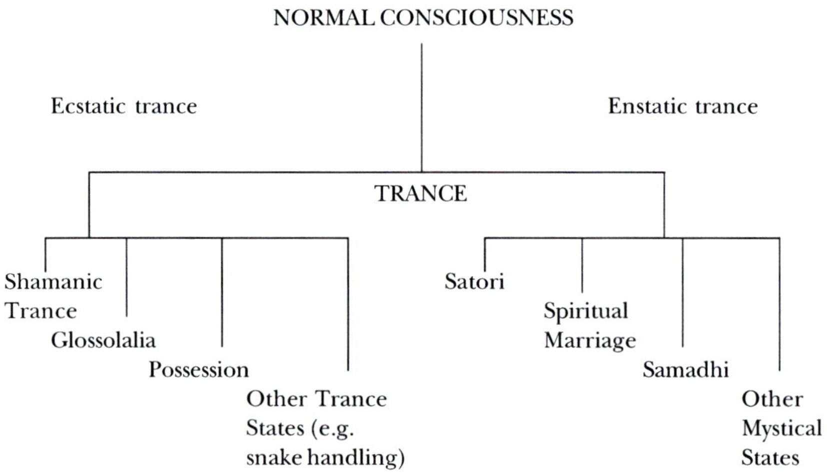


Trance states also vary across a spectrum of what we might call depth or profundity. At one end we have what is often called a light trance; examples would be daydreaming and watching television. At the other, we have much more focused states such as the hypnotically induced analgesia employed in the context of dental surgery and, beyond that, the experimentally induced states of complete mental blankness and intensely realistic hallucination. We might also add the states of possession by deities, spirits and the like that are recorded in many and disparate cultures.

Trances also vary in their orientation. Some are internally focused, sometimes to the point where there is no response at all to external stimuli. Others are externally focused, but perception, instead of being regulated by the consensus reality into which the person has been socialized, is guided by the imagination of the entranced person or by the suggestions of another person (hypnotists, storytellers, gurus, etc.). If a person's trance experience is created with the help of another then we call it hetero-hypnosis or hetero-trance. Clinical and stage hypnosis would be obvious examples. If, on the other hand, the trance is self-induced it is generally referred to as auto-hypnosis or auto-trance.

Another important distinction is that between trance induction and trance utilization. The former refers to the means of creating a trance state; the latter to what you do with it once you have it. Both manifest considerable variety. Trances can be induced by rhythmic and repetitive movement, bodily immobility, attentional absorption (e.g. on a fixed point, a person's voice or a process), intense stress, extended periods of solitude, balancing of muscle tonus, loss of bodily equilibrium accompanied by a loud noise and a host of other techniques.[16] They can be used to create analgesic and anaesthetic effects in most areas of the body, to eliminate conditioned responses to a variety of stimuli, to change memories, to enhance performance in various activities, to generate experiences of so-called 'former lives' and a whole host of seemingly veridical hallucinations. In short, there are many ways to create a trance state and many things you can do with it once you have it.

Given this variety, one might wonder whether there is anything that all trances have in common, anything that usefully distinguishes trance experience from other kinds of experience. This is a matter of current debate and, one might say, considerable controversy amongst trance researchers at the present time. There are, however, at least two features that, to me at least, seem to be constant. One is what Ronald Shor has called 'a fading of the Generalized Reality Orientation' (Charles Tart calls it the Consensus Reality Orientation). This is 'a structured frame of reference in the background of attention which supports, interprets, and gives meaning to all experiences'.[17] It is what sociologist Peter Berger would call our internalized socially constructed reality.[18] The other seemingly common feature of all trance states is attentional absorption, the sense of being caught up or totally involved in the phenomenon to which one is attending. Erika Fromm and Stephen Kahn found that these two features were the only ones common to all the cases of auto- and hetero-hypnosis that they studied.

Fromm and Kahn also noticed, and I mention it here because it is relevant to an understanding of what happens during yogic meditation, that the imagery generated in auto-hypnosis tended to be more vivid than that generated in hetero-hypnosis. They write, 'internal events at times took on a quality of verisimilitude comparable to the way in which one experiences external reality itself'.[19] It may be, however, that the hetero-hypnosis they employed was less than optimally effective because other writers, for example Charles Tart, have reported the same and even enhanced vividness in subjects experiencing trance via hetero-hypnosis.[20] The general point to be noted, therefore, is that in trance states people can experience mental creations being as real as or even more real than ordinary waking experience. Trances can facilitate what Joseph de Rivera and Theodore Sarbin call 'believed-in-imaginings'.[21]

Three other points are worth mentioning at this juncture. The first is that trance states often develop spontaneously; they do not always have to be cultivated. Michael Yapko claims that people can spontaneously enter trance states during conversations, watching television, reading and making love and in many other ways, for example highway hypnosis.[22] The second and related point is that trance experiences often have a quality of involuntariness about them. 'Things just seem to happen', as Gilligan puts it. The phenomenon of post-hypnotic suggestion is interesting in this connection because when a person engages in an action or thought process in response to a trigger stimulus that had been suggested during trance the trance state is re-evoked.[23] Many of our everyday behaviours are actually responses to trigger stimuli and a little self-reflection will reveal that most of these behaviours are little sequences which, once triggered, need to run to completion (e.g. vaulting horse gymnasts in the old Amicable Life advertisement, who kept on running towards the vaulting horse even though they could see that the previous vaulters were all crashing in to each other after vaulter number two had failed to make the vault—or even a simple handshake).

When such behaviours are disadvantageous to us but we have been unsuccessful in removing them we often experience that 'Oh here we go again' feeling every time they are triggered. Such sequences, often called conditioned behaviour patterns, have the involuntary character of many trance states and may even be kinds of trance states themselves. If this is the case, and it certainly seems that it might be, then for each of us our entire life is filled with entries into and exits out of trance states. Now the most effective way to modify behaviours that were laid down during trance states or are maintained through trance states, as every hypnotherapist knows, is by utilizing trance itself—because in trance states there is a loosening of previously conditioned patterns.

One analogy for this is the gearbox of a car. Once you are in a gear you are stuck in it unless you activate the clutch, which disengages the gear and allows a change to another gear. And when you want to get out of that gear you have to employ the clutch again. Trance is a bit like a clutch; it creates a state of mind in which mental programs put into place previously can be removed or modified.

Finally, we may note that not all experiences of trance involve vivid imagery. Many reports of deep trance show that people can experience deep stillness and complete blankness of mind, a state of 'no-thing-ness'. As Charles Tart points out, the typical response of a deeply hypnotized subject to the question 'What are you experiencing?' is 'Nothing'.[24] What seems to be the case, then, is that *both* tranquillity or emptiness of mind *and* vivid imagery are products of the intention of the person who induces and guides the trance (whether that be through auto- or hetero-hypnosis) and of the techniques employed to create the trance.

So, to summarize what has been said about trance states:

1. they all involve the inhibition or diminution of conscious processing;
2. all or most of them seem to share the qualities of attentional absorption and a fading of the generalized reality orientation;
3. they can be self-induced or induced by someone else;
4. they can be internally or externally oriented;
5. they can be induced by many different methods or events;
6. they can generate a wide range of experiences, from a complete blankness or emptiness of mind to vivid, reality-like images;

7. they can be cultivated or arise spontaneously;
8. they can be used to rework or remove existing mental sets and behaviour patterns.

When we turn our attention to yogic meditation and the experiences that arise from this we find many parallels with trance. The kinds of things yogins do are just the kinds of things that many trance-inducers would do in order to create a trance state. Both the rhythmic movement of āsana and the rhythmic breathing of prāṇāyāma would certainly facilitate the induction of a trance state, as would the physical immobility and attentional focus that is characteristic of pratyāhāra, dhāraṇā, dhyāna and samādhi. And in Buddhist yoga, certainly, a misunderstanding of the nature of things is deemed to be perpetuated by thought-construction or conceptualization (vikalpa) or concept-based beliefs (dṛṣṭi), whilst what is sought is nirvikalpa samādhi (concept-free absorption) and nirvikalpa jñāna (concept-free knowledge). Again, this is paralleled in trance experience where the conceptualization characteristic of conscious processing is reduced and replaced by what Gilligan calls 'experiential, nonconceptual involvement' in ongoing experience. In Buddhism the concept-free knowledge that arises out of meditational practice is also known as right knowledge (samyak jñāna). Of course, what makes it 'right' in this context is its content, but this is a metaphysical claim and cannot be evaluated from the outside. Right knowledge is the ninth step on the tenfold version of the eightfold path (aṣṭāṅga mārga), on the basis of which the Buddha claims that he sees the world as it really is (yathābhutam). Interestingly, when commenting on the 'experiential, nonconceptual involvement' that characterizes many trance experiences, Gilligan mentions that entranced individuals are more able to directly experience 'things as they are' than is possible outside of trance.[25] We can, I think, take this to mean that the nature of the experience leads the person to think of it as one of 'things as they are', rather than as a claim to completely veridical and certain knowledge, even though this is how it might seem to the person having the experience.

The yogic equivalent of Buddhist right knowledge is the truth-bearing insight (ṛtaṃbharā prajñā) that arises in the nirvicāra samāpatti described in Patañjali's *Yoga Sūtra*. The dharma-megha samādhi mentioned in book 4 of the same text might also be regarded as referring to the same kind of experience. These 'visions of the truth', like their Buddhist counterparts, follow on from the attainment of samādhi, an essentially contentless state of attentional absorption. What is more, among the effects of such experiences we find the eradication of conditioned patterns of perception and behaviour. Right view, we may recall, arose for many of the Buddha's disciples when he had provided them with a teaching in brief and enabled them to follow the path because the karmic conditioning that had so restricted their freedom was no longer operative.

In short, practitioners of yogic meditation do the kinds of things that are often done by people who seek to induce trance states, and they have subsequent experiences that are characterized by a sense of veridicality or reality—a combination that is highly reminiscent of reports of deep trance experiences. This statement of parallelisms is not particularly controversial in itself but controversy inevitably arises when we seek to determine the status of experiences that are claimed to reveal 'the truth'. Are they to be taken as literally true or as imaginative constructs that just seem to be true? Those who have the experiences and those who want what the experiencers say to be true will be inclined to favour the former interpretation, whilst those who come from the perspective of trance research will be inclined to favour the latter.

In support of the latter interpretation is the fact, mentioned above, that different yogic meditators, and indeed mystics from other religious traditions who do the same kinds of things, tend to experience quite different 'truths' as a result of their exertions. The Vedāntic yogin experiences the ultimate reality as all-embracing, undifferentiated being. A follower of Patañjali experiences kaivalya, the separation of the individual spirit (puruṣa/draṣṭṛ) from the psycho-physical world of prakṛti. The Buddhist experiences the dissolution of all forms of self-construct, the realization that the entire phenomenal world is dependently arisen and the indescribable bliss of the unconditioned nirvāṇa.

It is certainly possible that one of these accounts describes the ultimate nature of things and that the others are just inaccurate or incomplete. But since their claims, although similar, are mutually exclusive it is not possible for all of them to be accurate. It is equally possible that all of them are just plain wrong and that some other description corresponds more closely to the actual nature of things than does any of these. It is also equally possible that all of these accounts are accurate descriptions of experiences that were mistakenly accorded objective status. This is the kind of interpretation that would come naturally to most people acquainted with the research on trance states. For the trance researcher the value of such experiences would be assessed not by reference to their truth value (for this would be essentially unknowable) but by reference to their pragmatic value: do they lead to well-being and happiness?

There is a further feature of yogic meditation that brings it within the orbit of trance experience, and that is the location of yogic meditation within the broader category of mystical experience and the close parallels between the categories of mystical experience and of trance experience. Yogic experiences are regarded by many scholars as prime examples of mystical experiences, almost paradigmatically so in some cases. They exemplify with unrivalled clarity the classic pattern of mystical activity and experience that is found in many of the world's major religious traditions. Attention is focused down to a single point and directed inward to produce a deep state of mental tranquillity which is followed by a spontaneous or meditator-initiated acquisition of knowledge about the ultimate nature of things.

Not all mystical experiences conform to this pattern, however. Some arise spontaneously. Others produce a transformation of external rather than internal experience. William Stace calls these extravertive mystical experiences.[26] Yet others are prompted not so much by the individuals having the experiences or the situation in which they find themselves but by a third party. It has already been noted that the Pali Buddhist texts contain many accounts of the Buddha taking people to one side and giving them a talk about dhamma (the teaching or the truth of things).[27] As a result of this talk the recipient experiences a mental state that is described in the same terms as are elsewhere used to describe the fourth jhāna (Skt. dhyāna), the meditative state in which the Buddha obtained the knowledges that freed him from rebirth. This jhāna-like experience then gives way to an experience of knowing and seeing that has very similar results: the person becomes either a stream-enterer (who will be reborn no more than seven times), a once-returner, a non-returner or an arahat (liberated here and now).

We find, then, that mystical experiences, like trance experiences, are quite varied both in the means of their induction and in their content. When we put the patterns found in the two types of experience side by side the parallels are striking: mystical experiences may be cultivated or spontaneous, trance experiences may be cultivated or spontaneous; mystical experiences may be internally or externally oriented, trance experiences may be internally or externally oriented; mystical experiences may be self-induced or induced by another, trance experiences may be self-induced or induced by another; mystical experiences may be devoid of content or full of vivid, realistic content, trance experiences may be devoid of content or full of vivid, realistic content.

When these parallels are put alongside the similarities in the methods used to access these states it is difficult not to conclude that mystical experiences and trance experiences derive from some common set of processes and, since trance experiences go beyond the mystical in their scope, that the latter are variants of the former. This being so, it follows that yogic experiences are varieties of trance experience. Indeed, I would contend that explaining yogic and other forms of mysticism in terms of trance experience clarifies the nature of the relationship between these forms better than any other explanation proposed to date. If it is correct, then it frees us to abandon 'truth' as the primary criterion for judging the worth of yogic traditions and opens the way for evaluating them in terms of the benefits they can offer. Not all can be true, but all can offer real benefits—even if their metaphysics are inaccurate.

# NOTES

Introduction

1. As the Devanāgarī script does not distinguish capital letters, decisions about whether to capitalize certain terms are rather arbitrary. Throughout this book the term 'yoga' will only be capitalized when it refers to a particular school or body of teaching.
2 Rawlinson (1997) pp. 98-99.
3 From Connolly (1989).
4 Horner (1957) pp. 398-402.
5 *Gradual Sayings* 2, Woodward (1933) p. 200.
6 See Jayatilleke (1963) p. 200 for a discussion of this term.
7 Horner (1957) pp. 360-61.
8 For further details, see Rhys Davids (1899) pp. 27-35.
9 Horner (1957) pp. 176-80.
10 See Warder (1980) pp. 135ff. for a discussion of the unanswered questions and *Kindred Sayings* 2, Woodward (1922) pp. 9-11 for an example of redefinition.
11 See Tosh (2000) for a discussion of modern approaches to historical enquiry.

Chapter 1

1 Wilson H.H. (trans.) *The Vishnu Purana* Book 4, chapter 22. For further details on Hindu cosmology, see Gombrich (1975) and Jacobi (1908; 1911).
2 See Brown (1968) for an exegesis of this hymn.

Chapter 2

1 **A note on the term 'brahman'.** Two general classes of priests can be identified in Vedic religion: those who served exclusively at the public sacrifices, the ritvij priests, and those who were primarily domestic priests for kings and nobles, but who could also serve at public sacrifices, the purohita priests. A later and more general term that was employed to refer to all types of priest is 'brāhman'. This is the term used to identify the whole of the priestly class (varṇa). However, priests are also known as brahmāṇas, literally 'a descendent of a brāhman' (and one still often encounters the Anglicized form of brahmin). In itself, this does not present the student with too many problems. They only arise when we realize that 'brahman' has two spellings: one with a short first 'a' and one with a long first 'a' (brahman and brāhman). The first of these has a double meaning: priest and expansive (the sacred power believed to pervade the universe),

and hence can be a source of confusion. Likewise, the term 'brāhmaṇa/Brāhmaṇa' has a double meaning. It can refer to a priest and to a set of texts (the second component of the Veda—this meaning will be indicated with a capital B throughout). To complicate matters further, there is the creator god called Brahmā (also capitalized) and the adjectival usage with a meaning something like 'sublime', as exemplified in the Buddhist and yogic idea of brahmavihāra (sublime abodes), of which there are four: lovingkindness, compassion, sympathetic joy and equanimity. These ambiguities are inherent in the Sanskrit language itself and the way that its terminology evolved. We just need to be aware of them.

2 S. Dasgupta (1922) p. 31.

3 The dates of Vedic texts are a matter of considerable dispute. The prevalent view among scholars during the latter half of the twentieth century was that the Vedas were composed by people who called themselves *Aryan*, meaning 'noble', and who migrated from the central Asian steppes during the second millennium BCE. That the original Indo-Aryan homeland was located on the Ukranian steppelands has been argued most persuasively by Marija Gimbutas (1970); see Davies (1996) pp. 86 and 1143n for details. These nomadic pastoralists moved westwards into Europe and the Middle East, southwards into Iran (Persia) and southeastwards into India, where they encountered a declining agricultural and urban culture in the valley of the River Indus. This view has been challenged recently by writers such as Georg Feuerstein, David Frawley and Subhash Kak. These writers claim that the Indus civilization was founded by the Vedic Aryans and that 'most of the Vedas date from before 2500 B.C.'. Feuerstein, Frawley and Kak (1992), pp. 65-69 and 100-102.

This is controversial to say the least, and the debate is likely to go on for some time. Issues that these writers and their supporters will have to address include 1) the dating of the Zoroastrian Avestan texts, which have much in common with the Vedic Saṃhitās and which are dated by the Zoroastrians themselves around the eighth century BCE; and 2) the Vedic condemnation of phallus worship (*Ṛgveda* 7.21.5 and 10.99.3) by people who are described as snub-nosed, and dark-skinned dāsa/daśya, a word that later came to mean 'slave', and who are said to have lived in fortified cities (pura) that were destroyed by the Vedic god Indra.

4 See Ch. 5, note 2.

5 See, for example, Danielou (1964), and Werner (1989).

6 From Griffiths (1973) p. 130.

7 Brown (1968) p. 217.

8 Zaehner (1966).

9 Connolly (1992).

10 Keith (1970) p. 313.

11 See the references to women in the Laws of *Manu* [*Mānava Dharma Śāstra*], e.g. Bühler (1969), for examples of how this kind of thinking developed.

12 Griswold (1971).

13 Hopkins (1993) p. 28, comments that unlike Upaniṣads such as the *Kaṭha* and *Maitrī*, the *Śvetāśvatara Upaniṣad* is never unambiguously copied by the epic poets. The implication is that it did not exist for them to copy at that time. K.B.R. Rao goes even further, claiming that the *SU* postdates even the later portions of the *Mahābhārata* (Rao [1966], pp. 297-333).

14 From Hume (1971) p. 163.

15 Hume (1971) pp. 140-41.

16 Hume (1971) p. 233. We may note that a caṇḍāla is the offspring of a brahman mother and a śūdra father. The message to young brāhman women is clear: if you mate with śūdra males your children will be of a lower class than either of you. No doubt this was a powerful sanction, and the fact that it had to be created is suggestive.

17 The term 'jñāna' is generally employed in Indian mystical and metaphysical texts to mean something like insight into the truth of things. We need to recognize, however, that the content of jñāna varies from school to school, and, since the doctrines of different schools are often incompatible with each other, not every jñāna can be true. R.C. Zaehner (1957) p. 176 comments: '*Jnana* like *gnosis* derives from the Indo-European root √*gno-* "to know"... it means, according to derivation, "knowledge" or "science".... [however] the word, despite its etymology, does not mean "knowledge" as that word is commonly understood in the English tongue: it means simply "a strongly held opinion" or "conviction". It means what the Greeks, with their customary accuracy, called a "dogma".' This interpretation fits well with the later usage of the term 'jñāna yoga', where practitioners substitute their ordinary, 'deluded' way of viewing the world with the one advocated by the text or teacher, i.e. they come to see the world in the way that they are told they should see it. Each text, of course, regards its own jñāna as the truth and the jñānas of other schools as false or mistaken.

18 The term 'torso' is here a translation of the Sanskrit word 'ātman', which is most frequently understood to mean 'self' or spiritual essence, though its meanings in pre-Upaniṣadic Vedic literature range from 'body/trunk/torso through self/oneself to immortal essence/Self'. See Connolly (1992) pp. 32-37.

19 Werner (1986).

20 Ancient Indian war chariots were occupied by two people, the charioteer and the warrior. The latter was the superior, being of noble birth; the former was a servant, one of whose jobs was to narrate the exploits of his master after the battle.

21 Dasgupta (1922) p. 31.

22 Hume (1971) p. 241.

23 Hume (1971) pp. 368-69.

24 Diamond (1997) p. 105.

25 Wilkinson (1996) passim.

26 Throughout this book I shall be using the BCE/CE dating indicators. BCE stands for 'Before the Common Era' whilst CE stands for 'Common Era'. In terms of actual dates, BCE covers the same period as the traditional Western European BC and CE the same period as AD. The problem with the traditional Western dating system is that it is Christian based, the postulated birth of Jesus being the point of transition from BC to AD. The nomenclature is also Christian, BC = Before Christ and AD = Anno Domini (the year of the/our Lord). Other cultures and religions use quite different systems, e.g. Buddhists do their calculations for before and after the enlightenment of the Buddha, and Muslims do theirs for before and after Muhammad's migration from Mecca to Medina. No one system of dating can do justice to every tradition. BCE and CE is the solution offered by Western scholars. It keeps the time periods the same as those in the Christian calendar whilst removing the specifically Christian nomenclature. It is not an ideal solution, but then there is no ideal solution.

27 See *RV* 7.21.5 and 10.99.3.

28 There is also a political dimension to this debate. The self-esteem of śūdra communities is considerably enhanced if it was their ancestors who created the Indus civilization and could be a significant symbolic factor in their attempts to procure social justice. On the other hand, if writers like Frawley, Feuerstein and Kak are correct in their claims that the Vedic Aryans created the Indus civilization, then that particular source of śūdra self-esteem is taken away from them—a significant loss in a period of fundamentalist Hindu nationalism.
29 Bhattacharji (1970) p. 286.
30 But see Gombrich (1992).
31 Deussen (1980) p. 279.
32 Radhakrishnan (1953) pp. 642-43.
33 See Connolly (1992) pp. 64-66 for a discussion.
34 Hume (1971) p. 451.
35 Deussen (1980) p. 352.
36 The āśramas are student (brahmacārya), householder (gṛhastha), recluse (vanaprastha) and renouncer (sannyāsin).
37 See Connolly (1992) p. 155 for details.

Chapter 3

1 Pande (1974) p. 258.
2 My own understanding of this contentious term is a story that embodies some of the values of a group and is located outside of ordinary time, e.g. 'once upon a time', or 'when giants walked the earth'.
3 Dasgupta (1922) p. 190.
4 Kumar Jayakirti, *Everyman—The Frontiers of Peace*, BBC Wales, 1986.
5 See Kalghati, T.G. 'The Jaina Way' in Connolly (1986).
6 There is an interesting story recounted by Heinrich Zimmer in *Philosophies of India* where, at the time of his enlightenment, Pārśva's grace opened the mind of his (formerly) wicked brother Samvara (who had asked for forgiveness) to right vision and set him on the path to liberation. Zimmer (1969).
7 See Gombrich (1992).
8 Horner (1959) section 123.
9 D2.12. Rhys Davids (1910) p. 8ff.
10 Fausboll (1905) *Sutta Nipāta* 11.15-16 (Nalakasutta). A more elaborate account can be found in the Sanskrit *Lalīta Vistara.*
11 Horner (1957) Sutta 36. A more elaborate version can be found in the Sanskrit *Mahāvastu.* An interesting point about this episode is that Siddhatta's father was ploughing, suggesting that he might have been a headman rather than a king (as later accounts portray him), an interpretation that fits better with the fact that the Śakyans were a republican confederacy rather than a kingdom at the time.
12 *Gradual Sayings* 1 Woodward (1932) pp. 128-29.
13 Horner (1957) p. 184.
14 Rhys Davids (1910) pp. 17-18 (D.2.21.); and V.1.15 (Book of the Discipline 4, p. 23).
15 Horner (1954) pp. 206-207.
16 Horner (1954) pp. 210-11.
17 Horner (1954) section 36 (*Mahāsaccaka Sutta*).
18 Fausboll (1905) *Sutta Nipāta, Padhāna Sutta.* For a discussion of these Mara passages see Gombrich (1996) p. 77ff.

19 Thomas (1949) p. 81.
20 The *Mahāparinibbāna Sutta* in, for example, Rhys Davids (1881).
21 Horner (1957) p. 357.
22 Woodward (1922) p. 2.
23 Rhys Davids (1910) pp. 51-52.
24 Woodward (1922) pp. 59-60.
25 Quoted in Harvey (2001) p. 98.
26 *Dialogues of the Buddha:* Rhys Davids (1910) p. 128; (1921) pp. 117-18; (1921) pp. 201-49; *Middle Length Sayings:* Horner (1959) p. 31. These passages display considerable variation in their elaborateness. The simplest is found in the *Middle Length Sayings* version (Horner).
27 Rahula (1967) p. 46.
28 Harvey (2001) p. 91.
29 *Anguttara Nikāya* 5.244 (*Gradual Sayings* 5, pp. 165-70); *Digha Nikāya* 2.217, 122ff (*Dialogues of the Buddha* 2, pp. 250-51, 130-31); *Majjhima Nikāya* 2.75f., 3.76 (*Middle Length Sayings*); *Sanyutta Nikāya* 5.1f. (*Kindred Sayings* 5, p. 3). Quoted in Masefield (1986b) p. 172.
30 Masefield (1986a and b); see also Lamotte (1984) pp. 53-54.
31 Masefield (1986b) p. 165.
32 Masefield (1986b) p. 167.
33 Rhys Davids (1899) pp. 200-201.
34 Five kinds of rebirth are acknowledged in Buddhism: as a hell-dweller, as an animal, as a ghost, as a human, and as a god/divine being. In the first three there is more suffering than happiness, in the fourth suffering and happiness are deemed equal, whilst in the fifth there is more happiness than suffering.

The universe within which these rebirths take place is divided into three realms (loka/dhātu), beyond which is nirvāṇa. The lowest level is the Kāma Loka, the realm of desire, which contains all the hell worlds and the worlds of humans and animals as well as six heavenly worlds. Next comes the Rūpa Loka, the realm of form, which is divided into four levels corresponding to the four stages of meditative contemplation (jhāna/dhyāna). Only beings who have experienced jhāna can be born in the Rūpa Loka. Then comes the Arūpa Loka, the formless realm, again divided into four levels corresponding to the meditative attainments (samāpatti): infinite space, infinite consciousness, nothingness and neither perception nor non-perception. See Harvey (2001) p. 261 for a chart of these realms.

This scheme is probably quite late in origin. It seems likely that the jhānas and samāpattis were originally separate schemes, describing different states of consciousness. As a number of accounts describe the Buddha gaining enlightenment whilst in the 4th jhāna, the samāpattis came to be regarded as a spiritual dead-end. The situation is complicated, however, by the fact that nibbāna seems, according to some suttas, to be accessible via the samāpattis and a further stage called the cessation of perception and feeling (saññavadanāyitanirodha)—see Middle Length Sayings p. 219. In this version the samāpattis follow on from the jhānas, giving a nine-level scheme.
35 Masefield (1986a) p. 166.
36 Masefield, P. 'The Sāvakasaṅgha and the Sotāpanna.' Unpublished paper.
37 Werner (1983) p. 171. The three knowledges are: remembering former lives; knowledge of the destinations of beings according to their karma, and knowl-

edge of the destruction of the āsavas. The six are these three plus magical powers (iddhi [P]), divine ear and knowledge of the minds of others.

38 This is the goal sought by contemporary Buddhists who follow the path of insight (vipassanā) meditation.

39 This estimate is based on the traditional Theravāda dating of the Buddha: 563–483 BCE.

40 The *Sukhāvatī* (Pure Land) *Sūtras* have been thought to indicate Zoroastrian influence as (a) Buddhism was well-established in northwestern India and bordering on Persia; (b) the Pure Land Sūtras introduce the idea of a Pure Land to the west that was created by the Buddha of infinite light (Amitabha) from where beings can gain enlightenment easily. Ahura Mazda, the wise lord of Zoroastrianism, is also a being of infinite light.

41 See Williams (1989) for a more comprehensive treatment.

42 The four qualities developed in these meditations are: 1. lovingkindness (metta); 2. compassion (karunā); 3. sympathetic joy (muditā), and 4. equanimity (upekkhā). The meditator develops each by first of all feeling it towards him or herself, then towards friends, then towards enemies and finally towards all sentient beings.

43 Rūpa (form), vedanā (feeling), saṃjñā (perception), saṃskāra (volition) and vijñāna (consciousness).

44 See Reynolds (1977) for details.

45 *Kindred Sayings* 3, Woodward (1925) p. 103.

46 Fausboll (1905) p. 197.

47 *Kindred Sayings* 4, Woodward (1927) p. 29.

48 See Kochumuttom (1982) pp. 198-200 for details of scholars who interpreted the Yogācāra as an idealistic system. Ninian Smart also offers an idealistic interpretation in his otherwise excellent *Doctrine and Argument in Indian Philosophy*; see Smart (1964) p. 57.

49 Kochumuttom (1982) p. 5.

50 Malalasekera (1968–) p. 138.

51 Malalasekera (1968–).

52 Thomas (1949) p. 75.

Chapter 4

1 In Dimock et al. (1978) p. 54.

2 Sukthankar (1936–37).

3 See also Van Buitenen (1973) p. xxiii, who identifies a four-stage process.

4 See Khair (1969) and Minor (1982) for overviews.

5 Sinha (1986).

6 All quotations from the *Bhagavad Gītā* are taken from Edgerton's translation unless otherwise stated. Edgerton (1972).

7 A similar teaching can be found in various parts of book 12 of the *Mahābhārata*, the *Śānti Parvan*, and also the *Śvetāśvatara Upaniṣad*.

8 Vss 19 and 20 are from *KU* 1.2.18-19.

9 The practice (abhyāsa) mentioned here is differentiated from dhyāna, which is deemed to be superior to it. In 6.35 we find abhyāsa coupled with detachment (vairāgya) just as it is in Patañjali's *Yoga Sūtra*. Patañjali, however, seems to include dhyāna within abhyāsa (see Chapter 5 below).

10 Zaehner (1969) p. 393.

11 The term 'catur-varṇa' that is here translated as 'four-caste' refers to the four divisions of society that are described in *Ṛgveda* 10.90, the four varṇas or colours. 'Caste', from the Portugese *castas* (Latin *castus* meaning 'pure') is more commonly used to translate the Sanskṛit term 'jati', meaning birth. Social divisions in Brāhmanical society are maintained by notions of purity and pollution. These are expressed in many ways, the two most significant of which are commensality, eating together, and marriage. Briefly, one may only accept food from another person if they are of the same or a higher level of purity than oneself, and a woman may only marry men of a group with the same or a higher level of purity than herself. Jatis are far more numerous than varṇas. A crude rule of thumb is to place the various jatis within the varṇa divisions so that each varṇa is regarded as being comprised of a number of jatis. In fact, the two systems probably had different origins and only map onto each other imprecisely.

12 Van Buitenen (1981) p. 24, points out that 'bhakti' is an action noun derived from the root √bhaj, meaning to share, and that its 'basic connotation' is that of loyalty.

13 Traditional commentators and modern scholars interpret these passages in various ways. It seems to me that Kṛṣṇa is referring to the followers of Sāṃkhya-Yoga here, and his reference to the inexpressible or indefinable, unmanifest, imperishable, omnipresent, inconceivable, unchanging, fixed (anirdeśya, avyakta, akṣara, sarvatra-ga, acintya, acala, dhruva) provides a fine example of the blending of philosophies so characteristic of the *Gītā*. Avyakta is a term that the Sāṃkhyans consistently apply to prakṛti (nature, the creative), whilst akṣara is a term that the Upaniṣads apply to ātman/brahman (see, e.g., *MundU* 1.1.5-7). The reference is clearly to the self as described in ch. 2 and elsewhere, yet it also incorporates the Upaniṣadic ātman, which includes rather than excludes the world of change that in Sāṃkhya-Yoga is the domain of prakṛti.

14 Van Buitenen (1981) p. 121. I used Van Buitenen's translation here as I found Edgerton's literalism rather cumbersome.

15 Hopkins (1971) p. 74.

16 Zaehner (1966) pp. 9-10.

17 Bühler (1969) p. 24.

18 Bühler (1969) pp. 194-98, 327-32.

19 Bühler (1969) p. 35.

20 Here I would like to endorse Robert Minor's comments on v.61. He writes: 'If prior to this passage "free-will" had not been eliminated by the discussion of the actions of the strands of *prakrti* as determining one's own action (e.g. 3.5, 33; 9.8; 18.40, 58-61), or by the concept of the predetermining will of Kṛṣṇa (11.32-33; 16.6), or by the law of *karma* generally, this verse seems to exclude all claims to free choice. The metaphysics of the *Gītā* cause one to come to no other conclusion than that Kṛṣṇa is sovereign ordainer of all. *Such teachings, of course, bother modern commentators.*' (Emphasis mine).

21 References are to the translations by Roy/Ganguli (c.1883–96) and Dutt (1988), which are based on the northern recension. There are two primary editions of this, the Calcutta and Bombay versions. The differences between them are few. The southern recensions contain much more additional material than the northern ones, whereas the critical edition published by the Bhandarkar Institute is based mostly on material that is common to all versions.

22 Van Buitenen (1973) p. xxxiii, describes Hopkins's work on this issue as 'persuasive' and comments that most other scholars accept his arguments either explicitly or implicitly.
23 Hopkins (1993) p. 107n.
24 See above, pp. 158-60 for details of the *Pañcarātra* and pp. 181-82 for details of the *Paśupata.*
25 See above, p. 21 for details.
26 Hopkins (1993) pp. 97-99.
27 E.g. 306.19; 317.4.
28 E.g. 2.5.7; 3.2.15; 12.50.33, and 12.314.34.
29 Hopkins (1993) p. 106.
30 Hopkins (1993) p. 106. We may note here that early Jainism and Buddhism were also highly ascetic. The Jain ideal for leaving the world was to simply stand in the forest until the final karmic residues dropped away—sculptures show creepers twining up the legs of such stationary ascetics, whilst the Buddhist monk had only the 'four resources' to cushion his hardships: 1. alms collected in bits for food; 2. old rags for clothing; 3. cow's urine for medicine; 4. shelter of trees for residence.
31 Hopkins (1901).
32 The puruṣa of the Sāṃkhya-Yoga is quite different from the cosmic giant mentioned in *Ṛgveda* 10.90, a number of Upaniṣads and the Laws of *Manu.* This can be a source of considerable confusion for students, not least because writers of a Vedāntic persuasion often conflate them.
33 See 12.269.33; 12.316.11, and also 12.268.7-8.
34 The Buddha attempted a similar kind of redefinition of what it means to be a brāhman: good qualities rather than birth in a brāhman family. See the *Tevijja* and *Sonadaṇḍa Suttas* for details. Rhys Davids (1899).
35 See the section on Sāṃkhya (ch 5.) for further details.
36 Hopkins (1993) p. 157.
37 By 'this-worldly' I mean that the highest values are located here, e.g. wives, cattle, children, etc. By contrast, 'other-worldly' orientations locate the highest values beyond the world, in heaven, nirvāṇa, kaivalya, etc.
38 Translations from Hume (1971).
39 Bhīṣma—12.175; 177; 195; 217; 274 and 301; Yajñavalkya—12.317; Vyāsa—12.236; 240; 245; 251; and 265.
40 The yoginī Sulabhā enters into King Janaka by means of her yogic power in 12.321.
41 Hopkins (1993) p. 110.
42 See Connolly (1992) for a fuller treatment of this issue.
43 The translator, following the commentary of Nilakantha, explains that '**The place** should be a level spot, not impure (such as a crematorium, etc.), free from *kankars*, fire, and sand, &c.; solitary and free from noise and other-sources of disturbance. **Acts** include abstention from food and sports and amusements, abstention from all kinds of work having only worldly objects to accomplish, abstention also from sleep and dreams. **Affection** means that for good disciples or for progress in *yoga.* **Objects** refer to sacred fuel, water, and suppression of expectancy and anxiety, etc. **Means** refer to the seat to be used, the manner of sitting, and the attitude of the body. **Destruction** refers to the conquest of desire and attachments, i.e., renunciation of all attractive things. **Certainty** means the unalterable belief that what is said about *yoga* in the Vedas

and by preceptors is true, (The nom. sing. inflection stands for the instrumental plural). **Eyes** include the other senses. All these should be restrained. **Food** means pure food. **Suppression** refers to the subjugation of our natural inclination towards earthly objects. **Mind** here has reference to the regulation of the will and its reverse, *viz.*, irresolution. **Survey** means reflection on birth, death, decrepitude, disease, sorrow, faults, &c.' (Emphasis mine).

Chapter 5

1 Hein (1986) p. 308.

2 There are 18 major Purāṇas (Mahāpurāṇas) and a large number of minor ones (Upapurāṇas). Apart from the Mārkaṇḍeya Purāṇa, which is relatively unsectarian, the majority of Purāṇas can be classified as Brahma, Vaiṣṇava or Śaiva.

The earliest Purāṇas were compiled between 250 CE and 500 CE. Most of the remaining important ones were compiled between 500 and 1000 CE, with a few notable ones appearing after 1000 CE.

| Date | Title | Sect |
|---|---|---|
| 250 | Mārkaṇḍeya (but Devīmāhātmya section is later) (M) | Brahma |
| 250–500 | Matsya (M) | Śaiva |
| 350 | Vāyu (classed as (M) in some lists) | Śaiva |
| 350–950 | Brahmāṇḍa (M) | Brahma |
| 400–500 | Narasiṃha | |
| 450 | Visnu (M) | Vaiṣṇava |
| 450 | Harivamśa (not technically a Purāṇa) | Vaiṣṇava |
| 450–900 | Vāmana (M) | Brahma |
| 500–800 | Sāmba | |
| 550–650 | Devī | |
| 550–850 | Kurma (M) | Śaiva |
| 600–1000 | Liṅga (M) | Śaiva |
| 700–1150 | Skanda (M) | Śaiva |
| 750 | Padma (but Sṛṣṭi Khanda is earlier—around 600) (M) | Vaiṣṇava |
| 750 | Varāha (M) | Vaiṣṇava |
| 750–900 | Bṛhannaradīya (M) | Vaiṣṇava |
| 750–1350 | Śiva (M) | Śaiva |
| 750–1550 | Brahma Vivarta (M) | Brahma |
| 850 | Agni (M) | Śaiva |
| 850–1350 | Devībhāgavata | Śaiva/Śākta |
| 900 | Garuda (M) | Vaiṣṇava |
| 950 | Bhāgavata (M) | Vaiṣṇava |
| 950–1150 | Saura (sometimes called Brahma) | Brahma |
| 1100 | Mahābhāgavata | |
| Before 1200 | Bhaviṣya (M) | Brahma |
| 1250 | Bṛhaddharma | |
| Before 1350 | Brahma (M) | Brahma |
| 1350 | Kālikā | Śaiva |
| 1500-1700 | Kalki | |

(M) = Mahāpurāṇa

The reason why there are 19 Mahāpurāṇas on this list is that Vāyu is sometimes classed as (M) and Śiva is not, or Śiva is classed as (M) and Vāyu is not. Note, however, that the term Mahāpurāṇa first occurs in the *Bhāgavata* which, interestingly, mentions both the Bhavisya and Brahma Purāṇas and these, according to Wendy Doniger O'Flaherty (1975), from whom the chronology is taken, are supposed to be later than the *Bhāgavata*. Also, the *Matsya Purāṇa* gives Vāyu rather than Śiva and Agneya rather than Agni.

The sectarian classification of Purāṇas also differs in different Purāṇas and therefore both the chronology and sectarian classification of the above list are to be regarded as tentative only. For example the *Matsya Purāṇa* has both Śaiva and Vaiṣṇava chapters; the Brahmavivarta is really dedicated to Kṛṣṇa and the Brahma/Saura teaches the worship of both Viṣṇu and Śiva. As Winternitz points out, 'The texts which have come down to us, only partially agree with this artificial (sectarian) classification. All this is additional confirmation of the fact that none of the Purāṇas has come down to us in its original form.' Winternitz (1927) p. 532.

3 Hein (1986) p. 311.
4 Zimmer (1946) pp. 3-11.
5 The Cintāmaṇi was a mythical jewel that was believed to grant all wishes.
6 Larson (1979) pp. 78-79.
7 Larson (1979) p. 89.
8 Beidler (1975) p. 18.
9 Rao (1966) pp. 297-333.
10 Hopkins (1993) p. 27.
11 Hopkins (1993) p. 28.
12 Van Buitenen (1957b) p. 89.
13 Grierson (1909) pp. 540ff.
14 E.g. Pande (1974) and Zimmer (1969).
15 Hopkins (1993) p. 98.
16 Roy (n/d) Vol. 10, p. 453.
17 Roy (n/d) Vol. 10, p. 471.
18 Roy (n/d) Vol. 10, p. 621.
19 Hopkins (1993) p. 99.
20 Chakravarti (1975) p. 54.
21 Roy (n/d) Vol. 9, p. 406.
22 Roy (n/d) Vol. 10, p. 431.
23 Roy (n/d) Vol. 10, p. 422.
24 Roy (n/d) Vol. 10, pp. 470-71.
25 Roy (n/d) Vol. 10, p. 478.
26 Roy (n/d) Vol. 10, p. 487.
27 Van Buitenen (1957a) p. 16.
28 See Eliade (1969) note 1.3 for a discussion of this matter.
29 See Eliade (1969) p. 371.
30 Feuerstein (1979) p. 78.
31 Frauwallner (1973) p. 336.
32 Frauwallner (1973) p. 343.
33 Dasgupta (1922) pp. 229-30.
34 Woods (1966) p. 105.
35 Dasgupta (1922) p. 230.
36 See *KU* 6.11. 'Yoga arises and passes away.'

37 See *YS* 2.17 and 2.24.
38 A term that they share with Jainism in describing the liberated state.
39 See *YS* 2.25.
40 Feuerstein (1980) ch. 7.
41 This is how most interpreters seem to take 1.25. Indeed, if Patañjali had meant anything else by this sūtra it is far from clear what that might be.
42 Eliade (1969) p. 74.
43 Woods (1966) p. 52.
44 The late *Sāṃkhya Sūtras* make this claim (e.g. 6.59), as does Vijñāna Bhikṣu when commenting on sūtra 1.109. However, since such statements are not found in the *Sāṃkhya Kārikās* and the *Yoga Sūtras* we can only say that it is possible that this view was held by adherents of the Sāṃkhya and Yoga schools in the classical period.
45 Woods (1966) p. 42.
46 The term 'seed' (bīja) is used here as a synonym for 'karma formation' (saṃskāra)—the mental imprint of a former action which is stored in the mind and will, at some point in the future, 'sprout' to affect perception and behaviour.
47 1.17-18 reads as follows: *vitarka vicāra ānanda asmitārūpa anugamāt saṃprajñātaḥ / virāma pratyaya abhyāsa pūrvaḥ saṃskāraśeṣah anyaḥ.*
48 Nature (prakṛti) has three aspects or components (guṇa): sattva, rajas and tamas. The mind is composed mostly of sattva, but with some admixture of the other two. Not until the mind becomes pure (sattva) is the vision of the self possible (see 3.49).
49 Woods (1966) p. 42.
50 See *YS* 2.11.
51 Each of the four Vedas was preserved by a number of schools which composed or compiled supplementary texts for their own guidance. The Brāhmaṇas are the works deemed to offer, in the main, guidance or ritual matters whilst the Āraṇyakas supply guidance on doctrinal and philosophical issues. Not all śākhās have survived or left their supplementary texts for posterity. Those which have bequeathed Upaniṣads to us are the Aitareyins and the Kausitakins of the *Ṛgveda*, the Tāṇḍins and Jaiminīyas (or Talavakāras) of the *Sāmaveda*, the Taittirīyakas, Kaṭhas and Maitrayainiyas of the *Kṛṣṇa Yajurveda* and the Vājasaneyins of the *Śukla Yajurveda*. For further details see Deussen (1966) pp. 1-15 and (1973) pp. 1-19. The exception to this is the *Atharvaveda*, whose Upaniṣads do not, on the whole (the *Māṇḍūkya* and *Jabala* constituting what Deussen [1980] Vol. 2, p. 555 calls 'suspect exceptions'), have any clear connections with the śākhās of that Veda.
52 Nakamura (1983) dates the *Maitrī* around 200 BCE and the *Māṇḍūkya* somewhere between 1 and 200 CE. He also points out that when the writings of interpreters of the Upaniṣads are examined, the later the interpreter the more the number of Upaniṣads that are accepted as canonical. This tendency to indicate or circumscribe what is to be regarded as canonical began, he suggests, with the compliers of the middle period Upaniṣads: *Kaṭhaka*, *Muṇḍaka*, *Praśna* and *Śvetāśvatara*. He writes, 'the Upanisads of the middle period clearly state that they find a special significance in the "vedānta," and that they themselves are based upon it. Because the poets who composed the Old Upaniṣads of the middle period had no longer any concern with rituals, and must have differed also in their social lives from the authors of the early period Old Upaniṣads, I think that we can recognize that these were new Vedāntins de-

voted to the Sacred Upaniṣads ... not only did the Vedānta students follow the early period Upaniṣads as sacred canon, they were also continually producing Upaniṣads and they ascribed canonical authority to these as well. The history of the composition of the Upaniṣads is exactly the same as the history of the Vedānta school' (pp. 46-47). Whilst there is obviously much truth in this claim it is probably more accurate with regard to the earlier period than the later in so far as in the post-Bādarāyaṇa period the composers of the Upaniṣads appear to be different from the principal interpreters of the Vedānta tradition. In other words, there is no evidence I am aware of that Śaṅkara, Bhāskara, Rāmānuja or any of the other prominent Vedānta teachers of the Middle Ages composed Upaniṣads.

53 Thibaut (1962a) p. xviii.

54 Thibaut (1962a) p. xi.

55 Also called the *Vedāntasūtra*(s), the *Śarīraksūtra*(s), *Caturlakṣanī*, *Śarīraka-śāstra*, *Śarīraka* and *Vedānta-mīmāṃsā-śāstra*. For details see Nakamura (1983) pp. 425-28.

56 Dasgupta (1922) pp. 24-25.

57 Pandey (1983) pp. 114-77.

58 Radhakrishnan (1931) pp. 432-33.

59 Deussen (1973) pp. 24-25.

60 Winternitz, quoted in Nakamura (1983) p. 408.

61 Dasgupta (1922) pp. 418-22 and 429; Pandey (1983) pp. 114-77.

62 Nakamura (1983) pp. 429ff.

63 Mayeda (1979) p. 12.

64 Nakamura (1983) pp. 425-37.

65 Thibaut (1962a) pp. xiii-xiv.

66 Thibaut (1962a) p. xiv.

67 Śaṅkara's dates are a matter of some controversy but the consensus of scholarly opinion at the present time seems to favour 700–750 CE. For details see Mayeda (1979) pp. 3f.

68 Rāmānuja's dates are traditionally 1017 to 1137 CE. John Carmen (1974) suggests 1077 to 1157 (p. 27), but goes on to qualify this by saying that 'the most probable dates of the important events in Rāmānuja's life indicate that he lived to be at least 80, and he may well have lived to be much older than that' (p. 280).

69 For details see S. Dasgupta (1940), Vol. 3, pp. 1-11, Radhakrishnan (1960) pp. 39-45, and Srinivasachari (1972). Both Dasgupta (p. 3 n.) and Radhakrishnan (p. 39 n.) find Bhāskara in general agreement with the Pañcarātrins, from which Rāmānuja's Śrī Vaiṣṇava movement developed.

70 Srinivasachari (1972) pp. 287-92.

71 Thibaut (1962a) p. lxxxvi.

72 Srinivasachari (1972) pp. 287-92.

73 Mayeda (1979) p. 6.

74 Mayeda (1979) p. 6.

75 See Leggett (1990) p. 19.

76 Niranjanananda (1993) pp. 40-41.

77 Bader (1990) p. 46.

78 *Upadeśāsahasrī* (gadyabanda, prose section) 3.115. Quoted in Bader (1990) p. 79.

79 Bader (1990) p. 69.

80 Bader (1990) p. 40.
81 For an exploration of some of the factors lying behind Śaṅkara's position see Connolly (1992).
82 See Schraeder (1973) for details.
83 Dasgupta (1940) p. 55.
84 Mādhava, in his *Sarva Darśana Saṃgraha* (14th century), makes no mention of Nimbarka's system, suggesting that it was either not well-known or non-existent at the time.
85 See, for example, Bhatt (1980) p. 23. Also, see Dasgupta (1949) p. 382.
86 Agrawal (1983) p. 124.
87 Raju (1985) p. 474.
88 Raju (1985) p. 476.
89 Bhatt (1980) p. 19.
90 Bhatt (1980) p. 25.
91 See Connolly (1997) for a discussion of the reasons why prāṇa teachings were marginalized in mainstream Vedāntic theology.
92 Deussen (1980) p. 558
93 See Deussen (1980) pp. 562-65 for a discussion of this.
94 The reason that the *Cūlikā* is not included in the Adyar collection is presumably because it has little to say about yoga. Rather, it presents a doctrine of a god (īśvara) that is known in various forms, is referred to by various names in various texts and stands above the Sāṃkhya tattvas as a 26th and even a 27th principle. There is an interesting reference to followers of Sāṃkhya knowing īśvara as the guṇaless person, suggesting either a pre-*Kārikā* Vedic version of Sāṃkhya as described in the section on Sāṃkhya in Chapter 5 or a post-*Kārikā* form of theistic Sāṃkhya.
95 Roy (and Ganguli) Vol. 9, p. 56.
96 Roy (and Ganguli) Vol. 9, p. 57 n.
97 Roy (and Ganguli) Vol. 9, p. 58.
98 The *Dhyānabindu Upaniṣad* has the manas making this journey.
99 Snellgrove (2002) points out that these adepts are acknowledged as enlightened masters in both Hindu and Buddhist traditions. This is because tantric ideas were introduced into Buddhism by two main routes: Buddhists exploring new forms of yoga practice, and existing yoga teachings and practices being accepted as compatible with Buddhism (pp. 180ff.).
100 See the discussion of this and the *Maṇḍalabrāhmaṇa* in Mariau (1986).
101 Ayyangar (1952) p. 269.
102 Ayyangar translates prāṇasamrodha, pratyāhāra and dhāraṇā as complete control of breath, withdrawal of breath and the holding of breath respectively.
103 Zaehner (1978) p. 165.

Chapter 6

1 *Vājasaneyi Saṃhitā* (*White Yajurveda*), ch. 16; *Taittirīya Saṃhitā* (*Black Yajurveda*) 4.5.1ff.
2 *Vājasaneyi Saṃhitā* 16, 19 and 39.
3 The elements of this myth can be found in *Taittirīya Saṃhitā* 2.6.8, *Śatapatha Brāhmaṇa* 1.7.3ff. and *Gopatha Brāhmaṇa* 2.1.2.
4 Bhattacharji (1970) p. 124.
5 See Lorenzen (1972) for further details.
6 See Briggs (1938) ch. 10 for details.

7 Briggs (1938) p. 226.
8 See Yocum (1982) for a study of this text.
9 See section on tantric yoga for details.
10 Buddhism was the dominant religious force in northwestern India from the time of Aśoka (269–232 BCE) to the eighth century CE.
11 Taken from Chatterji (1981). Similar 36 tattva schemes, which unify puruṣa and prakṛti at a 'higher' level are common in the Vaiṣṇava Saṃhitās, the Śaiva Āgamas and the Śākta Tantras—recognizing that examples of each category: Āgama, Saṃhitā and Tantra can be found in the literature of each movement.
12 Bhattacharyya (1974) p. 1.
13 Bhattacharyya (1974) p. 51.
14 Bhattacharyya (1974) p. 71.
15 Quoted at Bhattacharyya (1974) p. 73.
16 Bhattacharyya (1974) p. 94.
17 Bharati (1975) pp. 16-17.
18 Quoted at Bharati (1975) p. 20.
19 Chang (1971) p. 165.
20 See Kinsley (1982) pp. 116-21 for details.
21 Masefield (1986a) p. xvi.
22 Hume (1971) pp. 284-86.
23 Snellgrove (2002) p. 142.
24 Eliade (1969) p. 263.
25 Hopkins (1971) p. 129.
26 Snellgrove (2002) p. 160.
27 Snellgrove (2002) p. 153.
28 Snellgrove (2002) pp. 158-59.
29 Snellgrove (2002) p. 152.
30 Snellgrove (2002) pp. 158ff.
31 Or in the navel area according to a number of Yoga Upaniṣads.
32 See Connolly (1982) for details.
33 Briggs (1973, ch. 11) dates Gorakhnāth, the founder of the Nātha/Kānphaṭa Yogi movement, early in the eleventh century.
34 Briggs (1973) pp. 150-51.
35 Sinh (1975).
36 Woodroffe (1973) p. 22.
37 Woodroffe (1973) p. 215.
38 Dasgupta (1973) p. 160.
39 Bharati (1975) p. 186.
40 Conze et al. (1954).
41 Singh (1975) p. 28.
42 Danielou (1954) p. 114.

Chapter 7

1 DeMichelis (2004) p. 2.
2 DeMichelis (2004) pp. 2-3.
3 For example, Carrico (2004) adds 'Tantra Yoga' in her article 'The Branches of Yoga'.
4 DeMichelis (2004) pp. 86-87.
5 DeMichelis (2004) pp. 151-52.

6 Described by Alter (2000) p. 57, as 'a middle class Bengali civil servant turned sannyāsi'.
7 The Yoga Institute was eventually established at a permanent location in Santa Cruz near Bombay.
8 DeMichelis (2004) p. 183.
9 Alter (2004) p. 28.
10 Rodrigues (1982) p. 72, quoted in Alter (2000) p. 65.
11 Alter (2000) p. 68.
12 The *Yoga Journal* website www.yogajournal.com (7.1.05) lists 26 different forms of yoga, and these constitute just a sample of those available. Almost all of them have the body and health as their primary focus.
13 DeMichelis (2004) p. 189.
14 See, for example, *MundU* 1.1.1-3.
15 Sjoman (1996) p. 51.
16 The titles he received were Sāṅkhya Yoga Śikhāmaṇi, Mīmāṃsā Tīrtha, Nyāyācārya, Vedānta Vagiśa and Veda Keśari. Desikachar (1998) p. x.
17 Desikachar and Cravens (1998) p. 141.
18 Desikachar (1982) p. 8, puts this in the 1920s; Sjoman (1996) p. 50, puts it in the 1930s. The school remained open until 1950.
19 Desikachar (1998) pp. xi-xii.
20 Desikachar and Cravens (1998) p. 81.
21 Desikachar and Cravens (1998) pp. 81-82.
22 See Flournoy (1994) for a discussion of such issues.
23 Sjoman (1996) p. 40.
24 Sjoman (1996) p. 51.
25 Caxton Press, Bangalore, 1895.
26 Sjoman (1996) p. 54. Vinyāsas, as explained by T.K.V. Desikachar and Cravens (1998) pp. 112-13, are activities that prepare the practitioner for a particular āsana and restabilize the person after it has been achieved. 'When applied to a particular posture, *vinyāsa* begins with a visualisation, proceeds to the starting position and the incorporation of the breath into the movement. The *asana* is performed with concentration on the flow of the movement and smoothness of inhalation, exhalation, and often retention of breath, and toward the prescribed completion. Each step is a preparation for the next. And so it is with the sequence of *asanas*. Each posture is part of a flow of exercise: a beginning, a building toward a posture that is the height of the program, and then a progression toward an ending.' Sjoman (1996) p. 65, draws attention to another aspect of vinyasa. It is a term, he points out, that is used in Vedic rituals. It 'refers to the subsidiary factors around a mantra that are required to make the mantra effective. The term does not have any meaning in yoga and appears to be used to imply some kind of vedic sanction to yoga practices. The term is developed and used in MIMAMSA, the ancient school in which Krishnamacariar was originally trained.'
27 Desikachar and Cravens (1998) pp. 95-96. Though we may note that *Yogarahasya* 1.11 states that aṣṭāṅgayoga is only for the twice-born (dvijata = brāhmans, kṣatriyas and vaiśyas); for padajas (śūdras) 'only sadanga [= prapatti, surrender] is possible'.
28 Sjoman (1996) p. 50.
29 This work is described by Krishnamacharya as 'one of the earliest texts on yoga' and, because it is early, 'there is emphasis on kundalini calanam [moving or

rousing the kuṇḍalinī]' Desikachar (2000) p. xxiii. Desikachar identifies the author of this text with the Yajñavalkya of the *Bṛhadāraṇyaka Upaniṣad* (loc. cit.), an identification challenged by Mohan (n/d, p. 37), who locates the origin of the text in the second century CE. All this is wishful thinking. The text shows many signs of lateness. Mohan takes the fact of verses in common between this and other yoga texts as borrowings by them from this. The opposite is equally likely to be true: the *Yogayajñavalkya* has borrowed from them. The works he identifies as having verses in common are the *Jabala Darśana*, the *Triśikhibrāhmaṇa, Yogakuṇḍalī, Yogatattva* and *Śandilya Upaniṣads*, the *Haṭha Yoga Pradīpikā*, Śaṅkara's commentary on the *Śvetāśvatara Upaniṣad*, Mummadideva's commentary on the smaller *Yogavāsiṣṭha* and Anandavardhana's commentary on the *Bhagavad Gītā*. If the *Yogayajñavalkya* did borrow from these texts then it cannot be earlier than the latest of them, which is probably the *Haṭha Yoga Pradīpikā* (15th century). Moreover, references to kuṇḍalinī and kuṇḍalinī as śakti (6.66), as well as 10 yamas, 10 niyamas, 14 nāḍīs and 10 vāyus all suggest affinities with the later, post-siddha forms of Śāktism and the later Yoga Upaniṣads.

30 Krishnamacharya's family is part of a lineage that has preserved the texts of the *Black Yajurveda*. Among the Upaniṣads, students of Desikachar are encouraged to pay particular attention to the *Taittirīya*.

31 Divine Life Society (1985) p. 18.

32 Śivānanda describes the event thus: 'I learnt fencing from a teacher who belonged to a low caste; he was a harijan. I could go to him for only a few days before I was made to understand that it was unbecoming of a caste-born Brahmin to play the student to an untouchable. I thought deeply over the matter. One moment I felt that the God whom we had all worshipped in the image in my father's puja room had jumped over to the heart of this untouchable. He was my guru, all right! So I immediately went to him with flowers, sweets and cloth, and garlanded him, placed flowers at his feet and prostrated myself before him. Thus did God come into my life to remove the veil of caste distinctions.' Divine Life Society (1985) p. 2.

33 Divine Life Society (1985) p. 21.

34 Divine Life Society (1985) p. 37.

35 Divine Life Society (1985) p. 46.

36 Divine Life Society (1985) p. 46.

37 Divine Life Society (1985) p. 56.

38 Divine Life Society (1985) p. 59.

39 Divine Life Society (1985) p. 87.

40 Divine Life Society (1985) pp. 102ff.

41 Divine Life Society (1985) p. 104.

42 Divine Life Society (1985) p. 129.

43 Divine Life Society (1985) p. 125.

44 Divine Life Society (1985) pp. 192-93.

45 Divine Life Society (1985) p. 200.

46 Divine Life Society (1985) p. 200.

47 The Society now has branches in Australia, Austria, Belgium, France, Germany, Hong Kong, Italy, Malaysia, Mauritius, Nepal, Netherlands, South Africa, Spain, United Kingdom, USA, Venezuela and the West Indies as well as India (see www.dlshq.org/branches for details).

48 Divine Life Society (1985) pp. 373-74.

49 Divine Life Society (1985) p. 401.
50 Divine Life Society (1985) pp. 401-402. This is clearly a distortion of the facts as it ignores the development of āsana practice found in tantric literature such as the later Yoga Upaniṣads and the nātha texts. This passage also claims that it was Śivānanda who initiated the practice of āsana, etc. for health reasons. Who really started the practice of employing āsana, etc. for health promotion? Was it Śrī Yogendra, Swami Kuvalyananda, Sri Krishnamacharya or Swami Śivānanda? In terms of absolute, recorded dates the honour would seem to go to Śrī Yogendra, though it seems that these trends were part of the spirit of the times and that 'modern yoga' was emerging in similar, though not identical, forms across India during the early twentieth century. As DeMichelis (2004) points out, the soil was prepared in the nineteenth century with the Hindu Rennaisance and the emergence of Neo-Vedānta. That seeds should sprout relatively independently in a number of locations is, therefore, to be expected. There may well have been some unacknowledged borrowing, but, given the context, multiple, parallel developments are hardly surprising.
51 Divine Life Society (1985) p. 206.
52 Divine Life Society (1985) p. 161.
53 Niranjananda (1993) pp. 91-92.
54 Niranjananda (1993) pp. 97-99.
55 Niranjananda (1993) p. 337.
56 Niranjananda (1993) p. 167.
57 Swami Vivekānanda Mā (Valerie Davies)—personal communication.
58 Niranjananda (1993) p. 108.
59 Swamis Chidānanda and Krishnānanda are currently in charge of the Śivānanda Ashram, Satchidānanda presides over Yogaville, an influential Ashram in the USA, and Swami Śivapremānanda is still teaching in South America (Swami Satchidānanda Mā—personal communication).

Chapter 8

1 Jahoda (1958) pp. 14, 18, 21.
2 Taylor (1989) p. 48.
3 Skynner and Cleese (1993) p. 334.
4 Skynner and Cleese (1993) p. 208.
5 Taylor (1989) p. 213.
6 Schumaker (1995; 1990).
7 See Mackie (1977).
8 See Bandler and Grinder (1982).
9 Skynner and Cleese (1993) p. 74.
10 Skynner and Cleese (1993) p. 75.
11 Skynner and Cleese (1993) p. 76.
12 Brown (1991) p. 223.
13 Brown (1991) p. 190.
14 Gilligan (1987) p. 23.
15 Temple (1989) p. 468, n. 32.
16 See Gilligan (1987) p. 42; Sargant (1957) pp. 12-13; and Jaynes (1993), but especially pp. 347-53ff.; Storr (1989) pp. 49-50; Will Macdonald, co-author of Bandler and Macdonald (1988)—personal communication.
17 Shor (1969) p. 242. See also Tart (1988) p. 81.
18 Berger and Luckmann (1967).

19 Fromm and Kahn (1990) p. 79.
20 Tart (1975) p. 81.
21 De Rivera and Sarbin (1998).
22 Yapko (1990) pp. 42-43.
23 See Weitzenhoffer (1989) pp. 258-62 for a discussion of this phenomenon.
24 Tart (1988) p. 81.
25 Gilligan (1987) p. 49.
26 Stace (1960) pp. 62-68.
27 See Masefield (1986a) passim.

# BIBLIOGRAPHY


Agrawal, M.M. 1983. *The Philosophy of Nimbarka.* 2nd edn. Chaukhamba Surbharati Prakashan, Varanasi.

Alter, J.S. 2004. *Yoga in Modern India: The Body Between Philosophy and Science.* Princeton University Press, Princeton, NJ.

—— 2000. *Gandhi's Body: Sex, Diet and the Politics of Nationalism.* University of Pennsylvania Press, Philadelphia.

Ayyangar, T.R.S. 1952. *The Yoga Upanishads.* The Adyar Library, Adyar.

Bader, J. 1990. *Meditation in Sankara's Vedanta.* Aditya Prakashan, Delhi.

Bandler, R. and Grinder, J. 1982. *Reframing: Neuro-Linguistic Programming and the Transformation of Meaning.* Real People Press, Moab, Utah.

Bandler, R. and Macdonald, W. 1988. *An Insider's Guide to Submodalities.* Meta Publications, Cupertino, CA.

Bechert, H. and Gombrich, R. (eds). 1984. *The World of Buddhism.* Thames and Hudson, London.

Beidler, W. 1975. *The Vision of Self in Early Vedanta.* Motilal Banarsidass, Delhi.

Berger, P. and Luckmann, T. 1966/1967. *The Social Construction of Reality.* Penguin, Harmondsworth.

Bharati, A. 1975. *The Tantric Tradition.* Rider, London.

Bhatt, G.H. 1980. *Sri Vallabhacharya and his Doctrines.* Butala & Co., Delhi.

Bhattacharji, S. 1970. *The Hindu Theogony.* Cambridge University Press, Cambridge.

Bhattacharyya, N.N. 1974. *History of the Sakta Religion.* Munshiram Manoharlal, New Delhi.

Briggs, G.W. 1938/1973. *Gorakhnāth and the Kānphaṭa Yogis.* Motilal Banarsidass, Delhi.

Brown, P. 1991. *The Hypnotic Brain: Hypnotherapy and Social Communication.* Yale University Press, New Haven.

Brown, W.N. 1968. 'Agni, Sun, Sacrifice and Vac: A Sacerdotal Ode by Dirghatamas (Rig Veda 1.164)'. *Journal of the American Oriental Society* 88, pp. 199-218.

Bühler, G. (ed.). 1969. *The Laws of Manu* (Reprint of the Clarendon Press 1886 edition: Sacred Books of the East, Vol. 25). Dover, New York.

Carmen, J.B. 1974. *The Theology of Ramanuja.* Yale University Press, New Haven.

Carrico, M. 2004. 'The Branches of Yoga'. *Yoga Journal,* http://www.yogajournal.com/newtoyoga/157_1.cfm

Chakravarti, P. 1975. *Origin and Development of the Sāṃkhya System of Thought.* 2nd edn. Oriental Books Reprint Corporation, Delhi.

Chang, G.C.C. 1971. *The Buddhist Teaching of Totality.* George Allen & Unwin, London.

Chatterji, J.C. 1981. *Kashmir Shaivism*. Galav Publications, Chandigarh.
Connolly, P. 2000a. 'Mystical Experience and Trance Experience'. *Transpersonal Psychology Review* 4.1, pp. 23-35.
—— 2000b. *A Psychology of Possession*, 2nd Series Occasional Paper 23, Religious Experience Research Centre, Oxford.
—— 1997. 'The Vitalistic Antecedents of the Ātman-Brahman Concept'. In P. Connolly and S. Hamilton (eds), *Indian Insights: Buddhism, Brahmanism and Bhakti*. Luzac Oriental, London.
—— 1992. *Vitalistic Thought in India*. Sri Satguru Publications, Delhi.
—— 1989. 'Epoche, Eidetic Vision and Beyond'. *Journal of Beliefs and Values* 10.2.
—— (ed.) 1986. *Perspectives on Indian Religion: Papers in Honour of Karel Werner*. Sri Satguru Publications, Delhi.
Conze, E. et al. (eds). 1954. *Buddhist Texts Through the Ages*. Harper & Row, New York.
Cowell, E.B. and Gough, A.E. 1981. *Sarva-Darśana-Saṅgraha of Mādhavāchārya*. Parimal Publications, Delhi.
Danielou, A. 1964. *Hindu Polytheism*. Routledge and Kegan Paul, London.
—— 1954. *Yoga: Method of Reintegration*. Christopher Johnson, London.
Dasgupta, S. 1922, 1932, 1940, 1949, 1955. *A History of Indian Philosophy* (5 vols). Cambridge University Press, Cambridge.
Dasgupta, S.B. 1950/1973. *An Introduction to Tantric Buddhism*. Shambhala, Boston.
Davies, N. 1996. *Europe: A History*. Oxford University Press, Oxford.
DeMichelis, E. 2004. *A History of Modern Yoga: Patanjali and Western Esotericism*. Continuum, London.
de Rivera, J. and Sarbin, T.R. (eds). 1998. *Believed-In Imaginings: The Narrative Construction of Reality*. American Psychological Association, Washington, DC.
Desikachar, K. 2005. *The Yoga of the Yogi: The Legacy of T. Krishnamacharya*. Krishnamacharya Yoga Mandiram, Chennai, India.
Desikachar, T.K.V. 1982. *The Yoga of T. Krishnamacharya*. Krishnamacharya Yoga Mandiram, Chennai, India.
—— (trans.). 2000. *Yogayajnavalkya Samhita: The Yoga Treatise of Yajnavalkya*. Krishnamacharya Yoga Mandiram, Chennai, India.
—— (trans.). 1998. *Sri Nathamuni's Yogarahasya—Presented by Yogacharya T. Krishnamacharya*. Krishnamacharya Yoga Mandiram, Chennai, India.
—— with Cravens, R.H. 1998. *Health, Healing and Beyond: Yoga and the Living Tradition of Krishnamacharya*. Aperture Foundation, Denville, NJ.
Deussen, P. 1980. *Sixty Upanishads of the Veda* (2 vols) (trans. V.M. Bedekar and G.B. Palsule). Motilal Banarsidass, Delhi.
—— 1912/1973. *The System of the Vedanta* (trans. C. Johnson). Dover, New York.
—— 1906/1966. *The Philosophy of The Upanishads* (trans. A.S. Geden). Dover, New York.
Diamond, J. 1997. *Guns, Germs and Steel: The Fates of Human Societies*. Jonathon Cape, London.
Dimock, E.C. et al. 1978. *Literatures of India*. University of Chicago Press, Chicago.
Divine Life Society. 1985. *Śivānanda, Biography of a Modern Sage*, Vol. 1. Divine Life Society.
Dutt, M.N. 1895–1905/1988. *Mahabharata* (7 vols), Vol. 6. Parimal Publications, Delhi.
Edgerton, F. 1972. *The Bhagavad Gita*. Rev. edn. Harvard University Press, Cambridge, MA.
Eliade, M. 1969. *Yoga: Immortality and Freedom*. Routledge and Kegan Paul, London.

Fausboll, V. 1881/1905. *The Sutta Nipāta*. 2nd edn. (Sacred Books of the East, Vol. 10, with Dhammapada). Motilal Banarsidass, Delhi.

Feuerstein, G. 1980. *The Philosophy of Classical Yoga*. Manchester University Press, Manchester.

—— 1979. *The Yoga Sūtra of Patañjali*. Dawson, Folkstone.

Feuerstein, G., Frawley, D. and Kak, S. July/August 1992. 'A New View of Ancient India'. *Yoga Journal*, pp. 65-69 and 100-102.

Flournoy, T. 1901/1994. *From India to the Planet Mars: A Case Study of Multiple Personality with Imaginary Languages*. Princeton University Press, Princeton, NJ.

Frauwallner, E. 1973. *History of Indian Philosophy* (2 vols) (trans. V.M. Bedekar). Motilal Banarsidass, Delhi.

Fromm, E. and Kahn, S. 1990. *Self-hypnosis: The Chicago Paradigm*. The Guildford Press, New York.

Gilligan, S. 1987. *Therapeutic Trances: The Co-operation Principle in Ericksonian Hypnotherapy*. Brunner Mazel, New York.

Gombrich, R. 1996. *How Buddhism Began: The Conditioned Genesis of the Early Teachings*. Athlone, London.

—— 1992. 'Dating the Buddha: A Red Herring Revealed'. In H. Bechert (ed.), *The Dating of the Historical Buddha, Part 2*, pp. 237-59. Vandenhoek and Ruprecht, Göttingen.

—— 1975. 'Ancient Indian Cosmology'. In C. Blacker and M. Loewe (eds), *Ancient Cosmologies*, pp. 110-42. Allen & Unwin, London.

Grierson, G.A. 1909. 'Bhakti Marga'. In J. Hastings (ed.), *Encyclopaedia of Religion and Ethics*, Vol. 2, pp. 539-51. T.&T. Clark, Edinburgh.

Griffith, R.T.H. 1973. *The Hymns of the Rgveda*. Rev. edn. Motilal Banarsidass, Delhi.

Griswold, H.D. 1971. *The Religion of the Ṛgveda*. Motilal Banarsidass, Delhi.

Gupta, S. 1972. *Laksmi Tantra*. E.J. Brill, Leiden.

Hare, E.M. 1935. *Gradual Sayings*, Vol. 4. Pali Text Society, London.

—— 1934. *Gradual Sayings*, Vol. 3. Pali Text Society, London.

Harvey, P. (ed.) 2001. *Buddhism*. Continuum, London.

Hein, N. 1986. 'A Revolution in Krsnaism: The Cult of Gopala'. *History of Religions*, Vol. 25 (4), pp. 297-317.

Hopkins, E.W. 1901/1993. *The Great Epic of India*. Motilal Banarsidass, Delhi.

—— 1901. 'Yoga-technique in the Great Epic'. *Journal of the American Oriental Society* 22, pp. 333-79.

Hopkins, T.J. 1971. *The Hindu Religious Tradition*. Dickenson, California.

Horner, I.B. 1954, 1957, 1959. *Middle Length Sayings* (3 vols). Pali Text Society, London.

Hume, R.E. 1931/1971. *The Thirteen Principal Upanishads*. 2nd edn. Oxford University Press, Oxford.

Jacobi, H. 1911. 'Cosmogony and Cosmology (Indian)'. In J. Hastings (ed.), *Encyclopaedia of Religion and Ethics*, Vol. 4, pp. 155-61. T. & T. Clark, Edinburgh.

—— 1908. 'Ages of the World (Indian)'. In J. Hastings (ed.), *Encyclopaedia of Religion and Ethics*, Vol. 1, pp. 200-202. T. & T. Clark, Edinburgh.

Jahoda, M. 1958. *Current Concepts of Positive Mental Health*. Basic Books, New York.

Jayatilleke, K.N. 1963. *Early Buddhist Theory of Knowledge*. George Allen & Unwin, London.

Jaynes, J. 1990/1993. *The Origin of Consciousness in the Breakdown of the Bicameral Mind*. 2nd edn. Penguin, Harmondsworth.

Kalghati, T.G. 1986. 'The Jaina Way'. In Connolly (1986) pp. 229-38.
Keith, A.B. 1925/1970. *The Religion and Philosophy of the Veda and Upanishads* (2 vols). Motilal Banarsidass, Delhi.
—— 1918/1975. *A History of Samkhya Philosophy*. Reprint. Nag Publishers, Delhi.
Khair, G.S. 1969. *Quest for the Original Gita*. Somaiya Publications, Bombay.
Kinsley, D. 1982. *Hinduism—A Cultural Perspective*. Prentice-Hall, Englewood Cliffs.
Kochumuttom, T. 1982. *A Buddhist Doctrine of Experience*. Motilal Banarsidass, Delhi.
Lamotte, E. 1984. 'The Buddha, His Teachings and His Sangha'. In Bechert and Gombrich (1984) pp. 41-58.
Larson, G.J. 1979. *Classical Sāṃkhya*. 2nd edn. Motilal Banarsidass, Delhi.
Leggett, T. 1990. *The Complete Commentary by Śaṅkara on the Yoga Sūtras*. Kegan Paul International, London.
Lorenzen, D.N. 1972. *The Kāpālika and Kālamukhas: Two Lost Śaivite Sects*. University of California Press, Berkeley.
Mackie, J.L. 1977. *Ethics: Inventing Right and Wrong*. Penguin, Harmondsworth.
Mahadevan, T.M.P. 1974. *Invitation to Indian Philosophy*. Arnold Heinemann (India) Pvt. Ltd.
Malalasekera, G.P. (ed.). 1968–. *Encyclopaedia of Buddhism*. Government of Sri Lanka, Colombo.
Mariau, D. 1986. 'Tāraka Yoga'. In Connolly (1986) pp. 45-52.
Masefield, P. 1986a. *Divine Revelation in Pali Buddhism*. Allen & Unwin and Sri Lanka Institute of Traditional Studies, Colombo.
—— 1986b. 'How "Noble" is the Ariyan Eightfold Path?' In Connolly (1986) pp. 161-74.
Mayeda, S. 1979. *A Thousand Teachings: The Upadeśasāhasrī of Śaṅkara*. University of Tokyo Press, Japan.
Minor, R.N. 1982. *Bhagavad Gītā: An Exegetical Commentary*. Heritage, Delhi.
Mohan, A.G. (trans.). n/d. *Yoga Yajnavalkya*. Ganesh and Company, Madras.
Nakamura, H. 1983. *A History of Early Vedānta Philosophy*. Motilal Banarsidass, Delhi.
Niranjanananda, Paramahamsa. 1993. *Samnyasa Darshan: A Treatise on Traditional and Contemporary Samnyasa*. Sri Panchadashnam Paramahamsa Alakh Bara Deoghar, Bihar, India.
Nyantiloka. 1972/1950. *Buddhist Dictionary*. AMS Press, New York.
O'Flaherty, W.D. 1975. *Hindu Myths*. Penguin, Harmondsworth.
Pande, G.C. 1974. *Studies in the Origins of Buddhism*. Motilal Banarsidass, Delhi.
Pandey, K.C. 1954/1986. *An Outline History of Śaiva Philosophy*. Reprint. Motilal Banarsidass Delhi.
Pandey, S.L. 1983. *Pre-Śaṃkara Advaita Philosophy*. Darshan Peeth, Allahabad.
Radhakrishnan, S. 1960. *The Brahma Sūtra*. George Allen & Unwin, London.
—— 1953. *The Principal Upanishads*. George Allen & Unwin, London.
—— 1929, 1931. *Indian Philosophy* (2 vols). George Allen & Unwin, London.
Rahula, W. 1978. *Zen and the Taming of the Bull*. Gordon Frazer, London.
—— 1967. *What The Buddha Taught*. 2nd edn. Gordon Frazer, London.
Raju, P.T. 1985. *Structural Depths of Indian Thought*. South Asian Publishers, Delhi.
Rao, K.B.R. 1966. *Theism of Pre-Classical Sāṃkhya*. University of Mysore, Mysore, India.
Rawlinson, A. 1997. *The Book of Enlightened Masters: Western Teachers in Eastern Traditions*. Open Court, Chicago.
Reynolds, F.E. 1971. 'The Several Bodies of the Buddha; Reflections on a Neglected Aspect of Theravāda Tradition'. *History of Religions* 16, pp. 374-89.

Rhys Davids, T.W. 1899, 1910, 1921. *Dialogues of the Buddha* (3 vols). Pali Text Society, London.

—— 1881. *Buddhist Suttas* (Sacred Books of the East, Vol. 9). Clarendon Press, Oxford.

Rhys Davids, C. and Surinagoda Sumangala Thera. 1917. *Kindred Sayings* I. Pali Text Society, London.

Rodrigues, S. 1982. *Life of Sri Yogendra, The Householder Yogi.* Yoga Institute, Bombay.

Roy, P.C. (and Ganguli, K.M.). n/d (c. 1883–1896). *The Mahabharata,* Vols 9, 10. Oriental Publishing Co., Calcutta.

Sangharakshita. 1957/1980. *Survey of Buddhism.* 2nd edn. Shambhala, Boston.

Sargant, W. 1957. *Battle for the Mind: A Physiology of Conversion and Brain Washing.* Heinemann, London.

Schraeder, F.O. 1973. *Introduction to the Pancaratra and the Ahirbudhnya Samhita.* 2nd edn. Adyar Library, Adyar.

Schumaker, J.F. 1995. *The Corruption of Reality: A Unified Theory of Religion, Hypnosis and Psychopathology.* Prometheus, Amherst, New York.

—— 1990. *Wings of Illusion: The Origin, Nature and Future of Paranormal Belief.* Polity Press, Cambridge.

—— (ed.) 1992. *Religion and Mental Health.* Oxford University Press, New York.

Shor, R. 1969. 'Hypnosis and the Concept of the Generalized Reality-Orientation'. (1959). Reprinted in C. Tart (ed.), *Altered States of Consciousness,* pp. 239-56. Doubleday, New York.

Singh, M. 1975. *Gorakhnāth and Mediaeval Hindu Mysticism.* Oriental College, Lahore.

Sinh, P. 1975. *The Haṭha Yoga Pradīpikā.* 2nd edn. Oriental Books Reprint Corporation, New Delhi.

Sinha, P. 1986. *The Bhagavad Gītā As It Was.* Open Court, Chicago.

Sjoman, N.E. 1996. *The Yoga Tradition of the Mysore Palace.* Abhinav Publications, New Delhi.

Skynner, R. and Cleese, J. 1993. *Life and How to Survive It.* Methuen, London.

Smart, N. 1964. *Doctrine and Argument in Indian Philosophy.* George Allen & Unwin, London.

Snellgrove, D. 2002. *Indo-Tibetan Buddhism: Indian Buddhists and their Tibetan Successors.* 2nd edn. Shambhala, Boston.

Srinivasachari, P.N. 1934/1972. *The Philosophy of Bhedābheda.* Reprint. Adyar Library, Adyar.

Stace, W. 1960. *Mysticism and Philosophy.* Macmillan, London.

Storr, A. 1989. *Solitude.* Harper Collins, London.

Sukthankar, V.S. 1936–37. 'Epic Studies'. *Annals of the Bhandarkar Oriental Research Institute* 18, pp. 1-76.

Tart, C.E.P. 1988. *Waking Up: Overcoming the Obstacles to Human Potential.* Element Books, Shaftsbury.

—— 1975. *States of Consciousness.* Dutton, New York.

Taylor, S. 1989. *Positive Illusions: Creative Self-Deception and the Healthy Mind.* Basic Books, New York.

Temple, R. 1989. *Open to Suggestion: The Uses and Abuses of Hypnosis.* Aquarian Press, Wellingborough.

Thibaut, G. 1962a *The Vedānta Sūtras of Bādarāyaṇa with the commentary by Śaṅkara* (2 vols). Dover, New York. (Corrected version of the Clarendon Press, 1890 and 1896 editions). Sacred Books of the East, Vols 34 & 38.

—— 1962b. *The Vedānta Sūtras of Bādarāyaṇa with the Commentary by Rāmānuja.* Motilal Banarsidass, Delhi. (Reprint of Oxford University Press, 1904 edition. Sacred Books of the East, Vol. 48.)

Thomas, E.J. 1949. *The Life of Buddha as Legend and History.* Routledge and Kegan Paul, London.

Tosh, J. 2000. *The Pursuit of History.* 3rd edn. Longman, Harlow.

Ueda, Y. 1967. 'Two Main Streams of Thought in Yogācāra Philosophy'. *Philosophy East and West* 17, pp. 155-65.

Van Buitenen, J.A.B. 1981. *The Bhagavad Gītā in the Mahābhārata.* University of Chicago Press, Chicago.

—— 1973. *The Mahābhārata,* Vol. 1. University of Chicago Press, Chicago.

—— 1957a. 'Studies in Sāṃkhya, Part Two'. *Journal of the American Oriental Society* 77.1, pp. 15-25.

—— 1957b. 'Studies in Sāṃkhya, Part Three'. *Journal of the American Oriental Society* 77.2, pp. 88-107.

—— 1956. 'Studies in Sāṃkhya, Part One'. *Journal of the American Oriental Society* 76, pp. 153-57.

Warder, A.K. 1980. *Indian Buddhism.* 2nd edn. Motilal Banarsidass, Delhi.

Weitzenhoffer, A.M. 1989. *The Practice of Hypnotism,* Vol. 1. John Wiley, New York.

Werner, K. 1989. 'From Polytheism to Monism—A Multidimensional View of the Vedic Religion'. In Glenys Davies (ed.), *Polytheistic Systems.* COSMOS—The Yearbook of the Traditional Cosmology Society, 5, pp. 12-27. Edinburgh University Press, Edinburgh.

—— 1986. 'Yoga in the Old Upaniṣads'. In Connolly (1986) pp. 1-8.

—— 1983. 'Bodhi and Arahattaphala: From Early Buddhism to Early Mahayana'. In P. Denwood and A. Piatagorsky (eds), *Buddhist Studies: Ancient and Modern,* pp. 107-81. Curzon, London.

Whitney, W.D. 1905/1971. *The Atharva Veda Saṃhitā* (2 vols). Reprint. Motilal Banarsidass, Delhi.

Wilkinson, R.G. 1996. *Unhealthy Societies: The Afflictions of Inequality.* Routledge, London.

Williams, P. 1989. *Mahāyāna Buddhism: The Doctrinal Foundations.* Routledge, London.

Wilson, H.H. 1980. *The Vishnu Purāṇa* (2 vols). Nag, Delhi.

Winternitz, M. 1927, 1932. *A History of Indian Literature* (2 vols). Russell & Russell, New York.

Woodroffe, J. 1973. *The Serpent Power.* Ganesh & Co., Madras.

Woods, J.H. 1914/1966. *The Yoga System of Patañjali.* Motilal Banarsidass, Delhi.

Woodward, F.L. 1932, 1933, 1936. *Gradual Sayings,* Vols. I, II, V. Pali Text Society, London.

—— 1922, 1925, 1927, 1930. *Kindred Sayings,* Vols II–V. Pali Text Society, London.

Yapko, M.D. 1990. *Trancework: An Introduction to the Practice of Clinical Hypnosis.* Brunner Mazel, New York.

Yocum, G. 1982. *Hymns to the Dancing Śiva.* Heritage, New Delhi.

Zaehner, R.C. 1969. *The Bhagavad Gītā.* Oxford University Press, Oxford.

—— 1966. *Hindu Scriptures.* Dent, London and New York.

—— 1957. *Mysticism—Sacred and Profane.* Oxford University Press, Oxford.

Zimmer, H. 1951/1969. *Philosophies of India.* (Reprint). Princeton University Press, Princeton, NJ.

—— 1946/1972. *Myths and Symbols in Indian Art and Civilization.* Harper & Row, New York.

# INDEX

Breinigsville, PA USA
21 October 2009
226266BV00003B/1/P

9 781845 531560